THE EMPIRE'S NEW CLOTHES

Barack Obama in the Real World of Power

PAUL STREET

Paradigm Publishers
Boulder • London

Copyright © 2010 by Paradigm Publishers

Published in the United States by Paradigm Publishers, 2845 Wilderness Place, Suite 200, Boulder, CO 80301 USA.

Paradigm Publishers is the trade name of Birkenkamp & Company, LLC,

Dean Birkenkamp, President and Publisher.

Library of Congress Cataloging-in-Publication Data

Street, Paul Louis.
    The empire's new clothes : Barack Obama in the real world of power / Paul Street.
        p.   cm.
    Includes bibliographical references and index.
    ISBN 978-1-59451-844-7 (hardcover : alk. paper) — ISBN 978-1-59451-845-4 (pbk. : alk. paper)
        1. United States—Politics and government—2009– 2. United States—Foreign relations—2009– 3. Obama, Barack. I. Title.
    E907.S74 2010
    973.932092—dc22   2010014744

Printed and bound in the United States of America on acid-free paper that meets the standards of the American National Standard for Permanence of Paper for Printed Library Materials.

Editorial production by the Book Factory.

14   13   12   11   10   1   2   3   4   5

"Barack Obama is a brand. And the Obama brand is designed to make us feel good about our government while corporate overlords loot the Treasury, our elected officials continue to have their palms greased by armies of corporate lobbyists, our corporate media diverts us with gossip and trivia and our imperial wars expand in the Middle East. Brand Obama is about being happy consumers. We are entertained. We feel hopeful. We like our president. We believe he is like us. But like all branded products spun out from the manipulative world of corporate advertising, we are being duped into doing and supporting a lot of things that are not in our interest.

" . . . President Obama does one thing and Brand Obama gets you to believe another. This is the essence of successful advertising."
—*Chris Hedges, May 3, 2009*[1]

"One benefit of the Obama presidency is that it is validating much of George W. Bush's security agenda and foreign policy merely by dint of autobiographical rebranding [and with] . . . artfully repackaged versions of themes President Bush sounded with his freedom agenda. We mean that as a compliment . . . "
—Wall Street Journal *editors, "Barack Hussein Bush," June 5, 2009*[2]

"Like Bush's America, Obama's America is run by some very dangerous people."
—*John Pilger, October 14, 2009*[3]

"As Obama came into office, Condoleezza Rice predicted that he would follow the policies of Bush's second term, and that's pretty much what's happened apart from a different rhetoric and style. But it is wise to attend to deeds, not rhetoric. Deeds commonly tell a different story."
—*Noam Chomsky, London, November 2009*[4]

"The U.S. has a machine that spans the globe, that has the capacity to kill, and Obama has kept it set on kill."
—*Allan Nairn, January 6, 2010*[5]

1. Chris Hedges, "Buying Brand Obama," Truthdig (May 3, 2009), read at http://www.truthdig.com/report/item/20090503_buying_brand_obama.

2. *Wall Street Journal,* December 5, 2009, read at http://online.wsj.com/article/SB124416109792287285.html.

3. John Pilger, "Media Lies and the Ware Drive Against Iran," October 14 2009, read at http://www.johnpilger.com.

4. Common Dreams, November 9, 2009.

5. Allan Nairn, "'Obama Has Kept the Machine Set on Kill' —Journalist and Activist Allan Nairn Reviews Obama's First Year in Office," *Democracy Now* (January 6, 2010), read transcript at http://www.democracynow.org/2010/1/6/obama_has_kept_the_machine_set.

Contents

Preface

In my 2008 book, *Barack Obama and the Future of American Politics*, I observed that every four years millions of Americans invest their hopes in an electoral process that does not deserve their trust. These citizens qua voters hope that a savior or at least a more effective manager can be installed in the White House—someone who will raise wages, roll back war and militarism, provide universal and adequate health care, rebuild the nation's infrastructure, produce high-paying jobs, fix the environmental crisis, reduce inequality, guarantee economic security, and generally make daily life more livable. But these dreams are regularly drowned in the icy waters of historical and political "reality." In the actuality of American politics and policy, the officially "electable" candidates are vetted in advance by what Laurence Shoup calls "the hidden primary of the ruling class." By prior establishment selection, all of the "viable" presidential contenders are closely tied to corporate and military-imperial power in numerous and interrelated ways. They run safely within the narrow ideological and policy parameters set by those who rule behind the scenes to make sure that the rich and privileged continue to be the leading beneficiaries of the American system. In presidential as in other elections, U.S. "democracy" is at best a "guided" one; at worst it is a corrupt farce, amounting to manipulation, with the larger population the project of propaganda in a controlled and trivialized electoral process. "It is an illusion," Laurence Shoup claims (correctly, in my opinion), "that real change can ever come from electing a different ruling class-sponsored candidate."[1]

This is especially true in the corporate-neoliberal era,[2] perhaps, when the Democratic Party has moved ever further away from its declared mission of representing workers, the poor, and minorities—the disadvantaged— in their continuing struggles with plutocracy, inequality, empire, racism, and indifference. But the deeper and darker truth is that American democracy has always been significantly constrained and compromised by the privileged and the propertied and power elite. Sixty years ago, historian Richard Hofstader, in his widely read book *The American Political Tradition*, scrutinized the nation's most significant national leaders, from Thomas Jefferson, Alexander Hamilton, and Andrew Jackson to Abraham Lincoln, William Jennings Bryan, Herbert Hoover, and both Theodore and Franklin Delano Roosevelt—liberals and Democrats as well as conservatives and Republicans. Hofstader found that "the range of vision embraced by the primary contestants in the major parties has always been bounded by the horizons of property and enterprise. . . . They have accepted the economic virtues of capitalist culture as necessary qualities of man. . . . That culture has been intensely nationalistic."[3] We might add that American political culture has also long observed narrow parameters of permissible debate and action surrounding skin color and sex type—barriers that have generally prevented leading politicians and officeholders from seriously attacking underlying structures and patterns of racial and gender disparity.

Throughout the century in which Hofstader wrote and into the present one, Howard Zinn noted, "We have seen exactly the same limited vision Hofstader talked about—a capitalist encouragement of enormous fortunes alongside desperate poverty, a nationalistic acceptance of war and preparation for war. Government power swung from Republicans to Democrats and back again, but neither party showed itself capable of going beyond that vision."[4]

Hofstader's and Zinn's observations remain strikingly relevant to a Barack Obama presidency that is one year in the making as I write today. Obama's careful, business-friendly handling of the economy (strong on bailouts for giant financial institutions and weak on support for the growing mass of unemployed and poor), the weakening of his "health reform" to a corporation-serving shadow of its original progressive promise, the passage of a record-setting Pentagon budget, and the related significant escalation of U.S. military violence in Afghanistan, Pakistan, Yemen, and Somalia are just some of the many indications (detailed in the chapters that follow) of how deeply beholden Obama is to existing dominant domestic and global hierarchies and doctrines.

This may at first strike some as an overly harsh and radical judgment, but I am far from alone among commentators and reporters (many quite "mainstream") in observing Obama's record of governing from the center-right since the election. Although some readers may not agree with my assessment of Obama's first year in power, I expect many who sift through the facts and developments I present will come to see things in a similar light.

The quantity of evidence is considerable, as we will see ahead; it can be expected to grow before the time this volume hits the bookshelves.

Even though this book is highly critical of the Obama presidency, this criticism is proffered with six caveats, or qualifications, as follows.

First, for all my harsh judgments, I always situate Obama's presidential conduct within the narrow institutional and ideological framework imposed by the U.S. profits system and Empire.

Second, this book maintains my previous book's insistence on seeing Obama's behavior within the context of the history of the Democratic Party and of the broader conservative electoral system and political culture of which that party is a key part.

Third, there are some things that President Obama has done that meets my approval and that of some other leftists: easing the ban on stem cell research, ending White House denial on climate change, scrapping the global gag rule on abortion counseling, setting aside some wilderness land for federal protection, signing a bill giving the federal government new power to regulate cigarette production and marketing, advancing and signing legislation that expands college access for many young Americans by overhauling the federal student loan system, and making it easier for women to sue for job discrimination.

Fourth, I think it is a historic sign of cultural and political progress that a black family now resides in a White House that was built by African American slaves.[5]

Fifth, I think it has been essential for U.S. voters and citizens, especially younger ones, to experience life under a Democratic presidential administration. The "corporate Democrats" (of which Obama is the new leader and epitome) are better able to deceptively pose as a progressive alternative to business class and imperial rule than the Republicans when they are out of office than when they are in power. Democrats are more effectively exposed as ultimately inadequate tribunes of the ordinary working people they claim to represent when they hold power and then quite naturally fail to deliver on popular hopes and dreams they've ridden and raised on the road to office. They are less able to hide their essential identity as the other business and Empire party (what former Richard Nixon strategist Kevin Phillips once aptly termed "history's second most enthusiastic capitalist party"[6]) when they sit atop the political system.

Most serious middle-aged and senior lefties haven't required yet another lesson from Obama (or, alternatively, a President Hillary Clinton) on the bipartisan nature of the U.S. profits system and the related American Empire Project. But many in a new and younger generation of real and potential left progressives can use such an education. They have come of political age in a time mainly of Republican rule, helping make them prone to the deadly illusion that party rebranding at the highest level of government constitutes a dramatic transformation

Sixth, I believe that the potentially left-leaning disenchantment that can result from that experience will not be effective unless and until popular forces develop considerably more capacity and willingness to organize for meaningful social and political change from the bottom up. More than being merely meaningless, popular disenchantment could become dangerous in the absence of such development. Mass resentment abhors a vacuum. Without truly progressive institutions and ideas in place to channel energy in positive and democratic directions, popular disquiet and estrangement under Obama and the Democrats could just as easily feed a dodgy right-populist (proto-fascistic) rebellion against supposed Obamaist "socialism." There is no shortage of powerful, high-wattage demagogues—Sean Hannity, Glenn Beck, Rush Limbaugh, Mark Levin, and Bill O'Reilly, to name a few—ready to appeal to anxious and oppressed people with real grievances.

The book has an introduction, six chapters, an afterword, and a postscript. Chapter 1 ("Business Rule as Usual") traces the Obama White House's corporate- and Wall Street–friendly policies through the late spring and early summer of 2009, placing special emphasis on the not-so-"socialist" (actually corporatist) president's continuation of the Bush administration's policy of granting massive taxpayer transfers to elite U.S. financial firms.

Chapter 2 ("Empire's New Clothes") turns to foreign policy. It traces the new administration's bold embrace and advance of militarism and Empire within and beyond the oil-rich Middle East and Southern Asia.

Chapter 3 ("Corporate-Managed 'Health Reform'") returns to Obama's business-captive domestic policy, extending the analysis advanced in Chapter 1 to "health reform," the new president's declared top domestic priority.

Chapter 4 ("Barack Obama, the Myth of the Postracial Presidency, and the Politics of Identity") turns to the racial and other identity-politicized meanings of the Obama presidency. Although this chapter focuses primarily on black-white tensions and issues, I also touch on related questions relating to Latino/a rights/status, women's rights, and gay rights.

Chapter 5 ("Big Brother Lives") details the Obama White House's disturbing continuation of repressive Bush administration "war on terror" practices and policies at home and abroad.

Chapter 6 ("We Were Warned") welcomes but also questions the disappointment that many on the left side of the American political spectrum expressed as Obama's allegiance, service, and captivity to reigning inequality and empire structures and doctrines became ever more apparent in 2009. Building on my previous book and reflecting my background as a historian, this chapter shows numerous and interrelated ways in which we were clearly warned about what to expect from Barack Obama in the world of capitalist and American power.

The Afterword offers some modest reflections toward authentic left revival under, beyond, and, where necessary, against Obama.

I completed most of the writing of this book (except for the May 2010 Postscript)

- nine days after Barack Obama had received the Nobel Peace Prize.
- eighteen days after Obama had told a national television audience that he would be escalating the U.S. war in/on Afghanistan for a second time.[7]
- two days after Obama had returned from high-stakes climate negotiations in Copenhagen where he made no serious effort to forge a meaningful binding agreement to reduce global carbon emissions to anything like the degree that most earth scientists were saying was urgently required.[8]
- two days after Obama had ordered air raids that were widely reported to have killed a large number of innocent civilians in southeast Yemen.
- as the White House and top Democrats were agreeing to strip down their business-friendly "health reform" efforts of any remaining progressive content to a degree that led mainstream Democrat Howard Dean to denounce their bill as a "gift to the insurance companies" and to recommend that U.S. senators "kill it."[9]
- one month before my sixth caveat was validated by the stunning victory of a little-known right-wing Republican state senator (Scott Brown) in a special election to fill the open U.S. Senate seat formerly held by liberal standard-bearer Teddy Kennedy—a victory that ended the Democrats' filibuster-proof "supermajority" in that legislative body and imperiled even the Democrats' watered-down health reform.

The Postscript (written in the first week of May 2010) details some of the main policy developments in the Obama administration between late December 2009, when I finished work on this book, and early May 2010, when this book went to press. Picking up on my sixth caveat, the Postscript records and reflects on what I call "the sorry surrender of the so-called radical Left" and notes the rise of angry right-wing fake populism in the void left by the abject pacification of left-progressive movements in the Age of Obama.

As I write these words on the morning of May 7, 2010, an essay in my e-mail inbox reflects on the conservative nothingness of the White House's recent fake-progressive claims to be responding to legitimate popular outrage by seriously regulating the leading archparasitic financial firms that crashed the economy in 2008 and 2009 and that can be expected to create another major financial meltdown in the not-so-distant future. As left economist Robin Hahnel noted:

> We are now witnessing the kind of political maneuvering you would expect . . . from the Obama Administration and the US Congress. *Speeches designed to assuage a furious public, followed by legislation designed to please their paymasters on Wall Street* [emphasis added]. When all is said and done the big holding banks will be even bigger and therefore less likely to be permitted to fail. Commercial and investment banking will still be tied at the hip. Trading in highly profitable, esoteric financial products, that have no social value whatsoever but put the financial system at great risk, will continue. And regulatory powers will be more concentrated in the hands of the Federal Reserve Bank, which Wall Street captured long ago. In short, financial reform will be a fig leaf in the US, leaving the financial system just as prone to crisis as it was before September 2008. The only question will be what the next asset bubble looks like, and how long it will take to grow and burst.[10]

Plus ca change plus c'est la meme chose.[11] Relevant left-progressive anger at this and other cold state-capitalist realities at the heart of the Obama administration is hard to find as more Americans support the right-wing Tea Party "movement" than the president on major issues and as America's resurgent right gears up for victory in the upcoming midterm elections of November 2010.[12]

Iowa City, IA
May 7, 2010

Introduction

"An Instant Overhaul for Tainted Brand America"

In 1985, the clever antitelevision writer Neil Postman dissected the authoritarian nightmare that is modern U.S. political advertising. The television commercial, Postman noted, is the antithesis of the rational popular consideration that leading early philosophers of Western economic life took to be the enlightened essence of capitalism. "Its principal theorists, even its most prosperous practitioners," Postman observed, "believed capitalism to be based on the idea that both buyer and seller are sufficiently mature, well-informed and reasonable to engage in transactions of mutual self-interest." Furthermore,

> the theory states, in part, that competition in the marketplace requires that the buyer not only knows what is good for him but also what is good. If the seller produces nothing of value, as determined by a rational marketplace, then he loses out. It is the assumption of rationality among buyers that spurs competitors to become winners, and winners to keep on winning. Where it is assumed that a buyer is unable to make rational decisions, laws are passed to invalidate transactions, as, for example, those which prohibit children from making contracts. In America, there even exists in law a requirement that sellers must tell the truth about their products, for if the buyer has no protection from false claims, rational decision-making is seriously impaired. . . . The distance between rationality and advertising is now so wide, that it is difficult to remember that there once existed a connection between them. Today, on television commercials, propositions are as scarce as unattractive people.

The television commercial, Postman noted, makes "hash" out of the capitalist assumption of intelligent and informed consumer sovereignty. It undercuts the notion of rational claims, based on serious propositions and evidence. In the place of cogent language and logical discourse, it substitutes evocative imagery and suggestive emotionalism.

When political success came to revolve largely around the same manipulative antienlightened methods prevalent in commodity advertising, Postman observed, the same sorry fate fell to "capitalist democracy's" assumption of rational and informed voters. Like the bamboozled commodity purchasers propagandized by radio and television ads, voters are subjects of persuasion through deception instead of through respectful and sensible communication. Candidate marketing makes hash out of the myth of voter sovereignty in "democratic" politics.[1]

"The Brand Relaunch of the Year"

This is why we didn't hear Barack Obama's many highly educated liberal supporters say much about the interesting fact that Obama was selected by Association of National Advertisers (ANA) as the "Marketer of the Year" on the eve of the 2008 presidential election. According to the ANA's trade journal *Advertising Age* two weeks before the presidential election, "Sen. Barack Obama has shown he's already won over the nation's brand builders."

Angus Macaulay, vice president of Rodale Marketing Solutions, told *Advertising Age* that Obama's campaign was "something we can all learn from as marketers." AOL "Platform A" president Linda Clalirizio praised Obama for doing "a great job of going from a relative unknown to a household name to being a candidate for president."[2]

Six days after the election, *Advertising Age* heralded "Brand Obama" as a "case study in audacious marketing." The journal praised Obama's "messaging consistency" and "communications success," placing special emphasis on the Obama campaign's "boldness, that trait that happens to be the most important for anyone trying to build a brand now, in a chaotic time when many will be tempted to shelve innovation and creativity to take up defensive postures."

"And at same time Mr. Obama was building his brand with grand gestures," the journal added, "his campaign demonstrated an understanding of ground-level marketing strategies and tactics, everything from audience segmentation and database management to the creation and maintenance of online communities."[3]

Advertising Age was taken with the next president's success in wrapping the authoritarian American System in more outwardly democratic and progressive clothing. Expecting Obama to repair the damage done to that system and the U.S. public relations image by the brutal and clumsy excesses of the brazenly imperial Cheney-Bush gang, the trade journal hailed the president-elect for producing "An Instant Overhaul for Tainted Brand America." The journal quoted David Brain, CEO of the global public relations firm Edelman Europe, Middle East, and Africa, on how "the election and nomination process is the brand relaunch of the year. Brand USA. It's just fantastic."[4] Nick Ragone, senior vice president of client development at the leading global advertising firm Omnicom Group's Ketchum (also a dilettante "presidential historian"), told *Advertising Age* that "we've put a new face on [America] and that face happens to be African-American." In Ragone's view, Obama's racial identity "takes a lot of the hubris and arrogance of the last eight years and starts to put it in the rearview mirror for us."[5] In a similar Orwellian vein, Harvard Business School professor and former WWP Group (a global advertising firm) board member John Quelch (co-author of a recent book bearing the oxymoronic title *Greater Good: How Good Marketing Makes for Better Democracy*) told the advertising trade journal that "the election result zero-bases the image of the United States worldwide. We have a clean slate with which to work," Welch added. "Let us hope the opportunity is not squandered the way it was after 9/11."[6]

Carolyn Carter, London-based president and CEO of Grey Group Europe, Middle East, and Africa (creator of the popular teeth-rotting "Coke Zero" ad campaign for northern Europe), told *Advertising Age* that "the last eight years broke faith in Brand America, and people want that faith restored."[7] Enter Obama, who is "almost like Che Guevera, in a good way," according to *Foreign Policy* magazine's Web editor Blake Hounshell. "He has icon status," Hounshell told *Advertising Age*, "with the all the art[work] around the world of his face." The difference is that Che boldly inspired radical challenges to the American Empire but Obama inspires captivation with the corporate-imperial United States and its supposed self-reinvention as a land of progressive democracy and endless possibility.

Scott Kronick, global marketing firm Ogilvy PR's Beijing-based president, put it all in idealistic terms for *Advertising Age*. Obama's triumph, he said, "sends a strong message to the world that despite what many people believe and feel, . . . America can be very open, democratic, and progressive."[8]

"Rebranding the U.S. with Obama"

Advertising executives weren't the only ones who saw Obama's ascendancy as useful for the project of giving the United States a public relations makeover. In an opinion piece titled "Rebranding the U.S. with Obama," just days before the election, "liberal" *New York Times* columnist Nicholas Kristof exulted over how the election of a black president with an Islamic name would enhance the ability of the United States to advance its supposedly noble and humanitarian ideas and essence abroad. "If this election goes as the polls suggest," Kristof opined, "we may find a path to restore some of America's global influence—and thus to achieve some of our international objectives—in part because the world is concluding that America can, after all see beyond a person's epidermis."[9]

In a column titled "The Obama Dividend," published three days after the election, Kristof celebrated the election for giving new substance to the notion of America as an equal opportunity society. "We Americans have periodically betrayed the idea of equality and opportunity," Kristof exulted, "but on Tuesday we powerfully revitalized it."[10]

Digging in the same vein, "liberal" *Times* columnist Gail Collins followed the election by saying that Americans "can bask in the realization that there are billions of people around the planet who loathed our country last week but are now in awe of its capacity to rise above historic fears and prejudices, that *again the United States will have a president the world wants to follow*" (emphasis added). Collins shared with Kristof the standard underlying imperial assumption that "we" (in reality the U.S. foreign policy establishment elite and the White House) *should be followed* because "we" have the best interests of the world at heart—a supposition most of the world has long rejected, however happy much of the planet may have felt about the imminent disappearance of the dangerous "cowboys" George W. Bush and Dick Cheney.[11]

"President Obama Does One Thing and Brand Obama Gets You to Believe Another"

Advertising Age and the two columnists at the "liberal" *New York Times* might have said more, of course. They might have added that image, public relations, marketing, words, speeches, symbolism, and rhetoric are only skin deep. They might have added that the real change hoped for by tens of millions of Americans who voted for Obama and by many who applauded his election around the world was significant and substantive improvement in their real-life circumstances and a related concrete increase in democracy and justice against the combined and interrelated policies and imperatives of empire, militarism, capitalism, and inequality. They might have noted the difference between an ethno-cultural identity change in a top political office and deep and meaningful social and material change in the real-life circumstances of ordinary people after the "brand overhaul." They might have mentioned the potential deadly illusion involved in the "rebranding"—the creation and encouragement of a childish and fantastic mass belief in democratic change that cloaks the persistence and even the deepening, under new, fake-progressive cover, of steep and oppressive social hierarchies and doctrines. They might have noted the fantastic, even childish nature of the notion that significant social and democratic change can come through the replacement of one set of corporate- and military-vetted officeholders with another such set.

They might have looked ahead—as some observers did—to the profound authoritarian danger posed by what left author Chris Hedges would soon call "Brand Obama." As Hedges, author of a recent book titled *Empire of Illusion*, would write in May 2009, four months into the "rebranding":

> Barack Obama is a brand. And the Obama brand is designed to make us feel good about our government while corporate overlords loot the Treasury, our elected officials continue to have their palms greased by armies of corporate lobbyists, our corporate media diverts us with gossip and trivia and our imperial wars expand in the Middle East. Brand Obama is about being happy consumers. We are entertained. We feel hopeful. We like our president. We believe he is like us. But like all branded products spun out from the manipulative world of corporate advertising, we are being duped into doing and supporting a lot of things that are not in our interest.
>
> . . . The Obama campaign was named *Advertising Age*'s marketer of the year for 2008 and edged out runners-up Apple and Zappos.com. Take it from the professionals. Brand Obama is a marketer's dream. President Obama does one thing and Brand Obama gets you to believe another. This is the essence of successful advertising. You buy or do what the advertiser wants because of how they can make you feel.

The Obama illusion was symptomatic, Hedges concluded, of a long-standing national "junk politics" that "personalizes and moralizes issues rather than clarifying them," emphasizing narrowly defined emotional response feelings over rational and honest confrontation with harsh, interrelated realities of socioeconomic disparity, corporate rule, and empire. Dedicated to "effectively mask[ing] the wanton internal destruction and theft being carried out by our corporate state," this junk politics is "about keeping us in a perpetual state of childishness."[12]

"Making the Burdens
Yet to Come More Bearable"

But, of course, none of these dark thoughts were mentionable within the pages of the openly capitalist *Advertising Age* or for that matter the supposedly liberal and even "left" (according to the American right) *New York Times*. The real-world ideological orientation of these and other leading opinion-forming U.S. institutions has nothing to do with empowering domestic and global masses over and against corporate elites and imperial masters.

Committed to the preservation of existing power relations, that orientation was suggested in a statement from the *Times* editorial board three weeks before Obama's inauguration. In a December 22, 2008, editorial entitled "The Printing Press Cure," the *Times* explained that Obama had to walk a fine line in relation to the badly damaged domestic business order and recession he was inheriting from George W. Bush. The next president would need, the *Times* felt, to embrace a level of government intervention that was adequate to save the profits system while distancing himself from democratic pledges that might encourage the citizenry to resist. "As president," the *Times* lectured, "Mr. Obama will have to convey optimism without over-promising. He will have to inspire confidence, even in the absence of a dramatic turnaround—which is simply not on the cards." The editorial ended on an interesting note: "While Mr. Obama must continue to level with the American people—the economy is unlikely to turn up until 2010 at the earliest, and even then it will probably rebound slowly—his near-term moves will go a long way towards *making the burdens yet to come more bearable*."[13] Translated, the *Times* felt it was Obama's job—on the model of Franklin Delano Roosevelt during the 1930s—to prevent the citizenry's anger and struggles (under a dramatically failing capitalism) from coalescing into popular rebellion. The *Times* editors felt that Obama's proper role would be to stop the deepening economic crisis (imposed by capital) from sparking a powerful new working class movement. To repeat the words of the *Times'* editorial, it was all about "*making the burdens yet to come more bearable* [emphasis added]."

Interestingly, the *Times* had a different take on Obama's duties to the American Empire. The editors' emphasis on Obama's need to "realistically" downsize popular hopes in regard to domestic policy stood in curious contrast to the grandiose expectations the paper's opinion authorities held for Obama's obligation to repair and expand the power of America's military. In a November 16, 2008, editorial entitled "A Military for a Dangerous World," the *Times* editors explained:

As president, Barack Obama will face the most daunting and complicated national security challenges in more than a generation—and he will inherit a military that is critically ill-equipped for the task.

Troops and equipment are so overtaxed by President Bush's disastrous Iraq war that *the Pentagon does not have enough of either* [emphasis added] for the fight in Afghanistan, the war on terror's front line, let alone to confront the next threats.

This is intolerable. . . . The Obama administration will have to rebuild and significantly reshape the military. We do not minimize the difficulty of this task. Even if money were limitless, planning is extraordinarily difficult in a world with no single enemy and many dangers.

The *Times* editors recommended:

- Provision of "sufficient troops, ships and planes to reassure allies in Asia, the Middle East, and Europe"
- Efforts to "ensure [the Pentagon's] ability—so-called lift capacity—to move enormous quantities of men and material quickly around the world and to supply them when necessary by sea"
- "A military that is large enough and mobile enough to deter enemies"
- "A significantly larger ground force"
- Provision of "new skills" to fight not just "traditional wars against hostile regimes" but also "guerilla insurgencies wielding terror tactics or possibly weapons of mass destruction"
- "Hiring more linguists, training more special forces, and building expertise in civilian affairs and cultural awareness" to more effectively conduct "counter-insurgency" wars and occupations that "protect the civilian population and legitimize the indigenous government" abroad
- The training of military forces to be "prepared to sustain long-term operations [occupations]"[14]

Taken together, these two postelection *Times* editorials were a striking example of what Dr. Martin Luther King Jr., during the middle and late 1960s, called America's "perverted priorities." The nation's leading newspaper called for cautious, conservative, and hope-chilling modesty when it came to addressing domestic pain and inequality. It advocated expansion of Superpower's already gargantuan capacity to deliver death and destruction across a world that is routinely described as "dangerous" in the standard paranoid parlance of imperial militarism.

So far, as of this book's writing (over the first year of Obama's presidency) the *Times* editorial board's hopes—not those of most of the American and global citizens who elected Obama and praised his ascendancy—have been met on the whole. The real-world President Obama has advanced the twisted priorities of empire, war, inequality, and oppression even as Brand Obama has helped make the burdens imposed by the ruling class and its global empire seem "more bearable" to suffering masses at home and abroad.

Nevertheless, the afterglow of the brand relaunch has faded considerably in the wake of one popular betrayal after another. The president-elect's and then new president's once practically messianic sheen has dulled considerably, along with his approval numbers. He has been increasingly revealed to be yet another in a long line of calculating, corporate-captive politicians who might talk a good game on behalf of "We, the People" but who is really a servant and indeed an agent of existing authoritarian domestic and global power structures and ideologies. This is a potentially positive development. It is essential for a large number of Americans to understand him in this light if U.S. citizens are going to open new and exciting possibilities for a kind of progressive politics that can bring about real, grassroots "change from the bottom up"—something very different from the corporate-crafted, candidate-centered, narrow-spectrum, and "two-party" "quadrennial electoral extravaganzas" that have for too long passed as the only politics that really matter in the United States.

1
Business Rule as Usual

People everywhere [have] learned a blunt lesson about power, who has it and who doesn't. They [have] watched Washington run to rescue the very financial interests that caused the catastrophe. They [have] learned that government has plenty of money to spend when the right people want it.
—*William Greider, March 2009*[1]

Everyone's back to business as usual. . . . Not a single CEO from a top bank attended. The [Obama] speech [to Wall Street] sank with scant notice because there has been so little action to back it up and because its conciliatory stance was tone-deaf to the anger beyond the financial district.
—*Frank Rich, September 20, 2009*[2]

I can't tell you how many foreign leaders who are heads of center-right governments say to me, I don't understand why people would call you socialist. In my country, you'd be considered a conservative.
—*President Barack Obama, Sept. 20, 2009*[3]

The architects of policy protect their own interests, no matter how grievous the effect on others.
—*Adam Smith, 1776*[4]

Getting Things Done
with a Plutocratic Violin

Two and a half weeks after Barack Obama's victory in the 2008 presidential election, David Rothkopf, a former Clinton administration official, commented with a musical metaphor on the president-elect's corporatist and militarist transition team and cabinet appointments. Obama, Rothkopf told

9

the *New York Times*, was following "the violin model: you hold power with the left hand and you play the music with the right."[5] In other words, "you" gain and hold the presidency with populace-pleasing progressive-sounding rhetoric, but you govern, you make policy, in service to existing dominant corporate, state, and military institutions and ideologies.

The Obama' administration's record over its first sixteen months has been richly consistent with Rothkopf's analysis. It's been "the violin model" with a vengeance. Obama has lectured Wall Street on the immorality of its bonuses and visited hard recession-hit towns such as Elkhart, Indiana, and Pomona, California, to show solidarity with downtrodden working people. And then he gave yet more of the public treasury and commons away to the privileged few, justifying the handouts as a noble expression of his "sensible," "realistic," and "pragmatic" commitment to rising above ideological divisions to "get things done" for the American people.

Funny how the nation's "pragmatist" in chief has kept getting things done for the rich and powerful above all. My mind and soul have recurrently gone numb as yet one more populist-, progressive-, and peaceful-sounding Obama campaign promise after another have been crushed by the cold imperatives of business and imperial rule during the first year of Obama's presidency. This chapter and Chapter 3 (the latter on "health reform" in the Age of Obama) focus on the administration's service to the dominant business class and financial elite in regard to domestic economic and social policy. Chapter 2 takes up the intimately related story of Obama's foreign policy. Chapters 4 and 5 look at similar themes of progressive betrayal and deceptive "rebranding" in relation to questions of race, ethnicity, gender, gay rights, and civil liberties.

Change Means More of the Same

Keeping Perpetrators Afloat

Consistent with his description of himself as a "New [that is, conservative and pro-corporate] Democrat" in March 2009,[6] Obama has spent more than $10 trillion of federal money on further taxpayer handouts to the giant Wall Street firms that spent millions on his campaign and that drove the economy over the cliff in the first decade of the new millennium. The new president was too attached to those firms and to their so-called free-market ideology to undertake the elementary bank nationalizations and public financial restructuring that were required to put the nation's credit system on a sound and socially responsible basis. Obama's plan to guarantee the financial, insurance, and real estate industries' toxic, hyperinflated assets while keeping existing Wall Street management in place amounted to a giant effort (according to liberal economist James K. Galbraith) to "keep perpetrators afloat" at a giant cost in taxpayer dollars.[7] Liberal economist and *New York Times* columnist Paul Krugman was "filled with a sense of despair" by Obama's bank rescue plan, which, Krugman noted, "recycles Bush administration policy—specifically the 'cash for trash' plan proposed, then abandoned, six months ago by then-Treasury secretary Henry Paulsen."[8]

The plan has rewarded reckless and selfish investor-class behavior with what is supposed to be the people's money. Under the scheme unveiled in March 2009, the public was put on the hook to the tune of $1 trillion. Krugman described this scheme as a coin flip in which "investors win if it's heads and taxpayers lose if it's tails."[9] As the *Times* noted while the full-blown Obama phase of the federal Wall Street bailout was being unveiled in the early spring, "The Treasury and the Federal Reserve will be offering a least a tablespoon of financial sugar for every teaspoon of risk that investors agree to swallow" by buying up the toxic mortgage assets that the investor class created in the first place.[10] The government ("identical to the people in a functioning democracy," as Noam Chomsky noted) was slated to take more than 90 percent of the risk, but private investors would reap at least half the reward.[11]

Meanwhile, the underlying insolvency of the banks went largely unresolved, a problem the new administration hoped citizens would forget about as they got dazzled and bamboozled by its fancy and obscure plan. "In the end," even the *Times* editorial board noted, "there is no getting around firing the executives at failing banks, acknowledging the losses, wiping out the shareholders and then deciding how the government can restructure the institutions."[12] Beneath claims of allegiance to "free-market" ideals and "private enterprise," the administration's "bank rescue" design—described by former U.S. labor secretary Robert Reich as a continuation of "the most expensive tax-supported fiasco in history"—boiled down to a traditional, if rather extreme, exercise in Wall Street welfare: socialism for the rich, market discipline and capitalism for the rest. As Reich also noted, the plan threatened to weaken "the public's confidence that its money isn't being thrown down a rathole," undermining Obama's ability to undertake "other ambitious undertakings such as health care or education or the environment."[13]

According to the *New York Times*, Obama's corporate-Democratic Treasury secretary Timothy Geithner's bailout plan reflected a triumph for unfettered capitalist prerogatives inside the new White House. *Times* reporters

Stephen Labaton and Edmund Andrews noted that Geithner "prevailed in opposing tougher conditions on financial institutions that were sought by presidential aides, including [top political and media expert] David Axelrod." Geithner fought successfully "against more severe limits on executive pay for companies receiving government aid." He overcame "those who wanted to dictate how banks would spend their money. And he prevailed over top administration aides who wanted to replace bank executives and wipe out shareholders at institutions receiving aid." According to administration and congressional officials, Geithner told Obama that "that plan would not work" if it was burdened with "too much government involvement in the affairs of the companies"—companies who deeply interfered with ordinary Americans' capacity to keep their heads above water. The new Treasury chief, whose nomination was applauded by Wall Street, "also expressed concern that too many government controls would discourage private investors from participating."

Geithner grave concern over the negative impact of government—the people in a functioning democracy—won out over more image-sensitive Obama aides who worried that "rising joblessness, populist outrage over Wall Street bonuses and expensive perks, and the poor management of last year's bailouts could feed a potent political reaction" if the new White House failed to "demand sacrifices from the companies that receive federal money."[14] "For all its boldness," Labaton and Andrews noted, the Obama bailout "largely repeat[ed] the Bush administration's approach of deferring to many of the same companies and executives who had peddled risky loans and investments at the heart of the crisis and failed to foresee many of the problems plaguing the markets."[15]

Reinventing the Same System

Early in April 2009, the *New York Times* published an article with an ironic title: "In Cuba, Change Means More of the Same." This "news" item reported that "rather than dismantling Cuba's socialist framework," Cuba's president Raul Castro "seems to be trying to make it work more efficiently."[16] Castro, the *Times* reported, sought to keep power concentrated "at the top."

But what had President Barack Obama—Mr. "Change" himself—tried to accomplish other than to make the American corporate profits system "work more efficiently" without "dismantling the [capitalist] framework" and with power (and wealth) still concentrated "at the top"? As the *Times* acknowledged in an article titled "English-Speaking Capitalism on Trial," Obama and his neoliberal partner Gordon Brown, the British prime minister, had "focused on ways of revitalizing the [existing] system. . . . Even as both men have embarked on enormous increases in public-sector spending," *Times* correspondents John Burns and Landon Thomas reported, "they have maintained that the solutions to the crisis lie in reawakening the markets and recapitalizing the banks rather than tearing at the system's foundations. And both, when they respond to private anger at the private sector, have seemed *more geared to managing anger than stoking it*"[17] [emphasis added]. As prolific Marxist geographer David Harvey observed on the left television news and commentary show *Democracy Now* in April 2009, "What [the Obama team is] trying to do is to reinvent the same system"—to "reconstitute the same sort of capitalism we have had over and over again over the last thirty years in a slightly more regulated, benevolent form" that didn't "challenge the fundamentals."[18]

The Banks "Own the Place"

Consistent with Harvey's judgment, the Obama White House's mild June 2009 plan to "re-regulate U.S. financial markets for the 21st century" left the extreme power of the nation's elite "bankster" class intact. While praising the Obama plan's efforts to create a strong consumer financial regulatory body, to reduce speculative betting with higher leverage standards, to prevent predatory and reckless lending, and to advance the White House's power to take over failing, systemically significant firms, liberal Washington, DC–based corporate and financial reform activist Robert Weissman noted that the administration's plan contained four basic flaws that would leave the financial sector and the broader economy vulnerable to future crises. First, it did "not propose to do anything serious about executive pay and top-level compensation for financial firms," failing thereby to address basic questions of economic justice and leaving intact a "Wall Street bonus culture" that "gives traders and executives alike an incentive to take big bets—because they get massive payoff if things go well, and don't suffer if they go bad, or go bad sometime in the future."

Second, Obama proposed no serious structural reform of the financial industry. His refusal to return to "Glass-Steagall" principles by reseparating (on the model of the 1930s Glass-Steagall Act, repealed under Bill Clinton) commercial banking from other financial activities, including the speculative world of investment banking, and to reduce the size of gargantuan ("too big and interconnected [and powerful] to fail") financial institutions, promised to leave the nation's economy (and politics) far too beholden to concentrated wealth and power.

Third, the plan's regulatory scheme included a dangerous "regulatory exemption for customized derivatives—a loophole that will create lots of business for corporate lawyers ready to change terms in derivative contracts so that they differ somewhat from standardized terms." It also failed to ban "classes of dangerous financial instruments that cannot be justified," such as the notorious credit default swap (denounced by international financial mogul George Soros as a "weapon of financial mass destruction") and "to require that exotic financial instruments be subjected to pre-approval requirements."

Fourth, Obama's financial plan contained no measure "for giving consumers the power to organize themselves to advance their own interests. Simply mandating that financial firms include in bills and statements (whether mailed or e-mailed) an invitation to join an independent consumer organization would facilitate tens of thousands of consumers—and likely many more—banding together to make sure the regulators do their job, and to prevent Wall Street from 'innovating' the next trick to scam borrowers and investors." Advocates like Weissman called for this basic mandate, to no avail.[19]

Other key deletions were noted by former Wall Street economist and Distinguished University of Missouri Research Professor Michael Hudson: proposals to repeal federal legislation used by the Bush administration to nullify the power of local state prosecutors to investigate and take legal action against financial malfeasance; measures to properly fund federal agencies charged with fraud reduction and other aspects of meaningful regulation; proposals to "counter extortionate credit-card practices by re-introducing anti-usury laws"; proposals to the "repeal of the pro-creditor reversal that Congress passed in 2005 [with then U.S. senator Barack Obama's support] in response to lobbying by the credit card and banking industry" (thereby making it more difficult for personal debtors to declare bankruptcy and preventing courts from "rolling back debt to the population's ability to pay"); proposals to "reform the tax system that has distorted the financial system to promote predatory extractive debt, not productive industrial credit."[20]

All of these critical omissions were highly predictable given that, as Senator Majority Whip Richard Durbin candidly noted in the spring of 2009, "The banks are still the most powerful lobby on Capitol Hill. And they frankly own the place."[21] Wall Street invested $5 billion in U.S. politics between 1999 and 2009 and was the leading campaign finance sponsor of Hillary Clinton, John McCain, and Barack Obama during the 2008 election cycle.[22] Hudson's essay on Obama's "false financial reform" (Greider's description) bore a depressing title: "Obama's (Latest) Surrender to Wall Street."

Revealingly enough, Obama's financial plan won approval from the leading neoliberal Anglo-American paper, the *Financial Times*. Praising Obama's proposals for "marry[ing] dynamism and safety," the financial organ noted that "they work largely with the grain of the market as it exists today, seeking to make it more stable and better at pricing risk by increasing capital. The plan does not ban dangerous financial products, break up complex financial institutions or enforce any structural division of the industry along the lines of the Glass-Steagall Act that followed the crash of 1929." According to *Financial Times* correspondent Edward Luce, the Wall Street–friendly Obama "reforms" "embodie[d] the art of what is politically possible," with the boundaries of acceptable change determined through "months of scrambled consultation between the administration of Barack Obama and industry representatives" and by "a skillfully threaded series of compromises between a diverse galaxy of regulators, Capital Hill barons, and industry lobby groups." Luce was pleased at the absence of any proposal to "return to a two-tier banking system" and of "any trace of the original plan to produce a drastic consolidation of banking regulators." The paper's editors praised Obama's regulatory reforms as "comprehensive and careful."

"Certainly," Luce exulted, "most of the financial sector lobby community is happy with what has emerged."[23] Speaking at Riverside Church in New York City's Harlem in June 2009, Noam Chomsky noted that the government controls required to prevent financial crises are "contrary to the deregulatory rage that was . . . carried forward by the Clinton administration, *under the leadership of those who Obama has now called upon to put band-aids on the disaster they helped create* [emphasis added]."[24]

Absolving the Agents of Crisis

The financial lobby was certainly also pleased with Obama's repetition of a key theme from his inaugural address in making his case for "meaningful financial reform." The president tried to make it seem as if all Americans were equally implicated in the nation's financial breakdown and that therefore there was no one in particular to condemn. "A culture of irresponsibility took root from Wall Street to Washington to Main Street," Obama claimed. "And a regulatory system basically crafted in the wake of a 20th century economic crisis—the Great Depression—was overwhelmed by the speed, scope and sophistication of a 21st century global economy."[25] But as liberal left journalist William Greider noted in mid-June 2009, Obama was here advancing a whitewashed history that egregiously deleted the very predominant role played by structurally superempowered economic and political elites, including top members of his own heavily Wall Street–minted economic team:

"That is not what happened, to put it charitably. . . . The regulatory system was not overwhelmed by historic forces. It was systematically gutted and dismantled by the government in Washington at the behest of the banking interests. If Obama wants details, he can consult his economic advisors—[Lawrence] Summers-[Timothy] Geithner—who participated directly as accomplices in unwinding the prudential rules and regulations." Obama's "version of events" reminded Greider "of what compliant politicians and opinion leaders said after the war in Iraq they had endorsed turned disastrous: 'Hey, we were all fooled.'"[26]

According to Obama, the day before the first version of his financial reform plan was rolled out, it was all about getting the best deal possible for the American people in the real world. "We want to do it right," Obama said. "But we don't want to tilt at windmills."[27] This was a graphic statement of his apparent belief that the lords of finance represent a higher power than the presidency, the federal government, and, dare we say, the American people. It reflected a rather cowardly view for a president who had campaigned on a promise to place the needs of ordinary working- and middle-class Americans above those of the elite financial firms and who claimed in his election night speech that his victory proved the strength of a powerful democracy in which "anything was possible."

It was all more typical eloquent evasion from Obama, consistent with the notion that his election was largely an elite-managed rebranding dedicated to the persistence of the old corporate-imperial regime in the deceptive new rebel's clothes of democratic "change." The new president may have gotten into the Oval Office with progressive- and democratic-sounding rhetoric, but once there he showed little interest in even remotely challenging what Edward Herman and David Peterson call the "unelected dictatorship of money," which exercises a permanent behind-the-scenes veto power over any who would foolishly seek "to change the foreign or domestic priorities of the imperial U.S. regime."[28]

If "Obama were to tell the truth now about what went wrong in the financial system," Greider noted, "he would face a far larger political problem trying to clean up the mess." He would also face the political hyperpotent disapproval of the nation's leading economic powers that be. Given his epic distaste for conflict and radical change, much less revolution—"deeply conservative" traits that were naturally downplayed during a campaign that sought to rally support from millions of understandably angry and "fighting mad" voters—Obama opted instead "for smooth talk and some fuzzy reforms that effectively evade the nasty complexities of our situation. . . . Obama's so-called reform," Greider observed, "is literally 'kicking the can down the road,' as he likes to say about other problems. In the long run, it will haunt the country because it fails to confront the true nature of the disorders."[29]

Screwing Labor

Obama's federal restructuring of the auto industry in the winter and spring of 2009 was richly consistent with his "financial reform." Reflecting the persistent victory of the "low-road" corporate-globalizationist agenda in national economic policy, it wiped out tens of thousands of livable wage union jobs and led to a wave of wage and pension cuts for current and retired autoworkers. The administration's refusal to impose such draconian restructuring on the elite financial firms that collapsed the economy and hence the auto industry reflected those firms' remarkable political power and economic reach. It likely also reflected the fact there were no great institutions of working-class power like the United Auto Workers (UAW) to be undermined on Wall Street.

"Ruining the Lives of the Workforce"

Consistent with the suspicion of a pro-capital and antilabor agenda under the new corporate-Democratic White House, President Obama quickly betrayed his campaign pledges to (1) advance an elementary and overdue labor law reform (the Employee Free Choice Act) that would have fundamentally boosted labor's chances of overcoming employer opposition to basic union organizing and collective bargaining rights and (2) pursue the renegotiation of the North American Free Trade Agreement to include stronger labor and environmental protections.[30]

Sadly, enough given the prolabor sentiments he expressed during the campaign and the strong union support he got before and during the election, Obama's auto bailout plan subsidized GM's efforts to move yet more of its manufacturing jobs abroad. As Greider explained:

> So this is how the auto bailout will work. American taxpayers pump tens of billions into rescuing General Motors from bankruptcy. Then GM pays us back by shipping more jobs overseas—the equivalent of four assembly plants. The federal money will directly subsidize more imports from abroad, enabling GM to double its car production in Mexico, South Korea and China and selling the cars into the U.S. market.

. . . GM's restructuring plan envisions a doubling of the vehicles it will import from overseas factories, from 372,000 to 737,000, in the next four years. GM's imported cars—already 15.5 percent of its domestic sales—will rise to 23.5 percent.

"The overall number of vehicles GM will be importing in 2014 represents the production of four assembly plants, the same number that GM plans to close in the United States," UAW legislative director Alan Reuther noted. People already outraged by the bank bailouts should save some anger for the carmakers. "GM should not be taking taxpayers' money simply to finance the outsourcing of jobs to other countries," the UAW insisted.

. . . The outlines of the auto deal suggest the president is sticking with Rubinomics. Will other Democrats be brave enough to stand in his way?[31]

No relevant example of such courage emerged.

Obama's betrayal of American autoworkers reached levels that struck Chomsky as "surreal." In the summer of 2009, the business press reported that Obama's transportation secretary was traveling abroad in pursuit of contracts with European manufacturers to construct high-speed rail projects with federal funds designated by Congress for U.S. economic stimulus! U.S. taxpayer funding for badly needed domestic infrastructural development would perhaps go to Spanish and other European corporations. "At the same time," Chomsky noted, "Washington is busy dismantling leading sectors of U.S. industry, ruining the lives of the workforce, families and communities. Surely," Chomsky reflected, "the auto industry could be reconstructed, using its highly skilled workforce to produce what the country and the world needs—and soon, if we are to have some hope of averting major catastrophe. It has been done before, after all. But all such matters are off the agenda."[32]

Also in the category of the corporate-authoritarian surreal: Under the terms of the bankruptcy that the Obama White House and its "Car Czar" Steven Rattner worked out with General Motors at the end of May 2009, the company was permitted to grab workers' pension funds to pay off Wall Street. As progressive muckraker and expert corporate malfeasance-chronicler Greg Palast explained in advance of the deal:

Screw the autoworkers.

They may be crying about General Motors' bankruptcy today. But dumping 40,000 of the last 60,000 union jobs into a mass grave won't spoil Jamie Dimon's day.

Dimon is the CEO of JP Morgan Chase bank. While GM workers are losing their retirement health benefits, their jobs, their life savings; while shareholders are getting zilch and many creditors getting hosed, a few privileged GM lenders—led by Morgan and Citibank—expect to get back 100% of their loans to GM, a stunning $6 billion.

The way these banks are getting their $6 billion bonanza is stone cold illegal.

I smell a rat.

Stevie the Rat, to be precise. Steven Rattner, Barack Obama's "Car Czar"—the man who essentially ordered GM into bankruptcy this morning.

When a company goes bankrupt, everyone takes a hit: fair or not, workers lose some contract wages, stockholders get wiped out and creditors get fragments of what's left. That's the law. What workers don't lose are their pensions (including old-age health funds) already taken from their wages and held in their name.

But not this time. Stevie the Rat has a different plan for GM: grab the pension funds to pay off Morgan and Citi.

Here's the scheme: Rattner is demanding the bankruptcy court simply wipe away the money GM owes workers for their retirement health insurance. Cash in the insurance fund would be replaced by GM stock. The percentage may be 17% of GM's stock—or 25%. Whatever, 17% or 25% is worth, well . . . just try paying for your dialysis with 50 shares of bankrupt auto stock.

Yet Citibank and Morgan, says Rattner, should get their whole enchilada— $6 billion right now and in cash—from a company that can't pay for auto parts or worker eye exams.[33]

"Not Something You Might Have Expected from an Administration Elected with Union Support"

Five and a half months later, the *New York Times* chief financial columnist, Floyd Norris, marveled at how the Obama administration was "teaching capitalism to the carmakers." Back "in the bad old days, when supposed capitalists were running Detroit," Norris wrote, the auto industry relied on expanding volume through price cuts and "sweet lease deals," all designed to maintain cash flows and preserve market share. Faced with a "powerful" union (the UAW), the big three automakers supposedly (by Norris's account) failed to focus on capitalist profitability, which would have required closing plants and firing workers. The situation was being corrected by the Obama administration, falsely accused of "socialism." As Norris explained:

One rap on socialism has always been that governments are much more worried about jobs than profits. No politician wants to be responsible for layoffs, so the government is happy to rely on optimistic assumptions to avoid painful decisions.

That is how the term "lemon socialism" was coined.

So what happened this year?

First, the Obama administration demanded G.M. and Chrysler come up with believable strategies for getting out of the mess they were in. When those plans came back with the usual rose-tinted perspective, the administration demanded changes.

The result was a lot of job cutting, *not something you might have expected from an administration elected with union support* [emphasis added]. The unions lost their generous pay for laid-off workers. To be sure, the union health plans were not treated as harshly as some creditors were, but in the end creditors and workers all paid for the sins of past managements.[34]

In the Obama administration version of state capitalism as applied to the auto industry, the state was *more ruthlessly capitalist than the capitalists themselves.*

Insult to Injury

Team Obama added insult to injury in regard to its many supporters in the labor movement. In mid-April 2009, Obama's aides defended him against the charge that he was "wimpy" in confronting powerful institutions by praising him for "picking fights" with "main components of the Democratic base, like organized labor"[35]—as if unions instead of capitalist corporations were the real source of money and power in Washington. At the same time, Obama's tepid and undersized stimulus plan was dysfunctionally overloaded with business-friendly tax cuts and was too short on labor-intensive projects to put people to work right away. The president said nothing or close to nothing about the overdue labor law reform he had campaigned on, the Employee Free Choice Act, which ought, as Noam Chomsky argued, to have been at the heart and center of any reasonably progressive economic recovery program.[36] Revealingly enough, Obama made a public visit (in support of his stimulus bill) to a Caterpillar factory in Illinois. It was a slap in the face of two groups—the Palestinians and U.S. organized labor. A provider of bulldozers equipped and used by Israel to raze Palestinian homes to make way for illegal Israeli settlements, Caterpillar had been the first large U.S. manufacturer in decades to break a major strike with scabs.

Assaulting Public Schools
in the Name of Reform

Praised by political and media elites for the skill with which he and his handlers were "managing [betrayed popular] expectations," President Obama failed to advance elementary and urgently needed progressive measures, such as a moratorium on foreclosures, a capping of credit card interest rates and finance charges, and a rollback of capital income tax rates to 1981 (not just 1993) levels. He wouldn't let the government enter into the business of making direct mortgage loans. Even before taking office, Obama committed himself to so-called entitlement reform, code language for claiming to cut the federal deficit by chipping away at Medicare and Social Security—by taking a pound of flesh from the incomes and health of senior citizens.[37] Both before and since his inauguration, moreover, Obama has warmed business hearts and betrayed progressive supporters by advancing a "market"-oriented corporate-neoliberal K–12 schools agenda.

Educational justice advocates were understandably displeased with his appointment of Chicago Public Schools (CPS) CEO Arne Duncan to the position of education secretary in the next White House. Describing schools as stock investments, Duncan told a posh, business-sponsored "school reform" conference in May 2008 that "I am not a manager of 600 schools. I'm a portfolio manager of 600 schools and I'm trying to improve the portfolio." Obama had selected a vacuously neoliberal ally of Chicago's interlocked elite business and political class to head his push for "school reform." As left education professors Kenneth Saltman and Henry Giroux noted in December 2008:

> Obama's call for change falls flat with this appointment, not only because Duncan largely defines schools within a market-based and penal model of pedagogy, but also because he does not have the slightest understanding of schools as something other than adjuncts of the corporation at best or the prison at worst.

> Duncan, CEO of the Chicago Public Schools, presided over the implementation and expansion of an agenda that militarized and corporatized the third largest school system in the nation, one that is about 90 percent poor and nonwhite. Under Duncan, Chicago took the lead in creating public schools run as military academies, vastly expanded draconian student expulsions, instituted sweeping surveillance practices, advocated a growing police presence in the schools, arbitrarily shut down entire schools and fired entire school staffs.

. . . Duncan's neoliberal ideology is on full display in the various connections he has established with the ruling political and business elite in
Chicago. He led the Renaissance 2010 plan, which was created for Mayor
Daley by the Commercial Club of Chicago—an organization representing
the largest businesses in the city. The purpose of Renaissance 2010 was to
increase the number of high quality schools that would be subject to new
standards of accountability—a code word for legitimating more charter
schools and high stakes testing. . . . Most of the new experimental schools
have eliminated the teachers union.[38]

The interrelated hallmarks of private school graduate Duncan's six and
one-half years at the helm of CPS included school privatization, union-
busting (charter and contract schools operate union free), excessive standardized testing, authoritarian rote-memorization pedagogy, teacher-blaming,
repressive "zero tolerance," military schooling, and the rollback of community input on school decisions. "In the last couple of years," Chicago school-
teacher and activist Jesse Sharkey noted in December 2009,

> Duncan has been turning public schools over to private operators—mainly in
> the form of charter and contract schools—at a rate of about 20 per year. Dun-
> can has also resuscitated some of the worst "school reform" ideas of the 1990s,
> like firing all the teachers in low-performing schools (called "turnarounds").
> At the same time, he's eliminated many Local School Councils (LSCs) and
> made crucial decisions without public input. . . . Charter schools and test-
> score-driven school "choice" have been have been the watchwords of Duncan's
> rule in Chicago.[39]

These are also the key characteristics of Obama's national K–12 schools
policy under Duncan. Upon his federal appointment, Duncan quickly announced his intention of closing 5,000 "underperforming" public schools (to
be replaced primarily with nonunion charter and private contract schools)
over the next five years, "introducing the market model into education at,
you'd think, an unpropitious time, when the market model has brought down
the house on people's heads."[40] When Obama and Duncan came into office,
they immediately created a $4.3 billion "Race to the Top" fund. States that
embraced what the new White House called school reform qualified for
federal payments, with reform defined as "standing up to teachers' unions"
by tying teacher pay to students' standardized test scores—themselves mainly
determined (contrary to the reigning conservative, schools- and teacher-
bashing ideology) by students' socioeconomic status[41]—and by handing

over more public schools to private, nonunion, and antiunion charter management and ownership. By the end of the summer of 2009, leading Republican pundit David Brooks approvingly reported, "states across the country [were] changing their laws" to encourage privatization, "competition," and "merit pay." To prove the excellence of Obama's commitment to business-friendly education reform, Brooks cited no less a Republican than former Florida governor Jeb Bush, who said Obama's education agenda was "deserving of Republican support."[42] Sadly, Duncan and Obama's educational "vision" portends "the end of schooling as a public good and a return to the discredited and tired neoliberal model of reform that conservatives love to embrace."[43]

Socialism for the Rich and Capitalism for the Rest

Meanwhile, a rising number of citizens in "the world's richest nation" all-too-quietly faced new challenges in the struggle to keep a roof over their heads and food in their bellies. Badly damaged by a vicious 1990s welfare "reform" (elimination) that Obama had repeatedly praised as a great policy success, the nation's public family cash assistance system was too weak to match the expansion of destitution across America even as the new president advanced a new level of Wall Street welfare. As the *New York Times* reported on its top page one in late March 2009, tent cities, modern-day "Hoovervilles" for the evicted and foreclosed, had sprung up in more than a dozen U.S. cities.[44] Foreclosures dipped briefly while the mortgage companies waited for the details on Obama's tepid housing plan. But foreclosures surged again and unemployment continued to rise dramatically as Obama spoke of "glimmers of [economic] hope" and while Fed Chief Ben Bernanke claimed to discern "green shoots" of recovery.

The deepening of misery at the bottom stood in stark contrast to the restoration of opulence at the top by Bush-Paulsen-Obama-Geithner's giant cash infusion for the rich and powerful. The *New York Times* reported on page one in late April 2009 that pay at the nation's leading investment banks, after falling off in 2008, bounced back to "stratospheric" heights. Wall Street paychecks and bonuses were soaring back to 2007 levels, the *Times* noted, thanks in no small measure to the fact that the bankers could now borrow cheaply, with all the federal guarantees they'd been given. It was already "party time" again on "the Street, thanks to the $600 billion committed under the TARP, the vast credit lines proffered by the Fed, expanded F.D.I.C. guarantees, the government bailout of AIG, and the like"[45]—thanks to what might ironically be called "Temporary Assistance for Not-So-Needy Banks."

Green as in Money

And then there was Obama's betrayal of his "green" (environmentalist) voting base in service to corporate interests. Already by the middle of spring 2009, the new, rebranded corporate-neoliberal administration had dealt "a series of anti-environmental blows." It gave the green light to mountaintop-removal coal extraction in Appalachia. It refused to kill plans for offshore oil drilling. It denied endangered species protection to the gray wolf. It pushed federal subsidies for nuclear power and advanced the loophole-loaded and market-driven "carbon cap and trade" legislations (so gutted to please polluters that it will barely limit carbon emissions, if at all) instead of pushing for serious and strict regulation of carbon emission. It advanced rapacious corporate plans to "replace oil with biofuels, which will push marginal agricultural lands into production of genetically engineered and pesticide-saturated monocrops, scalping topsoil and draining dwindling water supplies across the Great Plains and Midwest" as well as to assault national forests and the public's trees.[46] It dedicated only a tiny portion of the economic stimulus bill and budget proposals to mass transit and appointed "a mediocre, Republican time-server, Ray LaHood," as transportation secretary.[47] In true neoliberal fashion, Obama in late June 2009 cited the global recession and the alleged dangers of "protectionism" to justify opposing the imposition of trade penalties on nations that refused to accept limits on global warming pollution.[48]

This occurred as the latest climate science advanced an increasingly horrific prognosis for the planet, reflecting the disturbing fact that key predicted changes (such as the retreat of Arctic glaciers) were developing more quickly than expected and that "feedback loops" amplifying the impact of anthropogenic carbon emissions were more powerful than previously understood. According to a 2007 paper in the journal *Science*, a permanent drought, bringing Dust Bowl–type conditions to the American Southwest, was now imminent "within a time frame of years to decades."[49] A report released by MIT scientists in the spring of 2009 advanced the most comprehensive modeling ever constructed on the global climate change. The report showed that "without rapid and massive action, the problem will be about twice as severe as previously estimated six years ago—and could be even worse [because] the model does not fully incorporate other positive feedbacks that can occur, for example, if increased temperatures caused large-scale melting of permafrost in arctic regions and subsequent release of large quantities of methane." A prominent earth scientist heading the MIT report said that "there's no way the world can or should take these risks" and argued that "the least-cost option to lower the risk is to start now and steadily transform the global energy system over the coming decades to low or zero greenhouse-gas-emitting technologies."[50]

There was "little sign" of any serious White House effort in that direction within or beyond the United States in the dawning Age of Obama,[51] who as a candidate branded himself to be "a green president" and spoke eloquently on the problem of global warming to enthusiastic liberal and progressive audiences in 2007 and 2008. During his remarkably well-received campaign speech in Berlin in the summer of 2008, he cast himself as a "citizen of the world," promising to lead a global reduction in carbon emissions, telling the German masses that "all nations—including my own—[must] act with the same seriousness of purpose as has your nation, and reduce the carbon we send into our atmosphere. This is the moment to give our children back their future. This is the moment to stand as one."[52] After his election, Obama won accolades from environmental progressives for repudiating the Bush administration's rejection of global climate change.

But the Democrats' Obama-led climate bill, which was still working its way through Congress as I completed this chapter in early December 2009, proposed to reduce carbon emissions by a paltry 4 percent relative to 1990 levels. This despite the facts that serious climate researchers believed that reductions of at least 40 percent were required to stop irreversible environmental ruin and that U.S. per capita carbon emission was roughly twice that of other industrialized states and many times higher that of the developing world.[53]

Thanks to the collapse of the auto industry, Obama had what progressive author and journalist David Lindorff called "a unique opportunity to compel one of the industries most responsible for the looming global ecological catastrophe to start to fix it." The new White House could have undertaken a major green conversion to the "development and production of electric vehicles and mass transit." Instead, Lindorff noted, the administration "dropped the ball and just provided a taxpayer bailout with the goal of getting the domestic auto industry back into the business of cranking out gas guzzlers."[54]

"The Leader of the 'Haves' in Their Dispute with the 'Have-Nots'"

To make matters immeasurably worse, the "green president" effectively sabotaged the global effort to reach a new treaty to reduce greenhouse gas emissions. At global climate talks in Bangkok in late September and early October 2009, the Obama administration helped move the "advanced" capitalist world backward on this critical issue. During George W. Bush and Dick Cheney's reign, European governments set themselves apart from the United States with their strong commitment to the Kyoto Protocol on global warming. European Union (EU) nations reduced their carbon emissions by 2 percent from 1990 levels, while the United States increased its emissions by 20 percent. But in Bangkok, the Obama administration succeeded in persuading the EU and the rest of the "developed world" to tear up and replace the Kyoto Accords at much-ballyhooed climate meetings in Copenhagen in December. Kyoto mandated unmistakable and binding emission-reduction targets, placing the preponderant burden of responsibility squarely on the shoulders of the wealthy nations that had created the climate crisis in the first place. The new Obama plan, by contrast, left each country free to decide how much to cut and then to submit its plan to weak international monitoring. The plan treated all nations as the same, deleting the rich countries' special responsibility. In the end, it left the world with what Naomi Klein rightly called "nothing but wishful thinking to ensure" that the planet's temperature stays below "catastrophic levels."[55] As the climate talks in Denmark loomed closer, British columnist Johann Harri noted that Obama's "environmental team" was "vandalising the vital Copenhagen conference" by insisting the United States—the world's largest carbon emitter—would not agree to any legally binding restrictions on its release of warming gases.[56]

Three weeks before Copenhagen, Obama announced that there would be no binding carbon-emission rules. "It was the admission of a massive failure," wrote German environmental commentator Christian Schwagerl. Obama "came to office promising hope and change," Schwagerl noted. "But on climate change, he has followed in the footsteps of his predecessor, George W. Bush," refusing to "take a leadership role on a problem that could shake civilization to its very core."[57]

Thanks in no small part to Obama's lack of progressive leadership, the Copenhagen conference was something of a fiasco. The three-page accord he worked out with the leaders of China, India, Brazil, and South Africa and presented as a fait accompli to the conference did not even meet the "modest expectations that leaders set for this meeting." It failed to commit either industrialized states or developing nations to firm targets for midterm or long-term greenhouse gas emissions reductions. It failed even to set a 2010 goal for reaching a binding international treaty to seal the provisions of the accord. Obama added to a palpable sense of bitterness and frustration among most of the conference's global delegates, including those from poorer nations that had been frozen out of the negotiations and that represented the leading victims of a climate crisis the richer nations (with the United States in the lead) had created. As British newspaper the *Guardian* reported:

> Barack Obama stepped into the chaotic final hours of the Copenhagen summit today saying he was convinced the world could act "boldly and decisively" on climate change.
>
> But his speech offered no indication America was ready to embrace bold measures, after world leaders had been working desperately against the clock to try to paper over an agreement to prevent two years of wasted effort—and a 10-day meeting—from ending in total collapse.
>
> He offered no further commitments on reducing emissions or on finance to poor countries beyond Hillary Clinton's announcement yesterday that America would support a $100bn global fund to help developing nations adapt to climate change.
>
> He did not even press the Senate to move ahead on climate change legislation, which environmental organizations have been urging for months.
>
> In his address, Obama did say America would follow through on his administration's clean energy agenda, and that it would live up to its pledges to the international community.
>
> "We have charted our course, we have made our commitments, and we will do what we say," Obama said.
>
> . . . But in the absence of any evidence of that commitment the words rang hollow and there was a palpable sense of disappointment in the audience.[58]

It was a pathetic, business-captive performance.

According to leading British climate activist and intellectual George Monbiot:

> The immediate reason for the failure of the [Copenhagen] talks can be summarized in two words: Barack Obama. The man elected to put aside childish things proved to be as susceptible to immediate self-interest as any other politician. Just as George Bush did in the approach to the Iraq war, Obama

went behind the backs of the UN and most of its member states and assembled a coalition of the willing to strike a deal which outraged the rest of the world. This was then presented to poorer nations without negotiation; either they signed it or they lost the adaptation funds required to help them survive the first few decades of climate breakdown.[59]

According to the *Wall Street Journal*, Obama was a "Washington liberal" but "a Copenhagen conservative," functioning as "the conservative stalwart in Copenhagen" by "supporting the least-aggressive steps, advancing the conservative position of opposition to strict world-wide limits on emissions that ask much more of developed nations than of poorer countries." Obama was serving as "the leader of the 'haves' in their dispute with the 'have-nots.'"[60]

"In a Rational World"

"In a rational world," Paul Krugman noted in September 2009, "the looming climate disaster would be our dominant political and policy concern. But it manifestly isn't," mainly because "responding to climate change with the vigor that the threat deserves would . . . hurt some powerful vested interests" with "armies of lobbyists in place" and would violate the "dominant political ideology in America," which "has extolled private enterprise and denigrated government."[61]

Krugman wanted to believe that this ideology was advanced only by "the right," but the deeper truth was that the corporate lobbyists he rightly condemned worked the Democrats as well as the Republicans. The corporate neoliberal free-market ideology that claimed Krugman through much of the 1990s also claimed the neo-Clintonian "business liberal" Barack Obama.

The rebranding under Obama might have involved accepting the legitimacy of modern science's findings on climate change. It did not permit challenging elite corporate and financial prerogatives and doctrine to the degree required to save livable ecology.

Rewarding CropLife, Enemy of Michelle Obama's Organic Garden

An especially egregious betrayal of Brand Obama's green campaign promises and imagery took place in the fall of 2009 when Obama nominated Islam Siddiqui to be the chief agricultural negotiator in the office of the U.S. Trade Representative. Siddiqui was vice president of CropLife America, an alliance of the top corporate players in the pesticide industry, including Dow Chemical, Syngenta, and Monsanto. A former public official in President Clinton's Department of Agriculture and in the California Department of Food and Agriculture, he had previously worked as a lobbyist for CropLife, the pesticide industry's trade association. Nearly fifty corporate agribusiness groups signed a letter supporting his nomination, but a coalition of over eighty environmental, family farm, and consumer groups urged the Senate Finance Committee to reject his nomination, noting that Siddiqui's record and statements "show his clear bias in favor of chemical-intensive and unproven biotechnology practices that imperil both our planet and human health while undermining food security and exacerbating climate change."

As Marcia Ishii-Eiteman, a senior scientist at the Pesticide Action Network of North America, explained to Amy Goodman on *Democracy Now* in November 2009, "CropLife's agenda is . . . straightforward: opening new markets for pesticides and for the genetically engineered seeds that go with them. Their agenda is also to weaken international environmental treaties and any kind of environmental protections or regulations that might somehow get in the way or constrain the production, sale and export of their products."

Remarkably enough, as Ishii-Eiteman reported, CropLife had "infamously shuddered" at Michelle Obama's decision to plant an organic garden at the White House in the spring of 2009. "CropLife's regional partner in the Midwest sent a letter to Michelle Obama expressing their deep concern that she was setting a bad example for the rest of the country by not using their chemical pesticides," Eshii-Eiteman reported. "And then they organized a letter writing campaign to urge her to abandon this practice and start using pesticides as soon as possible." The scientist offered a telling critique of the "new" White House's basic continuation—beneath occasional symbolic and rhetorical flashes to the contrary—of the standard corporate "commitment to a fundamentally flawed industrial model of agriculture that is chemically intensive, energy and water intensive, and that is not the solution for the kinds of changes that the planet and US farmers, in particular, are facing in the coming years and decades with climate change, water scarcity and this rapidly diminishing supply of fossil fuels. What we really need to be doing," Ishii-Eiteman added, "is getting off the pesticide GMO [genetically modified organism] treadmill and moving as quickly as possible on to the right kind of agroecologically based farming that history and science now tells us is really the most robust way forward"—a path that might help save the planet and roll back the corporate assault on livable ecology (and democracy) but certainly stands well outside the parameters of Obama's "pragmatic" sense of practical "realism."[62] There were no reported comments from the First Lady on the Siddiqui nomination.

Business Liberalism

Blacklisting Progressives and Other Infidelities

There were other corporatist progressive betrayals. In June 2009, the White House decided to allow leading banks to make early repayments under the Troubled Asset Relief Program. This permitted top financial firms to pass on more wealth (in the form of excessive compensation) to top managers and reduce lending capacities even as unemployment and poverty spread across the nation and world. We learned that Obama was continuing the noxious, openly plutocratic Bush administration practice of handing top foreign diplomatic positions to leading campaign fund-raisers. Louis Susman, a former Citigroup banker and leading Obama moneyman, was appointed ambassador to England. Phil Murphy, a former Goldman Sachs banker and Democratic Party national finance chairman, became U.S. ambassador to Germany.[63]

In May, Obama disregarded numerous progressive defenders of civil liberties and human rights from consideration for appointment to succeed Justice David H. Souter of the Supreme Court and to thereby counter the hard-right leanings of the High Court's conservative majority.[64] He nominated instead Sonia Sotomayor, a centrist federal judge with close connections to leading Wall Street firms and a pro-corporate track record that was almost completely lost in the highly identity-politicized spring and summer debate over her Puerto Rican ethnicity and her onetime comment to the effect that a "wise Latina" judge might rule more justly in certain cases than a white male on the bench.[65]

These policy actions were consistent with the Obama's White House's pronounced preference for conservative and centrist economic thinkers and policy actors over even mildly progressive economists. As the veteran left-liberal Washington- and Obama-watcher David Sirota noted two weeks after the inauguration, President Obama and his team had "blacklisted progressives" from key policy roles in his administration. "Amid a stable of eminently qualified and well-respected progressives like James Galbraith, Joseph Stiglitz, Dean Baker, Robert Reich, Paul Krugman and Larry Mishel," Sirota observed that "Obama has chosen [corporate neoliberal] Rubin sycophants like Larry Summers and Tim Geithner to run the economy—the same Larry Summers who pushed the repeal of . . . Glass-Steagal . . . , the same Geithner who masterminded the kleptocratic bank bailout, the same duo whose claim to fame is their personal connections to Rubin, a disgraced Citigroup executive at the center of the current meltdown. And the list of Rubin sycophants keeps getting longer, from Peter Orszag to Jason Furman."

Sirota noted that venture capitalist Leo Hindery—a top economic advisor to presidential candidates John Edwards and (later) Obama—was banned from serious consideration for a top economic post in the new administration because he was "one of the few business leaders to use his wealth to challenge deregulation, corporate trade deals, and anti-worker policies." Hindery "dared to clash with the same Wall Street Democrats whose corporate-backed policies destroyed the economy." He committed the unpardonable sin of standing "in opposition to Obama's top [corporate-neoliberal] economic advisors, many of whom were associated with The Hamilton Project, an economic think-tank that was the inheritor of former Treasury Secretary [and former Goldman Sachs CEO Robert] Rubin's generally pro-trade positions."[66] As Hindery's case showed, it wasn't just progressive intellectuals and activists who were considered too radical for the administration's concept of "Change We Can Believe In." Even capitalists who preferred a slightly more equitable and high-road model of development were considered "too far left" for the country.[67] Never mind that the majority of U.S. citizens hold progressive policy opinions well to the left of the business class and the nation's two dominant business parties.[68]

It is true that the black environmentalist and left-progressive Van Jones was appointed by Obama as "special advisor for green jobs" in March 2009. Powerfully linking the interrelated issues of racism, poverty, and climate change, the highly accomplished and charismatic Jones (a Yale Law School graduate who had previously founded key civil rights organizations in Oakland, California) advocated a "clean energy revolution" that "would," in James's words, "put literally millions of people to work, putting up solar panels all across the United States, weatherizing buildings so they don't leak so much energy. . . . You could put Detroit back to work not making SUVs to destroy the world, but making wind turbines." Jones told left broadcaster Amy Goodman in October 2008, "We think that you can fight pollution and poverty at the same time."

Leftists and liberals who hoped against hope for a serious progressive presence in the Obama administration had reason to be pleased by Jones's presence in the administration. But Jones was already gone by early September, hounded out of his job by the far-right FOX News talk-show host Glenn Beck, who claimed that Jones was a "communist" and "black nationalist," emblematic of what Beck insanely called Obama's "deep-seated hatred for white people." Beck's charges against Jones were false, but Beck's campaign against Jones—echoed across the still-powerful "right wing noise machine" in the summer of 2009—were taken seriously enough by the Obama administration (notwithstanding Beck's reckless charge of racism against the president) for the White House to ask for and receive Jones's resignation.[69]

"To Tamp Down Populist Anger"

Despite the occasional "populist"-sounding outburst required to contain widespread popular anger over grotesque economic disparities and corporate corruption, Obama as president has not repeated Obama the candidate's habit of telling giant crowds to proclaim that (in a frequent Obama campaign refrain) "change doesn't happen from the top down. Change happens from the bottom up." After having mobilized citizens to vote out the old Republican regime in the name of progressive and democratic transformation, the in-power Obama team has had a different message for the people: *Calm down and let the experts from the political class do their work.* A T-shirt I saw worn by a young, white professional Iowa City resident at that town's Saturday morning farmers market in early September 2009 said it all: Above a broadly grinning Obama were the words "CHILL, I'VE GOT THIS."

"This," the message coming from the rebranded probusiness administration in Washington ran, was no time for "anger" and "ideology," which stand in the way of "getting things done." Now that people had played their role in the transition from one administration and party in power to another, they were supposed to return quietly and, hopefully, to remote, divided, and private realms, dutifully executing their paid work assignments (if they still have jobs), buying stuff (largely on credit thanks to the continuing lag of wages behind productivity in the United States), investing their modest savings (if they have any) in the stock market again (as Obama had recently admonished Americans to do), and watching their Telescreens while the new system-maintaining coordinators (including supposedly "pragmatic" and "nonideological" technicians like Summers and Geithner) did the serious and sober work of putting back on its feet the profits system (described by Obama in his 2006 campaign book *The Audacity of Hope* as "our greatest asset, . . . a system that for generations has encouraged constant innovation, individual initiative and efficient allocation of resources"). Condescendingly counseling Americans on their need to avoid (supposedly dysfunctional) resentment over Wall Street practices and Wall Street–friendly policies, and the deeper socioeconomic disparities White House actions both reflected and reinforced, Obama told CBS's

Steve Kroft in late March 2009 that "we cannot govern out of anger"—a consistent White House theme.[70]

In the first week of the new administration, Obama's top economic advisor Lawrence Summers lectured Americans to heed "President Obama['s] call for an age of responsibility" by agreeing to dutifully "manage [their] own finances" and "do [their] own jobs. . . . People," Summers told NBC's David Gregory, "need to work hard, they need to play by the rules, and those of us with responsibility for economic policy need to do everything we can to make the economy work." Appearing on the "Public" Broadcasting System's *NewsHour*, Summers said that Obama "recognize[s] and he share[s]the outrage that people feel at what has happened, at some of the bonuses that have been paid, about some of the irresponsibility that brought us to this point. But he also," Summers added, "urge[s] that we can't govern out of anger, that we can't let our rage, our legitimate anger, stop us from the necessary steps."[71]

A front-page *New York Times* "news analysis" in March noted that Obama political and public relations team was "increasingly concerned" about "a populist backlash" that could target the new bailout-friendly White House as well as the investor class. According to *Times* correspondent Adam Nagourney, "A shifting political mood challenges Mr. Obama's political skills, as he seeks to acknowledge the anger without becoming a target of it. A central question for Mr. Obama is whether his cool style will prove effective *when the country may be feeling more emotional* [emphasis added]." Nagourney cited unnamed Obama advisors on how the new White House "risks . . . backlash as Mr. Obama tries to signal that he shares American anger but pushes for more bail-out money for banks and Wall Street." Consistent with that contradictory and manipulative goal, Obama expressed calculated indignation against "excessive" executive bonuses at AIG (originally approved by Geithner) and made carefully orchestrated visits expressing concern about poverty and job loss. These were well understood by political and media elites to be public relations ("expectation-managing") efforts to "get ahead" of "populist rage" over the corporate agenda that continued to hold sway in Washington in the Age of Obama.

The "backlash" risk was exacerbated by the new president's perceived need to raise money from the wealthy few to support his "reform" agenda. A brief page sixteen report in the *Times* near the end of March 2009 noted the irony of Obama's appearance as "a featured guest at a fund-rising dinner that cost donors $30,000 per couple." This appearance did not fit well with what the *Times* described as "Mr. Obama['s effort] to pull the nation together, using his platform as president *to tamp down populist anger at Wall Street* [emphasis added] and expressing sympathy for people who are losing their homes and jobs." The same-day issue of the *Times* contained the afore-mentioned front-page story on "the arrival of modern-day Hoovervilles."[72]

"A Blunt Lesson About Power"

A glowing *Los Angeles Times* assessment of Obama's first hundred days re-produced an interesting statement from Obama to the leaders of the bank-ing industry in March. As the financial chieftains began to complain to him about the public's failure to understand their industry's need for high levels of compensation, Obama cut them off. "Be careful how you make those statements, gentlemen" Obama said. "The public isn't buying that. My administration is the only thing between you and the pitchforks."[73]

A student who told me about this *Los Angeles Times* report wrote me with an interesting comment. "The question for me (and I assume for many left-ists) is why is Obama using his administration to protect the bankers from the angry rabble (us)? Why doesn't his administration simply address the people's needs and leave the bankers to their fate? These are, of course, rhetorical questions. We know that he is serving to protect and legitimate the highly undemocratic and destructive class system of state capitalism through another crisis."

But one didn't need to be a Marxist like David Harvey or another sort of left anticapitalist radical like my student to be concerned about Obama's service to economic royalty during his first year in the White House. As giant financial bailouts exposed the chasm between the investor and polit-ical classes and the broad citizenry in March, William Greider made a telling observation in a *Washington Post* column titled "Obama Asked Us to Speak, but Is He Listening?":

> People everywhere [have] learned a blunt lesson about power, who has it and who doesn't. They [have] watched Washington run to rescue the very financial interests that caused the catastrophe. They [have] learned that gov-ernment has plenty of money to spend when the right people want it. "Where's my bailout," became the rueful punch line at lunch counters and construction sides nationwide. Then to deepen the insult, people [have] watched as establishment forces re-launched their campaign for "entitle-ment reform"—a euphemism for whacking Social Security benefits, Medi-care and Medicaid.[74]

The previous month, liberal economist Robert Kuttner, who had hoped passionately for a "progressive" Obama presidency and was sorely disap-pointed, told a television interviewer that the new chief executive was advancing "conservative solutions to a radical crisis."[75] And as Obama rolled out his bailout plan, John R. MacArthur, the president of *Harper's* magazine, noted that both the right and left had collaborated in the creation of a "fantasy"—in "an absurd reading of Obama" as a social-democratic progressive. MacArthur, no anticapitalist, saw the new chief executive as "a moderate with *far too much respect for the global financial class* [emphasis added]" and as "surely the unleft, unradical, president."[76]

"The Quiet Coup"

In the May 2009 edition of the centrist public affairs magazine the *Atlantic,* Simon Johnson, former chief economist of the International Monetary Fund (no Marxist), observed that the Obama administration was for all intents and purposes in Wall Street's pocket. In an article titled "The Quiet Coup," Johnson argued that, in the words of the *Atlantic*'s editors, "the finance industry has effectively captured our government—a state of affairs that more typically describes emerging markets, and is at the center of many emerging-market crises. If the IMF's staff could speak freely about the U.S., it would tell us what it tells all countries in this situation: recovery will fail unless we break the financial oligarchy that is blocking essential reform. And if we are to prevent a true depression, we're running out of time." By Johnson's account, "Throughout the crisis, the government has taken extreme care not to upset the interests of the financial institutions or to question the basic outlines of the system that got us here. . . . [The] elite business interests [that] played a central role in creating the crisis . . . with the implicit backing of the government" [are] "now using their influence to prevent precisely [the] reforms that are needed, and fast, to pull the economy out of its nosedive. . . . The government seems helpless, or unwilling, to act against them."[77]

Chomsky rightly saw this as chilling confirmation of the great eighteenth-century economist and philosopher Adam Smith's warning that "the architects of policy protect their own interests, no matter how grievous the effect on others." "And they are the architects of policy," Chomsky added. "Obama made sure to staff his economic team with advisors from [the financial] sector."[78]

"Punked" by Fake "Pragmatism" Masking "Surrender to the Usual Corporate Interests"

In a *Harper's* article that appeared on news-shelves right before Obama's June 2009 financial regulation proposals were made public, Kevin Baker provided some interesting historical reflections on Obama's distinctly "unradical" taste for deliberation, compromise, and incrementalism. In Baker's view, it all amounted to false realism and fake pragmatism in "one of those rare moments in history when the radical becomes pragmatic, when deliberation and compromise foster disaster." Like the Republican U.S. president Herbert Hoover (1929–1933), Baker argued, "Barack Obama is a man attempting to realize a stirring new vision of his society without cutting himself free from the dogmas of the past—without accepting the inevitable conflict." Furthermore,

> just as Herbert Hoover came to internalize the "business progressivism" of his era as a welcome alternative to the futile, counterproductive conflicts of an earlier time, so has Obama internalized what might be called [Bill] Clinton's "business liberalism" as an alternative to useless battles from another time—battles that liberals, in any case, tended to lose.
>
> Clinton's business liberalism, however, is a chimera, every bit as much a capitulation to powerful and selfish interests as was Hoover's 1920s progressivism. [It] espous[es] a *"pragmatism" that is not really pragmatism at all, just surrender to the usual corporate interests* [emphasis added]. The common thread running through all of Obama's major proposals right now is that they are labyrinthine solutions designed mainly to avoid conflict [with big business].
>
> . . . Barack Obama is moving prudently, carefully, reasonably toward disaster.[79]

In mid-August 2009, *New York Times* columnist Frank Rich, something of an Obama fan in 2008, wrote an editorial noting the absurdity of Republican claims that Obama was a "socialist." The "bigger fear," Rich felt, was that "Obama might be just another corporatist, punking voters much as the Republicans do when they claim to be for the common guy." It was a clever if overly tenuous and cautious formation: There was no "might be" about it, which careful progressive Obama-trackers had been suggesting for quite some time by the summer of 2009.

Back to Business As Usual

"Mistaking the Health of Wall Street for the Health of the American Economy"

In a critical mid-September essay in the liberal monthly magazine *Mother Jones*, Nomi Prins responded in a highly critical vein to a September 2009 speech Obama gave at Federal Hall on Wall Street to mark the anniversary of Lehman Brothers' collapse and to promote his still-to-be passed milque-toast financial reform package. Prins began by noting that the new president was "still making the grave error of mistaking the health of Wall Street for the health of the American economy." Obama, Prins observed, "chose not to deliver his speech on, say, the streets of Bend, Oregon, or Fresno, California, which provide different indicators of our economic predicament. That's because Washington's approach to the crisis has been to focus on the banking system, throw a few crumbs to citizens, and hope everything else will magically work itself out." In Prins's view, "'Obama's reforms do not strike deeply enough. The banking crisis has been subdued, not fixed, because of enormous amounts of government assistance. Ignoring that fact, and failing to overhaul the sector, leaves us open to another crisis. And the next round will be worse, because there is now so much more federal money invested in the banks."

"Simply funding the banking system without reforming it is an expensive and dangerous game," Prins noted. Obama is capable of truly fixing things—by dividing up the Wall Street mega-banks with a new Glass Steagall Act, thereby enabling the success of more extensive regulatory reforms. Or, he could introduce a set of cosmetic changes that allow banks to keep doing what they did before last year's crisis and that put us on the path for the next one." Obama opted for the latter path—a perilous decision as national unemployment headed to 10 percent, as Wall Street bonuses reached precrisis levels (Goldman Sachs's bonus levels were actually higher), as the number of foreclosures (2 million in the first six months of 2009) was higher than in 2008, as risky bank borrowing was rising again, and as a large number of small and medium-sized banks continued to fail while the "too-big-to-fail" giant banks were "bigger than they were last year. Since the Fed blessed more mergers last fall," Prins observed, "the nation's three largest banks—Bank of America, JPMorgan Chase and Wells Fargo—hold the maximum percentage of legally permissible US deposits or more." To make matters yet worse, Prins noted, the government still lacked "detailed information on the trillions of dollars of loans the Fed handed out to the banking sector or about the quality of the collateral banks provided in return."[80]

Handed out, Prins might have added, to an ever more hyperconcentrated financial elite. Between 1990 and 2008, the percentage of U.S. financial assets held by the largest U.S. financial institutions rose spectacularly, from 10 to 50 percent. During the same period, the number of banks in the United States fell by nearly 50 percent, from 15,000 to 8,000. By the time Obama won his first Democratic Caucus, just fifteen giant financial institutions had together swallowed up a combined shareholder equity of $857 billion, total assets of nearly $14 trillion. With "off-balance sheet commitments" of $5.8

trillion, these institutions had a combined leverage ratio of 23 to 1 even as they underwrote derivatives with a "gross notional value" of $216 trillion. "These institutions had become so big," distinguished financial historian Niall Ferguson noted, "that the failure of just one of them would pose a systemic risk." To make matters worse, the crisis that occurred in 2008 wiped out three of the top fifteen Wall Street giants and came so close to crashing the U.S. and global financial systems as to certify the remaining firms' official status as "too big too fail"—what Ferguson called "TBTFs."[81]

Between Bush II and Obama, Prins noted, the federal government, from the Federal Reserve to the Treasury Department, had flooded the private financial sector with no less than $17.5 trillion worth of loans, guarantees, and other forms of support. About another $1 trillion—trifling by comparison—had been granted to citizens through the stimulus package, first-time homeowner tax benefits, auto purchase credits, and approximately $800 billion to help guarantee the loans of certain lenders—"which somewhat helps borrowers, but helps lenders more." The massive taxpayer payouts brought back the surviving reconcentrated top financial firms (now minus Lehman Brothers, Merrill Lynch, and Bear Stearns), but they did not bring the real economy inhabited by ordinary working Americans back to anything approximating economic security, and they hardly abolished the specter of renewed financial crisis. Hence the chant at "populist" rallies on Wall Street and across the nation in late 2009: "They Got Bailed Out, We Got Sold Out."

"The Wise Guys of Wall Street . . . Licking Their Fat-Cat Chops"

Arguing against the notion that racism was the main or leading substance behind Obama's rising unpopularity among Americans at the end of the summer of 2009, Frank Rich noted in mid-September that Obama had failed to convince "critics on the left or right that he will do as much for those Americans who are suffering as he has for the corporations his administration and predecessor's rushed to rescue." Obama's Lehman Brothers memorial address at Federal Hall may have promised reform, Rich noted, but little had changed in the corridors of high financial power. "Everyone's back to business as usual," Rich noted. "The *Wall Street Journal* reported that not a single CEO from a top bank attended. The speech sank with scant notice because there has been so little action to back it up and because its conciliatory stance was tone-deaf to the anger beyond the financial district."[82]

Exactly one month later, Rich's fellow *Times* columnist Bob Herbert wrote in shocked terms about "how passive the population has remained"

in response to "another orgy (with taxpayers as the enablers) of [Wall
Street] bonuses" inflicted while a rising sea of Americans struggled to keep
jobs and homes. Referring to recent *Times* headline proclaiming "Bailout
Helps Revive Banks, and Bonuses," Herbert issued a passionate call for basic social and democratic decency:

> We've spent the last few decades shoveling money at the rich like there was
> no tomorrow. . . .
> . . . Meanwhile, Wall Street is living it up. . . . Even as tens of millions of
> working Americans are struggling to hang onto their jobs and keep a roof
> over their families' heads, the wise guys of Wall Street are licking their fat-
> cat chops over yet another round of obscene multibillion-dollar bonuses—
> this time thanks to the bailout billions that were sent their way by Uncle
> Sam, with very little in the way of strings attached. . . .
> Enough! Goldman Sachs is thriving while the combined rates of un-
> employment and underemployment are creeping toward a mind-boggling
> 20 percent. . . .
> We cannot continue transferring the nation's wealth to those at the apex
> of the economic pyramid—which is what we have been doing for the past
> three decades or so—while hoping that someday, maybe, the benefits of that
> transfer will trickle down in the form of steady employment and improved
> living standards for the many millions of families struggling to make it from
> day to day.
> That money is never going to trickle down. It's a fairy tale. We're crazy
> to continue believing it.

Herbert was struck by a dark sense of "deja voodoo" as he recalled a
column he had written on the exact same topic—the sharp disconnect between Wall Street elites "harvesting a record crop of bonuses" and "order-
ing up record shipments of Champagne and caviar" and working families
struggling to survive—three days before Christmas in 2007. A liberal and
black columnist who had greeted Obama's election with notable enthusiasm, Herbert now clearly saw the new president as an agent and symbol
of plutocratic continuities reaching back decades and through the Reagan
and Bush administrations. He did so with good reason.[83]

"A New Gilded Age"

One didn't even need to be from the liberal or progressive side of the spectrum to be concerned about the not-so-"new" White House's excessive

closeness to the elite Wall Street financial interests he had run against. In a late September 2009 commentary in *Newsweek*, Ferguson, a noted conservative and former fellow of the right-wing Hoover Institute, remarked on the White House's pronounced failure to address "the most important flaw in our financial system"—the existence of giant TBTF financial institutions. "On the contrary," Ferguson felt that the emergency measures taken in 2008 had made the TBTF problem "significantly worse" and that the Obama administration's proposed "regulatory reforms" had failed to "do anything to address the central problem of the TBTFs." Ferguson saw the Obama administration and the Democrats involved in a useless "charade in which politicians claim they are going to regulate the big banks more tightly" when what was really required was "a serious application of antitrust law to the financial services sector and a speedy end to institutions that are 'too big to fail.'" Thanks to both the Bush and Obama administrations' failures to undertake the sort of "radical reform" indicated by recent terrible employment and growth projections, Ferguson argued, all Americans were getting now were policies creating a "new gilded age" for Wall Street giants that were "effectively guaranteed by the full faith and credit of the United States. Yes, folks, now it's official: heads, they win, tails, we the taxpayers, lose. And in return we get . . . a $30 charge if we inadvertently run up a $1 overdraft on our debit card. Meanwhile, JP Morgan and Goldman Sachs executives get million-dollar bonuses. What's not to dislike?"

"Tinkering Around the Edges"

Less than one month later, *New York Times* financial editor and columnist Gretchen Morgenson noted that Obama's recently re-unveiled "financial reform" efforts amounted to little more than "tinkering around the edges." Morgenson, no radical, formerly worked for the openly plutocratic *Forbes* magazine and for the equally aristocratic, archcapitalist presidential candidate Steve Forbes. She concluded that the White House's weak efforts at "regulation" might actually increase the likelihood of another financial disaster because they failed to address "the most significant issue of all: how to make sure that companies do not grow to the point where they become too big or interconnected to be allowed to fail." According to Neal Barofsky, special inspector general of the U.S. Treasury's Troubled Asset Relief Program (TARP), the Bush and Obama administrations' sponsorship and support of several mergers at the top of the financial sector meant that the risk of a major collapse was alive and well. "If anything," Barofsky told CNN in mid-October, "we could be in more danger than we were a year ago," thanks to the increased size and power of the surviving uppermost financial firms. This dark reality went largely unacknowledged in "mainstream" media reports that focused heavily on Obama's superficially progressive proposal in October to (briefly) rein in runaway executive pay at seven federally bailed-out companies. "The white-hot focus on pay," Morgenson noted, "*looks like a way for the government to reassure an angry public that they are making genuine changes* [emphasis added]. Meanwhile, compensation is a trivial matter compared to, say, true reform of derivatives trading"– or to the urgent necessity of breaking up gargantuan banks.[84] She might have added that the big banks remained—contrary to the Obama administration's public relations rhetoric of a strong bank recovery—highly fragile in part because they continued to be burdened with trillions of dollars worth of toxic financial assets, which were never actually purchased by the Bush or Obama Treasury Department.[85] Beneath the Obama rebranding the same old dangerous financial regime was largely in place.

"Obama's Presidency Isn't Too Big to Fail"

Nomi Prins's and other progressives' sentiments were echoed by the liberal-left Obama supporter Robert Scheer in the pages of the liberal-left weekly magazine *The Nation* in mid-September 2009. "Obama, who raised questions before his election about the propriety of a plan that would rescue the banks but ignore the plight of ordinary folks, has," Scheer noted with sadness, "adopted that very approach as president. He elevated Lawrence Summers and Timothy Geithner, the two Democrats most closely aligned with Paulson's policy, to top positions in his government." Furthermore,

> Obama's proposed new regulations, while containing some kind words about better informing consumers, do not portend any breakup of the "too big to fail companies" whose problems were permitted to fester by previous deregulatory measures. His answer is to increase the regulatory capacities of the Federal Reserve, which failed to use its already existing and considerable powers to avoid the debacle. The promise is that next time the Fed will behave better. As Obama put[s] it . . . "Our plan would put the cost of a firm's failures on those who own its stock and loaned it money. And if taxpayers ever have to step in again to prevent a second Great Depression, the financial industry will have to pay the taxpayer back every cent."
>
> Why not now? And why has he accepted the Wall Street line that all this represents a "collective failure," as if the con men and the conned had equal responsibility?

. . . Hogwash. The chicanery of the financial system, securitizing highly suspect mortgages, was codified into laws that made the hustle legal.

That insistence on equating the swindled with the swindlers is also what is wrong with the evolving health care reform plan.[86]

The title of Scheer's essay was "Obama's Presidency Isn't Too Big to Fail." It was an apt heading in light of shifting public opinion data. Obama's public approval rating fell from 69 percent to 50 percent between January and late August 2009. That was a very rapid decline by comparative historical standards. Obama had reached his low more quickly than most of his White House predecessors, according to Gallup, which has surveyed presidential approval since the late 1940s.[87]

Obama's "honeymoon" was already over. According to surveys, most U.S. citizens now disapproved of his economic policies and of his (very weak and corporate-friendly) efforts at "health reform." A growing number opposed his determinations to escalate the U.S. war in (maybe I should say "on") Afghanistan.

The fall in Obama's popularity over the summer of 2009 largely reflected a growing sense that he was unable and/or unwilling to undertake policies and actions necessary to stem increasing unemployment and to provide universal affordable and high-quality health care to citizens. Obama remains a great public speaker and a highly charismatic and intelligent, telegenic personality. But a silver tongue and good looks went only so far when the U.S. official unemployment rate headed toward 10 percent and thousands were losing their health insurance and homes each day—all this as the "defense" (empire) budget (at least $1 trillion per year and responsible for nearly half the military spending on earth) actually increased under Obama, while an increasing number of U.S. soldiers died (needlessly) in Afghanistan, and as the biggest banks got bigger and richer thanks to the actions of the Obama economic team, which was itself made up largely of Wall Street insiders.

Of course, one of Obama's problems was that his campaign and the media built an almost messianic aura around him. The democratic and social expectations surrounding his election were inordinately high, particularly in the wake of the Bush-Cheney administration, possibly the most incompetent and grossly plutocratic White House in U.S. history. The higher the expectations for "change" from a president are, the steeper is the decline in popularity and credibility when that president is revealed to be another all-too-mortal and limited politician who functions in service to existing dominant domestic and global hierarchies and doctrines. The bigger you are, the harder you fall.

At the same time, as Scheer noted, Obama was "presented with a series of crises not of his making but for which he is now being held accountable." He inherited "the legacy of a president who raised the military budget to its highest level since World War II despite the end of the Cold War and the lack of a formidable military opponent—a legacy of debt compounded by Bush's decision to first ignore the banking meltdown and then to engage in a welfare-for-Wall-Street bailout."

Nevertheless, Obama the "not Bush" was not without fault. "What is nerve-racking about Obama," Scheer noted, "is that even though *he campaigned against Bush's follies he has now embraced them.*" Scheer failed to note that this is exactly what one would expect for a president hired and promoted to the nation's top elected job by its "unelected dictatorship of money" with the purpose of creating the illusion and managing popular expectations for change and providing a profitable public relations makeover— a rebranding—for the same old American system of empire and inequality and "democracy incorporated."

"Actually Accomplishing Something"

To be sure, the administration had a different story line. As *New York Times* columnist Maureen Dowd noted in mid-October 2009, "White House advisors don't seem worried yet that Obama's transformational aura could get smudged if too much is fudged. They say it is the normal tension between campaigning on a change platform and actually accomplishing something in office."[88] In other words, it may have made "pragmatic" sense in terms of attaining the presidency to run on the notion of questioning elite business power, but it made no such "get things done" sense to act on populist-sounding promises when it comes to governing. Predictably enough from a realistic power-centered analysis of how policy and politics work under "the unelected dictatorship of money," the White House's concept of "actually accomplishing something" reduced again and again to enacting measures favorable to the rich and powerful and generally governing in accord with the needs of the few.

As I completed this chapter in early December 2009, the nation's official unemployment rate passed 10 percent. An honestly calculated rate would have been closer to 20 percent. One in four of the nation's children now depended on Food Stamps.[89] Economic misery haunted the United States as it entered what was clearly going to be a lean and mean Christmas season for many millions of Americans. The president himself told interviewers of his fear that the country was undergoing "a corporate recovery without job growth."[90]

"We Just Don't Have the Money"

"If you're looking for a job right now," Paul Krugman noted at the end of November 2009, "your prospects are terrible." There were six times as many Americans seeking work as there were job openings in the United States, Krugman reported. The average job-seeker was spending more than six months looking for work, the highest level since the Great Depression.

"You might think," Krugman reasoned, "that doing something about the employment situation would be a top policy priority." And not just anything: The extreme levels of joblessness and poverty being experienced across the country as it headed into the Christmas season called for an emergency federal jobs program—one in which "the federal government would provide jobs . . . by providing jobs" on an at least small-scale version of the 1930s New Deal Works Progress Administration. But there was little in the works and nothing on the scale to match the crisis. "Now that total financial collapse has been averted," Krugman noted, "all the urgency seems to have vanished from policy discussion, replaced by a strange passivity. There's a pervasive sense in Washington that nothing more can or should be done, that we should just wait for the economic recovery to trickle down to workers."[91]

Speaking at a White House forum prior to an administration "jobs summit" in early December of the same year, Obama fed this sense when he "offered no promise that he could do much to bring unemployment down quickly even as he comes under pressure from his own party to do more." Obama said he would consider "every demonstrably good idea" for creating jobs, but he cautioned that "our resources are limited."

"While liberals are calling for ambitious job-creating measures along the lines of the New Deal," the *Times* reported in early December, "Obama talked of limited programs that he suggested could provide substantial bang for the buck when it comes to job creation."[92] "Moving forward," the president told *USA Today* and the *Detroit Free Press*, "it is not going to be possible for us to have a huge second stimulus, because, frankly, we just don't have the money."[93]

Citizens were left to wonder how true this statement was in a time when Obama's federal government had the money to spend trillions on the rescue of corrupt, for-profit financial institutions. Liberal policy wonks like Krugman were left to argue that the federal government could both raise more revenue and discourage the sort of excessive speculative activity that had ended up creating the financial crisis and bailouts of 2008–2009 by modestly taxing financial transactions—an idea that Obama economic officials were "dead against," reflecting the fact that the new White House was deeply in "Wall Street's thrall" (Krugman).[94]

It was all very consistent with Obama's own ironic observation in an interview with CNN in September: "I can't tell you how many foreign leaders who are heads of center-right governments say to me, I don't understand why people would call you socialist. In my country, *you'd be considered a conservative.*"[95]

A conservative of the corporatist variety, he might have added. In late April of 2009 the liberal political scientist Thomas B. Edsall noted on *Huffington Post* that Obama had earned the label "King of Corporate Welfare." "No matter what else he achieves or where he falls short," Edsall wrote, "Barack Obama can lay claim to the title of King of Corporate Subsidies. . . . Using any variety of measures, the Obama administration has broken all records in the distribution of tax dollars to American business, primarily banks, automobile manufacturers, and insurance companies. . . . The tidal wave of dollar bills has stunned folks on all sides of the political spectrum."[96]

There was another problem, one that Krugman and other liberals failed to mention. Insofar as it was true that "we just don't have the money," no small part of that could be attributed to the nation's monumental "defense" or, more accurately, empire budget and to the federal government's continuing engagement in vastly expensive colonial wars and occupations even as many millions lacked adequate food and medical resources—not to mention employment—both abroad and at home, in "the world's richest nation" and supposed "greatest democracy." In Obama's America no less than George W. Bush's America, the specter of what Dr. Martin Luther King called "spiritual death"[97]—the privileging of military over social expenditures— continued to hang over the nation like a ghostly pall.

Those "defense" expenditures were themselves state-capitalist gifts to a certain segment of the ruling business class. High-tech corporate military contractors such as Boeing, Raytheon, Xe Services, Halliburton, and Lockheed Martin have continued to make out like bandits, reaping the hidden profits of empire.

The following chapter turns to the persistent imperial militarism that has continued to feed corporate profits under Obama.

2

Empire's New Clothes
Deeds and Words in Obama's Foreign Policy

Barack Obama is a brilliant supporter of empire who has figured out a way to essentially trick a lot of people into believing they're supporting radical change. . . . Obama is an incredibly Orwellian character. He can make people think that war is peace.

—*Jeremy Scahill, June 2009*[1]

As Obama came into office, Condoleezza Rice predicted that he would follow the policies of Bush's second term, and that's pretty much what's happened apart from a different rhetoric and style. But it is wise to attend to deeds, not rhetoric. Deeds commonly tell a different story.

—*Noam Chomsky, November 2009*[2]

If you would only give more than words. Perhaps from where you stand, Mr. President, you don't hear how hollow they sound.

—*Soja Karkan, October 2009*[3]

If you closed your eyes during much of the President's speech on Afghanistan Tuesday night and just listened to the words, you easily could have concluded that George W. Bush was still in the Oval Office.

—*Matthew Rothschild, December 2, 2009*[4]

Like Bush's America, Obama's America is run by some very dangerous people.

—*John Pilger, October 15, 2009*[5]

Nobel-Winning Obama Defends War in Call for Peace

—*News headline, December 10, 2009*[6]

Join the Antiwar Movement
by Voting for Barack

Of all the different Democratic presidential candidates' supporters I canvassed in my role as a volunteer for John Edwards—himself very problematic (from a left perspective) on foreign policy, including the Iraq War[7]—in eastern Iowa during the late summer, fall, and early winter of 2007 and 2008, none were more tight-lipped and hostile than Barack Obama's followers. During my many hours as a voter-contact volunteer, I would ask non-Edwards Democrats whom they were backing and why and if they'd be willing to hear some brief reflections relating to issues and policies and why they might consider my candidate. Obama's folks were not interested and not willing.

If the person I reached by phone or in person supported Bill Richardson, Joe Biden, Dennis Kucinich, or Chris Dodd, the results were generally quite congenial. A polite and productive conversation would often ensue. When I asked why they were supporting their candidate, they took no offense and typically mentioned two or three policy areas where they felt he had a made a special mark or held special promise. Often I would determine that Edwards was their second choice—a critical thing to know under the rules of the Iowa caucus system. The results with Hillary Clinton supporters were more mixed but generally good-natured and similar.

Things were very different with most of the "Obamanists" (as I came to call Obama's supporters by mid-December) I encountered. The great majority of Obama supporters I spoke with seemed offended at the notion that anyone would seek to engage them on candidate differences. They did on the whole not connect on policy issues. Many of them left me with the impression that they found something highly unpleasant and boorish—crypto-racist, perhaps—about daring to question their Great Leader.

It was quite pronounced. One middle-class lady with a poster saying "HOPE—Obama '08" on her front lawn became positively enraged when I asked her a simple question: "*So why are you supporting Obama?*"

Wondering if there was something wrong with my own approach to Obama's supporters, I related my experience to other Edwards volunteers. It turned out that my encounters with Obamanists were commonplace. A staffer explained it to me in the following terms: "Oh, you can't talk policy and issues with the Obama people. Don't even try. There's no discussion with them. They already know everything. It's a cult."

The judgment struck me as a little overly harsh but more accurate than not. It also struck me as ironic, for Obama's supporters were the most highly educated and academic of all the different Democratic candidates' constituents.

This is not to say that I never encountered some open and amiable Iowa Obamanists willing to explain at least their candidate allegiance. I found seven of them—four in my Iowa City precinct, one in the small rural town of Wilton, and two in Muscatine. And even though my sample of seven is not exactly a statistically significant survey, it interesting to note that each one of them gave special and pivotal credit to Obama for having "opposed the war on Iraq from the start." Obama struck them as a militantly antiwar candidate who was rejecting the foreign policy of both the Bush administration and the Democratic Party establishment—the latter identified with Hillary Clinton.

Four of my Obamanist voters also claimed that Obama's technical non-whiteness and vaguely Islamic-sounding name (Barack Hussein Obama) would prove highly useful in repairing America's relationship with the rest of the world in the wake of George W. Bush's disastrous policies. They clearly connected their favorite candidate's allegedly antiwar and anti-imperial foreign policy credentials to his black and multicultural identity.

My seven friendly and forthcoming Obamanists were emblematic of a broader opinion band in the white middle class. Along with a hope that Obama was a specially charismatic leader with the capacity to "get things done with people across the aisle" and a sense that his technical blackness represented progressive "change," the image of Obama as an antiwar and anti-imperial candidate was critical to his support.[8]

The image of Obama as the antiwar candidate was naturally cultivated by his campaign in 2007 and early 2008. Team Obama made their candidate's "opposition to the war from the start" the *single leading policy-specific selling point in repeatedly stated contrast* to Edwards and Clinton, both of whom rushed to authorize Bush's fateful invasion of Mesopotamia in the fall of 2002. In speeches and advertisements and mailings from coast to coast, Obama regularly cited his October 2002 speech against the impending war as an example of his foreign policy superiority over his chief rivals. In appearances across Iowa and New Hampshire, he made sure to refer to the "Iraq mess" as a war that "should have never been launched and"— throwing in a direct shot at Edwards and Clinton—"never been authorized." On the very last day before the Iowa caucus, Obama staffers and volunteers put copies of his October 2002 speech inside the screen doors of tens of thousands of potential caucus-goers.

His campaign even said this in a mass mailing sent across Iowa in the winter of 2007: "From the very beginning," the mailing went, "Barack

Obama said No to the War in Iraq. Join the movement to end the war and change Washington."[9] Barack Obama was asking me and other Iowans to *equate caucusing for the junior senator from Illinois with joining the antiwar movement.* It was a profoundly disingenuous request that was coldly contradicted by his own as record as a U.S. senator and by his comments to the foreign policy establishment during the campaign.[10]

Continuing the Iraq Occupation

Barack Obama's record as president has not jibed very well with Brand Obama's antiwar gloss, to say the least. The Iraq deception has continued into the Obama presidency. Obama won his epic primary battle with Hillary Clinton largely because he was able to convince much of the Democratic Party's liberal base to believe in the fairy tale that he was a strong and consistent opponent of George W. Bush and Hillary's archcriminal invasion of Iraq. But if we read the fine print on Obama's Iraq plan, however, we will see that he intends to sustain the occupation of that country into the indefinite future. He will keep at least 50,000 troops in Iraq well after the August 2010 combat troop withdrawal date he campaigned on. Many of the troops who stay will be in combat units redesignated as "advisory" brigades, a new classification that George Orwell would appreciate. As left activist, author, and journalist Anthony Arnove noted in March 2009, Obama's "withdrawal" plan "says nothing about the private contractors and mercenaries that are an essential part of the occupation and whose numbers may even be increased to cover functions previously provided by active-duty troops. . . . It will leave in place the world's largest foreign embassy, as well as the world's largest CIA foreign station, in Baghdad."[11] The United States will maintain critical control over Iraqi skies and a significant naval and air presence "over the horizon."

Fighting Forces in Iraq for as Long as a Decade

In May 2009, one of Obama's leading military officials, Chief of Staff of the Army General George Casey, announced that the Pentagon was ready to leave fighting forces in Iraq for as long as a decade. "Global trends are pushing in the wrong direction," Casey said in an invitation-only briefing of a dozen journalists and policy analysts from Washington-based think tanks. According to one reporter present at the briefing, Casey said that his planning "envisions combat troops in Iraq and Afghanistan for a decade as part of a sustained U.S. commitment to fighting extremism and terrorism in the Middle East."[12]

Resisting Popular "Anti-American" Iraqi Input on the Occupation

A June 10, 2009, *New York Times* article reported that Obama was pressuring the Iraqi government not to permit a popular referendum on U.S. withdrawal required by the Status of Forces Agreement (SOFA)—the withdrawal document forced on the Bush administration by the Iraqi resistance. As the *Times* explained, the Obama administration feared that the Iraqi population might insist on the immediate removal of all U.S. troops, rejecting the SOFA provision that delays full withdrawal until 2012. Such insistence, described as "anti-Americanism" by U.S. officials, would have been consistent with longstanding majority Iraqi opinion, recorded in Pentagon-run polls and other Western surveys. The legally required referendum (described by the *Times* as a "potent poison pill approved at the same time as the security agreement as a way to appease political factions that did not want to be tarred with the accusation that they had voted for a measure that allowed American soldiers to stay on Iraqi soil until 2012") was scheduled for July 30, 2009. In likely "deference to American concerns," the *Times* reported in June, the Iraqi cabinet declared its wish to delay the vote for six months so that it could be held at the same time as national elections in January "to save money and time."[13]

The popular referendum was in fact rescheduled to coincide with national Iraqi elections on January 16, 2010. In August, the *Washington Post* reported that Obama's military had "quietly lobbied against the plebiscite," oddly adding that American officials had "assumed the plebiscite was a dead issue" because it had not taken place as originally scheduled in July. Washington was upset that Iraq's prime minister Nouri al-Maliki had "appeared to disregard the wishes of the U.S. government" by endorsing the January referendum, which, Pentagon officials "worried," would likely go against "U.S." wishes.[14]

The worries were well founded. A poll commissioned by the U.S. military earlier in 2009 had found that Iraqis had far less confidence in American troops than in the Iraqi government. Just more than one-quarter (27 percent) of Iraqis polled said they had confidence in U.S. forces, according to a Pentagon report presented to Congress. By contrast, nearly three-fourths (72 percent) expressed confidence in the national government.[15]

Defiant of majority Iraqi (not to mention majority U.S.) opinion, Obama's efforts to prolong the imperial occupation of Iraq were an excellent example of what left-liberal journalist Robert Scheer in mid-September 2009 called Obama's "nerve-racking" penchant for "embracing" the very Bush administration "follies" he "campaigned against."[16]

Mercenaries on the Rise as
Uniform Troops (Slightly) Decline

Meanwhile, the Pentagon under Obama and his Republican defense secretary Robert Gates hired and deployed 250,000 private military contractors—half the force fighting U.S. colonial wars in Iraq and Afghanistan—and increased the number of mercenaries in those countries by more than 25 percent.[17] It was an important and commonly ignored development that helped the "new" administration cloak persistent occupation as withdrawal. During the second quarter of 2009, uniformed U.S. military personnel levels fell by 15 percent, but corporate mercenary troops employed by the United States rose by 23 percent. By the end of June 2009, private contractors accounted for nearly half (47 percent) of the U.S. force presence in Iraq and 57 percent of U.S. military forces in Afghanistan, where there were 73,968 contractors relative to 55,107 uniformed personnel.[18] Neither Obama nor Gates (carried over from the highly militaristic Bush-Cheney administration to demonstrate the new president's bipartisan spirit and safety to the military establishment) showed any interest in supporting legislation proposed by progressive Democrats to ban private mercenary firms from war-theater activities.

The Doctrine of Good Intentions

Less then two months into his presidency, Obama added occupation insult to injury during a "surprise" visit to so-called Camp Victory in Iraq. Consistent with his longstanding support for the standard U.S. doctrine of America's good and democratic intentions on the global stage, Obama said that it was time for the Iraqis to step up to the plate and "take responsibility" for the "democracy" and "sovereignty" the noble United States had granted them.[19] These were revealing comments more than six years into a brazenly imperial and petro-colonial invasion that Obama was finding ways to continue against the expressed will of the Iraqi people. Beyond the fact that Iraqis had in fact been standing up against the foreign invaders in the name of national sovereignty since the beginning of the criminal U.S.

occupation, Obama's claim of benevolent U.S intent was offensive in light of the almost unimaginable havoc the United States has wreaked in Mesopotamia. Holocaust. As left journalist, author, and editor Tom Engelhardt noted in mid-January 2008:

> Whether civilian dead between the invasion of 2003 and mid-2006 (before the worst year of civil-war level violence even hit) was in the range of 600,000 as a study in the British medical journal, *The Lancet* reported, or 150,000 as a recent World Health Organization study suggests, whether two million or 2.5 million Iraqis have fled the country, whether 1.1 million or more than two million have been displaced internally, whether electricity blackouts and water shortages have marginally increased or decreased, whether the country's health-care system is beyond resuscitation or could still be revived, whether Iraqi oil production has nearly crept back to the low point of the Saddam Hussein-era or not, whether fields of opium poppies are, for the first time, spreading across the country's agricultural lands or still relatively localized, Iraq is a continuing disaster zone on a catastrophic scale hard to match in recent memory.[20]

According to respected journalist Nir Rosen in the December 2007 edition of the mainstream journal *Current History*, "Iraq has been killed, never to rise again. The American occupation has been more disastrous than that of the Mongols who sacked Baghdad in the thirteenth century. Only fools talk of solutions now. There is no solution. The only hope is that perhaps the damage can be contained."[21]

Obama's "Good War": Expanding Imperial Violence in "Af-Pak"

Karzai's Irritating Request: Stop Killing Afghans

It is, of course, Afghanistan, that has emerged as "Obama's War" and perhaps as "Obama's Vietnam." From the onset of his presidency, Obama has increased the level of imperial violence in Afghanistan and in nuclear Pakistan. He coldly brushed off Afghanistan president Hamid Karzai's early plea for the United States to stop killing Afghans and for the United States to propose some sort of timeline for ending its illegal occupation of that country.[22] Karzai's minimal assertions of national independence irked Obama, who quickly increased the U.S. force presence in Afghanistan, a legendary graveyard of empires.

It would be nice to report that the real source of Obama's irritation with Karzai was that the Afghan president in late March 2009 signed a law that worsened the already terrible oppression of women in Afghanistan.[23] The legislation codified sharia, or Islamic law, creating restrictions on when women could leave their homes—saying they could do so only "for a legitimate purpose." It forbade wives from either being educated or employed without the express permission of their husbands. "Unless the wife is ill, the wife is bound to give a positive response to the sexual desires of her husband," the law stated. The law applied to Shiites, who make up 15 percent of the Afghan population.[24]

When asked about the terrible legislation while in Prague in April 2009, Obama made it clear that women's rights had little to do with his "new strategy" for Afghanistan. The legislation was "abhorrent," he said, but would not change the U.S. mission in association with the client state headed by Karzai. That mission, Obama said, was all about "defeat[ing] al Qaeda" and denying it a "safe haven" in Afghanistan.[25]

Obama's "Crackpot" Domino Theory

Beyond continuing and expanding the U.S. military's presence in Afghanistan, President Obama has significantly expanded the not-so-covert U.S. war in Pakistan. According to distinguished Middle East expert and University of Michigan historian Juan Cole at the end of March 2009, Obama bought into a recycled version of the "crackpot" cold war conspiracy and "domino theory." In Obama's "updated, al Qaida version" of the domino thesis, Cole noted, "the Taliban might take Kuna Province, and then all of Afghanistan, and might again host al-Qaida, and might then threaten the shores of the United States." The new president added Pakistan onto Afghanistan just as Richard Nixon had added on Cambodia to Vietnam. This time however, the dangerous territorial expansion was openly acknowledged, with Obama explicitly and eagerly merging the two nations "into one theater of war, called Af-Pak."[26] Even U.S. senator John Kerry (D-MA), an enthusiastic Obama backer, complained that this term was too provocatively and explicitly expansionist.[27]

In late March 2009, Obama ominously proclaimed that "the future of Afghanistan is inextricably linked to the future of its neighbor, Pakistan. Make no mistake: Al Qaida and its extremist allies are a cancer that risks killing Pakistan from within."[28] But by Cole's analysis, Obama's call to arms in South Asia was no more credible than Dick Cheney and John McCain's ravings about the danger of an "al-Qaida victory in Iraq":

This latter-day domino theory of al-Qaida takeover in South Asia is just as implausible as its earlier iteration in Southeast Asia (ask Thailand or the Philippines). . . . There are very few al-Qaida fighters based in Afghanistan proper. What is being called the 'Taliban' is mostly not Taliban at all. . . . The groups being branded 'Taliban' only have substantial influence in 8 to 10 percent of Afghanistan, and only 4 percent of Afghans say they support them. . . . Moreover, with regard to Pakistan, there is no danger of militants based in the remote Federally Administered Tribal Areas (FATA) taking over that country or "killing" it. . . . The FATA areas are smaller than Connecticut, with a total population of a little over three million, while Pakistan itself is bigger than Texas, with a population more than half that of the entire United States. A few thousand Pashtun tribesmen cannot take over Pakistan, nor can they "kill" it. . . . Over three quarters of Pakistanis said in a poll last summer that they had an unfavorable view of the Taliban.[29]

"Offending the Pakistani People's Deepest Sensibilities"

If anything, Cole noted, the greatest thing working on the Pakistani Taliban's behalf was the occurrence of U.S. Central Intelligence Agency (CIA) Predator drone strikes on Pakistani territory. "The danger is that that the U.S. strikes may make the radicals seem victims of Western imperialism and so sympathetic to the Pakistani public." Even establishment *New York Times Magazine* writer James Traub noted in early April 2009 that the "American policy has arguably made the situation even worse, for [Obama's] Predator-drone attacks along the border, though effective, drive the Taliban eastward, deeper into Pakistan. And the strategy has been only reinforcing hostility to the United States among ordinary Pakistanis."[30]

This was for reasons that were less than surprising. In mid-May 2009, CIA expert David Killcullen wrote a *New York Times* Op-Ed piece titled "Death from Above, Outrage Down Below." As Killcullen explained, the "not moral" use of remote-controlled drones (with "a hit rate of two percent on 98 percent collateral"[31]) was very disproportionately killing civilians, not militants, with predictable outcomes for Pakistani public opinion vis-à-vis the so-called U.S. war on terror:

> The drone war has created a siege mentality among Pakistani civilians. While violent extremists may be unpopular, for a frightened population they seem less ominous than a faceless enemy that wages war from afar and often kills more civilians than militants.

Press reports suggest that over the last three years drone strikes have killed about 14 terrorist leaders. But, according to Pakistani sources, they have also killed some 700 civilians. This is 50 civilians for every militant killed, a hit rate of 2 percent—hardly "precision." . . . Every one of these dead noncombatants represents an alienated family, a new desire for revenge, and more recruits for a militant movement that has grown exponentially even as drone strikes have increased.

. . . The strikes are now exciting visceral opposition across a broad spectrum of Pakistani opinion. . . . The persistence of these attacks on Pakistani territory offends people's deepest sensibilities, alienates them from their government, and contributes to Pakistan's instability.[32]

Five months later, a remarkable essay in the mainstream, upscale weekly magazine the *New Yorker* reported that the U.S. government maintained two drone programs. The first was run by the military and was publicly acknowledged. It operated in "recognized war zones" in Afghanistan and Iraq, functioning as "an extension of conventional warfare." The second was run by the CIA and classified as "covert" and therefore impervious to questions about operations, outcomes, and targets. It was against "terror suspects" the world over, even in countries where no U.S. troops were based. "It was initiated by the Bush administration," *New Yorker* writer Jane Mayer wrote, but "Obama has left in place virtually all the key personnel."[33] Beyond being largely beyond public inquiry, this second program relied heavily on private mercenary corporations (themselves responsible for more than half the U.S. troop presence in Afghanistan), including XE Services—formerly named Blackwater (whose abuses were so legendary as to call for a relabeling)—for a number of tasks, including flying the drones and maintaining and loading them with Hellfire missiles.

By Mayer's account, Barack Obama had embraced and deployed the controversial killer drone program with remarkable zest. "During his first nine and a half months in office," Mayer noted, "*he has authorized as many CIA aerial attacks in Pakistan as George W. Bush did in his final three years in office* [emphasis added]. . . . So far this year, various estimates suggest, the CIA attacks have killed between three hundred and twenty-six and five hundred and thirty-eight people. Critics say that many of the victims have been innocent bystanders."[34]

The first two Obama administration CIA Predator assaults occurred on the morning of January 23, 2009—the president's third day in office. The second strike ordered by the "peace" president on that day mistakenly targeted the residence of a progovernment tribal leader, killing his entire family, including three children. In keeping with U.S. policy, "there was no official acknowledgement of either strike." Thanks to the CIA/XE Services/ White House program's official secrecy, Mayer added, "there is no viable system of accountability in place, despite the fact that the agency has killed many civilians inside a politically fragile, nuclear-armed country with which the U.S. is not at war."[35] In May 2009, Mayer reported, Obama's handpicked CIA director, Leon Panetta, referred to this unaccountable, mass-murderous program as "the only game in town" when it came to fighting al Qaeda.[36]

"Hated Far More . . . Than Are the Taliban"

When we further consider that the Obama-escalated U.S.-Pakistani assault on the Swat Valley in the northern section of Pakistan's FATAs had created at least 2 million refugees by the fall of 2009,[37] it was hardly surprising that "the United States is hated far more in Pakistan than are the Taliban."[38] Asked by the *Al Jazeera*/Gallup Pakistan Poll in late July 2009 who they "think is the greatest threat for Pakistan" 59 percent of Pakistanis named the United States, 18 percent pointed to traditional national enemy India, and only 11 percent picked the Pakistani Taliban. Two thirds of Pakistanis said they "oppose drone attacks by the United States against Taliban and al-Qaeda targets in Pakistan."[39]

Six and a half months later, during a visit to Pakistan meant to bolster that nation's public support for the U.S. invasion, Secretary of State Hillary Clinton helped demonstrate why masses of Pakistanis might be alienated from the United States in the Age of Obama as well as of Bush. The following exchange took place during a carefully staged quasi–town hall meeting—what the State Department strangely labeled a "Townterview"— with female Pakistani journalists in Peshawar University, where a questioner asked the top U.S. diplomat if she thought that attacks that kill innocent civilians amounted to terrorism—the "execution of people without a trial" in, as another questioner said, "violation of international law":

QUESTIONER: What is actually terrorism in U.S. eyes? Is it the killing of innocent people in, let's say, drone attacks? Or is it, again, the killing of— a vengeful killing of innocent people in different parts of Pakistan, like the bomb blast in Peshawar two days ago? Which one is terrorism, do you think?

HILLARY CLINTON: I only heard your second one about the—

MODERATOR: Okay, basically the question was that victims of drone attacks, is that terrorism, or people being killed in a marketplace in Peshawar,

is that terrorism? In the United States—do you perceive both victims as victims of terrorism?
HILLARY CLINTON: No, I do not. I do not.[40]

As Justin Raimondo noted on Antiwar.com, "The audience of Pakistani women sat there in stunned, horrified silence."[41]

"Body Counts Are Back"

At the same time as it increased U.S. troop casualties and civilian "collateral damage" in Afghanistan and Pakistan, the Obama-era U.S. military command brought back the once-controversial tabulation and advertisement of body counts as part of the public relations of colonial war. As the *Wall Street Journal* reported from the Bagram Air Force base in June 2009:

> Body counts are back—reigniting the decades-old debate about whether victory in war can be judged measuring the stack of enemy dead.
>
> In recent months, the U.S. command in Afghanistan has begun publicizing every single enemy fighter killed in combat, the most detailed body counts the military has released since the practice fell into disrepute during the Vietnam War. . . .
>
> U.S. officers say they've embraced body counts to undermine insurgent propaganda, and stiffen the resolve of the American public.
>
> "It's a concern that at home, the common perception is this war is being lost," says Lt. Col. Rumi Nielson-Green, spokeswoman for the 101st Airborne Division, which initiated the policy.[42]

As *Wall Street Journal* reporter Michael M. Phillips explained, U.S. military planners originally came up with the chilling "body count" idea when the U.S. "found itself mired in a guerilla war in Vietnam, where front lines were blurred and villages taken or lost didn't indicate who was winning." Denied the past and simple "success metric" of "territory held" (the classic measure during World Wars I and II), the Pentagon opted for "enemy body counts" as a gauge of supposed triumph. Facing the U.S. public's perception that America was "losing" in Afghanistan and a related growing sense that the White House had no clear or precise, measurable war aims or exit strategy in that country, the Obama Pentagon calculated it might be useful to return to the practice of reporting the exact number of "insurgents"—an interesting term for militants fighting an illegal imperial invasion of their "sovereign" country—it had liberated from biological existence.[43]

(The Vietnam-era body count practice was abandoned because it tended to create a false impression of success and because it offended domestic moral sensibilities against the taking of human life. It became well known among antiwar activists and many U.S. citizens that Vietnam commanders inflated body counts to appear more "successful" than they were and that many of the officially reported "enemy" dead included innocent civilians counted under the notorious rule that "any dead gook is Viet Cong.")

Regret Without Apology:
Killing Afghans Versus Scaring New Yorkers

Dead civilians—the topic Karzai so impolitely raised with his new boss in Washington—have been a real problem for Obama. The new president's escalation of deadly attacks on insurgents who live intermingled with civilians has brought a predictable increase in "collateral damage" in South Asia. An especially graphic and politically difficult episode came in the first week of May 2009. That's when U.S. airstrikes killed more 140 civilians in Bola Boluk, a village in western Afghanistan's Farah Province. Ninety-three of the dead villagers torn apart by U.S. explosives were children. Just twenty-two were males eighteen years or older. As the *New York Times* reported:

> In a phone call played on a loudspeaker on Wednesday to outraged members of the Afghan Parliament, the governor of Farah Province, Rohul Amin, said that as many as 130 civilians had been killed, according to a legislator, Mohammad Naim Farahi. Afghan lawmakers immediately called for an agreement regulating foreign military operations in the country.
>
> "The governor said that the villagers have brought two tractor trailers full of pieces of human bodies to his office to prove the casualties that had occurred," Mr. Farahi said.
>
> "Everyone at the governor's office was crying, watching that shocking scene."
>
> Mr. Farahi said he had talked to someone he knew personally who had counted 113 bodies being buried, including those of many women and children. Later, more bodies were pulled from the rubble and some victims who had been taken to the hospital died, he said.[44]

The initial response of the Obama Pentagon to this horrific incident— one among many such mass U.S. aerial killings in Afghanistan since October 2001—was to absurdly blame the civilian deaths on "Taliban grenades." Clinton expressed deep "regret" about the loss of innocent life, but the administration refused to issue an apology or acknowledge U.S. responsibility for the blasting apart of civilian bodies in Farah Province.[45] By sharp contrast, Obama had just offered a full apology and fired a White House official because that official had scared New Yorkers with an ill-advised Air Force One photo-shoot flyover of Manhattan that reminded people of 9/11.[46] The disparity was extraordinary: Frightening New Yorkers led to a full presidential apology and the discharge of a White House staffer. Killing more than one hundred Afghan civilians did not require any apology. Nobody had to be fired. And the Pentagon was permitted to advance preposterous claims about how the civilians died—stories that were taken seriously by "mainstream" (corporate-imperial war and entertainment) media. George Orwell, Kurt Vonnegut, and Franz Kafka would have been impressed. The United States subsequently conducted a dubious "investigation" of the Bola Boluk slaughter that reduced the civilian body count drastically and blamed the Taliban for putting civilians in the way of U.S. bombs.[47]

Going for Broke:
A Death Squad Leader
Promoted to Chief of the Af-Pak War

Any doubt that Obama intended to go "full bore" without concern for human rights and other niceties in South Asia should have been erased when he decided in May 2009 to promote a notorious assassin and death-squad leader to the position of commander of U.S. Forces in Af-Pak. Obama's new Af-Pak chieftain was Lieutenant General Stanley A. McChrystal—former chief of the military's special Joint Special Operations Command in Iraq who was involved in a prisoner abuse scandal in Baghdad's Camp Nana and who played a key role in covering up the "friendly fire" death of professional football star and U.S. Army ranger Pat Tillman. By journalist Alexander Cockburn's account, "McChrystal's expertise is precisely in assassination and 'decapitation.' As commander of the military's Joint Special Operations Command (JSOC) for nearly five years starting in 2003, McChrystal was in charge of death squad ops, with its best advertised success being the killing of Abu Musab al-Zarqawi, head of al-Qaida in Iraq."[48] According to Tom Engelhardt, Obama's elevation of McChrystal, "a legacy figure from the worst days of the Bush-Cheney-Rumsfeld era," was emblematic of the new administration's "growing desperation and hysteria over the wars it inherited." By Engelhardt's chilling description:

Stanley McChrystal is the general from the dark side (and proud of it). . . . McChrystal's appointment as the man to run the Afghan War seems to signal that the Obama administration is going for broke. It's heading straight into what, in the Vietnam era, was known as "the big muddy."

General McChrystal comes from a world where killing by any means is the norm and a blanket of secrecy provides the necessary protection. For five years he commanded the Pentagon's super-secret Joint Special Operations Command (JSOC), which, among other things, ran what Seymour Hersh has described as an "executive assassination wing" out of Vice President Cheney's office.

. . . In the Bush years, McChrystal was reputedly extremely close to Secretary of Defense Donald Rumsfeld. The super-secret force he commanded was, in fact, part of Rumsfeld's effort to seize control of, and Pentagonize, the covert, on-the-ground activities that were once the purview of the CIA.

Behind McChrystal lies a string of targeted executions that may run into the hundreds, as well as accusations of torture and abuse by troops under his command.

. . . All of this offers more than a hint of the sort of "new thinking and new approaches"—to use Secretary of Defense Robert Gates's words—that the Obama administration expects General McChrystal to bring to the evolving Af-Pak battlefield.[49]

Interestingly enough, Obama has resorted to off-the-books, so-called supplemental funding of the colonial Iraq and Afghanistan Wars—a deceptive war-financing method that Bush pioneered and that candidate Obama said he would abandon.[50]

"The Safe Haven Myth"

On September 11, 2009, nearly nine months into his presidency, Obama marked the eight anniversary of the historic September 2001 jetliner attacks by justifying his escalation and expansion of the U.S. war in South Asia in a speech to New Yorkers.[51] After making the standard, obligatory statements of compassion for the "nearly 3,000 lives [that] were lost in the deadliest attack on American soil in our history," Obama moved toward the case for his increasingly unpopular escalation:

No one can guarantee that there will never be another attack; but what I can guarantee—what I can promise—is that we will do everything within our power to reduce the likelihood of an attack, and that I will not hesitate to do what it takes to defend America.

That is why we are providing the necessary resources and strategies to take the fight to the extremists who attacked us on 9/11 and who have found safe haven in Pakistan and Afghanistan.

We are investing in the 21st century military and intelligence capabilities that will allow us to stay one step ahead of our enemies, including increasing the size of the Army and Marine Corps.[52]

The reference to expanding the scale of the army and marines was intriguing to hear from a supposed peace president. At the same time, as numerous establishment experts pointed out in the summer of 2009, Obama's claim, inherited from George W. Bush, that the war in Afghanistan was required to protect Americans from another 9/11 was and remains a highly dubious assertion. As Harvard Kennedy School of Government professor Stephen Walt noted in an August 2009 *Foreign Policy* essay, Obama's "safe haven myth" rested on the fundamentally flawed premise that al Qaeda or its many and various imitators couldn't just as effectively plot and conduct future terror attacks from any of a large number of other locations, including Western Europe and the United States itself. At the same time, Walt noted, Obama's expanded engagement in the ambitious social and political reconstruction and reengineering of Afghanistan and perhaps even Pakistan, trying, with slight chances of success, to create a centralized democratic state in the former country, was reinforcing al Qaeda's core claim that the Western and, above all, the U.S. presence in South Asia was about imperial control. The more the United States was seen as "trying to restructure their societies along lines that we think are appropriate," Walt noted, "the more we play into the narrative that they use to try and attract support and recruit people in Afghanistan itself."[53]

Five days after Obama's war-rationalizing 9/11 speech, Georgetown professor and former deputy chief of the CIA's counterterrorist center Paul Pillar seconded Walt's critique in the editorial pages of the *Washington Post.* "By utilizing networks such as the Internet," Pillar noted, "terrorists' organizations have become more network-like, not beholden to any one headquarters." A significant jihadist terrorist threat to the United States was still very much alive, Pillar acknowledged, adding, however, that "that does not mean it will consist of attacks instigated and commanded from a South Asian haven, or that it will require a haven at all. Al-Qaeda's role in that threat is now less one of commander than of ideological lodestar, and for that role a haven is almost meaningless."[54]

As Promised:
Bush's (and Now Obama's) Good and Proper War

There was and remains a critical difference between Obama's actions on Iraq and those in regard to Af-Pak: Whereas his Iraq policy arguably contradicts critical aspects of his campaign rhetoric and imagery, his bloody actions in South Asia have been largely consistent with what he said he was going to do as president. Throughout his U.S. Senate career and presidential campaign, peace candidate Obama reassured the U.S. foreign policy establishment of his willingness to stay firmly within the spectrum of acceptable imperial opinion by voicing strong support for the U.S.-led bombing and invasion of Afghanistan that followed in the wake of the 9/11 attacks. According to Obama throughout the electoral contest, one of the main problems with George W. Bush's "mistake" (the Democratic presidential front-runners never called it criminal or immoral) of invading Iraq was that it "diverted" U.S. military resources that should have been dedicated to the supposed smart and just war in (on) Afghanistan. Like many other official "doves" on the "bad war" in Iraq, Obama was a hawk on Afghanistan. Speaking on ABC Television's *Nightline* the night before the four critical primaries of March 4, 2008 (Ohio, Texas, Vermont, and Rhode Island), Obama argued that Afghanistan was George W. Bush's worthy and necessary war. Then President Bush "responded properly when it came to Afghanistan," Obama told ABC, but "he responded ideologically when it came to Iraq"[55]—not criminally but "ideologically," according to a candidate who deceptively claimed to stand above "ideology." On February 21, 2008, in Austin, Texas, Obama used the platform of a CNN Democratic presidential candidates' debate to criticize the Bush administration for dropping the ball of the good and smart war on terror in (on) Afghanistan by choosing to wage its "dumb" and "ideological" war in (on) Iraq.[56]

Throughout the national debate over Obama's "Afghanistan options" in the summer and fall of 2009, there was no discussion outside marginal left media and circles of the fact that the initial, heavily Democratic Party-supported bombing and invasion of Afghanistan took place in bold defiance of international law forbidding aggressive war. Sold as a legitimate defensive response to the jetliner attacks, the campaign was undertaken without definitive proof or knowledge that that country's Taliban government had been responsible in any way for 9/11. It occurred after the Bush administration had rebuffed offers by that government to extradite accused 9/11 planners to stand trial in the U.S. With no legal claim to introduce regime change in another nation, the bombing and invasion sought to destroy the Taliban government. It took place over the protest of numerous Afghan opposition leaders and against the warnings of aid organizations that expected a U.S. attack to produce a humanitarian catastrophe. U.S. claims to possess the right to bomb Afghanistan—an action certain to produce significant casualties—raised the interesting question of whether Cuba and Nicaragua were entitled to set off bombs in the United States given that this country had provided shelter to well-known terrorists who had conducted murderous attacks on the Cuban and Nicaraguan people and governments.[57]

The U.S. attack on Afghanistan met none of the standard international moral and legal criteria for justifiable self-defense and occurred without reasonable consultation with the UN Security Council. As prominent legal scholar Marjorie Cohn noted in July 2008, "The invasion of Afghanistan was as illegal as the invasion of Iraq." As Cohn explained, the UN Charter requires member states to settle international disputes by peaceful means. Nations are permitted to use military force only in self-defense or when authorized by the Security Council. After 9/11, the council passed two resolutions, neither of which authorized the use of military force in Afghanistan. Assaulting that country was not legitimate self-defense under article 51 of the UN Charter because the jetliner assaults were criminal attacks, not "armed attacks" by another country. Afghanistan did not attack the United States, and fifteen of the nineteen 9/11 hijackers came from Saudi Arabia. Furthermore, there was no "imminent threat of an armed attack on the United States after September 11 or Bush would not have waited three weeks before initiating his October 2001 bombing campaign." As Cohn added, "The necessity for self-defense must be 'instant, overwhelming, leaving no choice of means, and no moment for deliberation.' This classic principle of self-defense in international law has been affirmed by the Nuremberg Tribunal and the U.N. General Assembly."[58]

Many defenders of the invasion, Democrats as well as Republicans, upheld Bush's right to attack prior to such consultation by making the analogy of a maniac who had broken into your house and already killed some residents: "Do you sit around and negotiate with the murderers while they kill more, or do you go in and take them out?" But as left author and antiwar activist Rajul Mahajan argued, "The analogy to the U.S. action would have been better if the maniac had died in the attack, and your response was to bomb a neighborhood he had been staying in, killing many people who didn't even know of his existence—even though you had your own police force constantly on the watch for more attacks."[59]

Not surprisingly, an international Gallup Poll released after the bombing was announced showed that global opposition was overwhelming. In

thirty-four of the thirty-seven countries Gallup surveyed, majorities opposed a military attack on Afghanistan, preferring that 9/11 be treated as
a criminal matter rather than as a pretext for war. Even in the United
States, just 54 percent supported war.[60] "In Latin America, which has some
experience with U.S. behavior," Noam Chomsky noted, "support [for the
U.S. assault] ranged from 2% in Mexico, to 18% in Panama, and that support was conditional on the culprits being identified (they still weren't eight
months later, the Federal Bureau of Investigation reported) and civilian
targets being spared (they were attacked at once). There was an overwhelming preference in the world for diplomatic/judicial measures, rejected out of hand by [Washington, claiming to represent] 'the world.'"[61]

U.S. Public Opinion Turns Against
Campaign for Escalation in Afghanistan

By the middle of summer 2009, one didn't have to be a left antiwar activist
or intellectual like Cohn, Mahajan, Chomsky, or the author of the present
volume to oppose Obama's "good war." A *Washington Post*/ABC News Poll
conducted between August 13 and 17 of that year found that a majority of
Americans now saw the war in Afghanistan as "not worth fighting." Just a
fourth believed that "more U.S. troops should be sent to the country." Public opinion had shifted significantly against the war since Obama's inauguration, when the new president had majority support for his decision to
send 17,000 more troops into Afghanistan. The new poll came as Mc-
Chrystal prepared to request more troops for his stepped-up efforts to "re-
move the Taliban from Afghan towns and villages." Overall, seven in ten
Democrats told the *Washington Post* and ABC News that the war had not
been "worth its costs," and fewer than one in five supported an increase in
troop levels. "Should Obama embrace his general's call for even more
forces," *Post* reporters Jennifer Agiesta and Jon Cohen argued, "he would
risk alienating some of his staunchest supporters" because "majorities of
liberals and Democrats alike now, for the first time, solidly oppose the war
and are calling for a reduction in troop levels."[62] A CNN/Opinion Research Council Poll late in August 2009 found that nearly three fourths
(74 percent) of Democrats and more than half (57 percent) of Independents opposed Obama and Bush II's "good" war, leaving the overall support
for the conflict at a very disproportionately Republican 42 percent. The
leading Democratic Afghan war skeptics included Representative John
Murtha (D-PA), chairman of the House Appropriations Committee's defense subpanel; Senator Carl Levin (D-MI), chairman of the Senate Armed
Services Committee; and even Speaker of the House Nancy Pelosi.[63] By

contrast with Obama's declining support on Afghanistan from Democrats and Independents, 70 percent of Republicans told the *Post* and ABC that the war was worth fighting, and conservatives (at 58 percent) remained the war's strongest backers.[64]

A front-page story in the *Wall Street Journal* in mid-September 2009 noted a remarkable irony: In his apparent determination to deepen U.S. involvement in Afghanistan "despite flagging support from the public and top Democrats in Congress," Democratic peace president Barack Obama was relying on "Republican allies," including leading neoconservative war hawks such as archreactionary pundit William Kristol and former Bush II political director Karl Rove. With his Joint Chiefs of Staff chairman (Admiral Mike Mullen) and his defense secretary (Robert Gates) speaking to Congress on behalf of McChrystal's request later this month for at least as many as 40,000 new troops in Afghanistan, Obama's Af-Pak commander and his escalation agenda were embraced by the highly placed archconservative, ultramilitarist pressure group, the Foreign Policy Initiative (FPI). FPI's director explained that his group was trying to make McChrystal the "public face" of an expanded Afghan war under Obama in the same way that President George W. Bush had "used General David Petraeus as an effective public surrogate" to advance the troop "surge" (escalation) in Iraq in 2006–2007. "What we're trying to do here is raise the visibility of Gen. McChrystal," the director reported. "It is in some case part of *a branding* of a credible general."[65]

In early September 2009, *New York Times* reporter Peter Baker offered an interesting report. "On at least one of his major policies," Baker observed, "President Obama is getting support, and a nudge, from an unlikely quarter—Sarah Palin," signer of a recent letter "praising [Obama] for his management of Afghanistan." The letter's other signatories included Kristol, Rove, and "a variety of veterans from the Bush administration" and the McCain campaign. "We urge you to continue on the path you have taken thus far and give our commanders on the ground the forces they need to implement a successful counterinsurgency strategy."[66]

"Boxed in" and Stumbling to Disaster

In mid-September 2009, the White House and *New York Times* claimed that Obama was seriously considering alternatives to a major troop increase in Afghanistan in a "wholesale" strategy review. According to some top White House aides and *Times* reporters Peter Baker and Elizabeth Bumiller, the new options being reviewed included Vice President Joe Biden's call to scale back "counterinsurgency" forces in Afghanistan and to focus more on a counterterrorism effort to "root out Al Qaeda there and in Pakistan." At best however, Obama was merely testing—or claiming to test—assumptions to try to mollify liberals in his own party before quite predictably acceding to General McChrystal's call for significantly more "boots on the ground" in Afghanistan. As hawkish U.S. senator Joe Lieberman (I-CT) suggested to *New York Times* columnist Ross Douthat at the end of September, "Obama's ultimate decision" was "a foregone conclusion—not least because the president's past statements allow for no alternative."

Throughout a discussion with the militarist senator, Douthat reported, "Lieberman repeatedly cited Obama's own arguments ('as the president said the other day . . . ') to buttress the case for sending more troops to Afghanistan. And he suggested, more than once, that the president's choice essentially amounts to deciding whether to abandon a strategy to which Obama has already committed himself." Douthat "heard a similar themes, in public and private, from many counterinsurgency advocates. . . . However serious his doubts about escalation," Douthat concluded, "Obama seems boxed in—by the thoroughness of McChrystal's assessment and the military's united front, by his own arguments across the last two years and by his party's long-running insistence on painting Afghanistan as the neglected 'good war.'"[67]

Douthat worried with reason that Obama was taking "us deeper into war out of political necessity," with "results" that "could be disastrous." Veteran prolific left U.S. historian Gabriel Kolko predicted that the president's unwillingness to buck the military establishment, Washington's reluctance to lose "credibility" by appearing to have suffered defeat, and the Vietnam-like mind-set of the chief executive would translate into an intensification of the "war" effort. "Obama," Kolko wrote, "thinks he will win the war by escalation—an illusion that also marked the futile war in Vietnam. He also believes he can 'Afghanisise' the war—as Nixon thought he could 'Vietnamise' that conflict—even though recruits for Karzai's army have little motivation apart from collecting their salary, and are scarcely a match for the Taliban."[68]

Kolko, a legendary left chronicler of U.S. foreign policy overreach and failure,[69] was certain that the "few officers, mostly lacking influence," who warned of a "disaster" were correct. Obama struck Kolko as too full of imperial hubris and illusion to heed the alarms. The weakness of the existing U.S.-supported regime in Afghanistan, the insistence of the Pakistani military that its prime enemy is India (and not the Taliban or Al Qaeda), and the continued fueling of extremist Islam by the Israel-Arab conflict combined with the growing unpopularity of the Bush-Obama "good war" in

Europe and inside the United States itself made it seem likely that Obama was headed for a true disaster in Af-Pak. Like Bush before him, Obama would be continuing the longstanding U.S. imperial pattern of reacting to global complexity "with overwhelming firepower rather than realistic political response and negotiation," a path strewn with bloody disasters and "baleful consequences for America and the world."[70]

Of course, one reasonable policy response was beyond remote consideration in either the Obama White House or the news and editorial sections of the *New York Times*:

> They can't or won't consider the most obvious solution which would accommodate the Taliban's often-stated position for a cease-fire: end the occupation.
>
> Solution: withdrawal with an Organization of Islamic Conference–backed peacekeeping force filling in the power vacuum, while turning the puppet government into an interim government towards a democratic election, in which the Taliban would disarm and become a party, ala Northern Ireland.
>
> But the US couldn't control the outcome so it can't be considered.[71]

Not that Obama wasn't given an opportunity to stand down from disaster in "Af-Pak." In September 2009, McChrystal undertook a shockingly public campaign on behalf of the assignment of 40,000 new troops to Afghanistan. His case for increased force levels was sent to *Washington Post* columnist Bob Woodward, and McChrystal advanced this case in a brazen speech to the Institute for Strategic Studies in London, where the "Af-Pak" commander said that Vice President Joe Biden's "small footprint counterterrorism strategy" would turn Afghanistan into "Chaosistan."

McChrystal's insolence was astonishing. Obama could have fired him—on the model of President Harry Truman's discharge of General Douglas MacArthur—for insubordinate disrespect of the civilian control over military policy that is codified in the U.S. Constitution. But McChrystal was let off with little more than a terse comment from Obama's national security advisor, General James Jones, who said that it would have been preferable for McChrystal's comments to have been voiced "through the chain of command." Obama then proceeded to aggravate his "progressive base" and defied irrelevant majority public opinion by proclaiming that "withdrawal is not an option."[72]

A Decision That Was Never in Doubt

Inevitably, Obama's extended "Afghan policy review" ended as left commentator Alexander Cockburn predicted. "He'll shoot," Cockburn wrote in early October, "for some kind of lethal semi-compromise on reinforcements, thus feeding the right and angering his liberal supporters."[73]

Cockburn's prediction was dead-on. On December 1, 2009, speaking to a prime-time national television audience from the U.S. Military Academy at West Point (George W. Bush also liked to announce military escalations from military settings), the commander in chief announced plans to send 30,000 more troops to Afghanistan over six months, on an accelerated timetable that would dispatch several hundred marines by Christmas. As the Associated Press noted on the morning before the president's war address, "Obama will try to sell a skeptical public on his bigger, costlier war plan by coupling the large new troop infusion with an emphasis on stepped-up training for Afghan forces that he says will allow the U.S. to leave."[74] Although he spoke vaguely of an "exit strategy" in order to mollify the nation's antiwar majority, Obama was clearly escalating in accord with the wishes of McChrystal and other top civilian and uniformed military officials and with his own record on Af-Pak. As David Lindorff observed, Obama had consistently "proceeded to ramp up the Afghanistan War from a small-scale operation to a full-fledged war, with no prospect of ending it, and every sign pointing to an ever wider and bigger war in that region."[75]

Obama used the phrase "safe haven" six times in his oration, trying to convince Americans that they would be endangered in their own daily lives if the United States did not send more troops to kill and die in remote Afghan hills and valleys. The president said nothing in his address about the tens of thousands of private military contractors deployed by the Pentagon in Afghanistan or about the secret drone war he had already dramatically escalated against Pakistani "terrorists" and civilians.

Empire and Inequality 2.0:
"The United States Is Broken . . . Yet
We're Nation-Building in Afghanistan"

He also failed to mention the absurdity of his decision to spend untold billions more dollars on a futile, massively expensive colonial operation abroad as misery and destitution expanded at home. The domestic social uplift and opportunity cost of his imperial policy—the very twisted misplacement of resources that Martin Luther King Jr. described as symptomatic of "spiritual death"[76]—was certainly enormous. By the best White House calculations, the Afghan escalation was going to cost $1 million a year per every single new soldier deployed[77]—a giant investment that could have been diverted to meet growing unmet social needs across the United States. Echoing

Dr. King's late-1960s sermons and speeches against the U.S. military state's "perverted priorities," *New York Times* columnist Bob Herbert marked the day of Obama's West Point Address with an eloquent lament:

> The president has arrived at a decision that never was much in doubt, and that will prove to be a tragic mistake. It was also, for the president, the easier option.
>
> It would have been much more difficult for Mr. Obama to look this troubled nation in the eye and explain why it is in our best interest to begin winding down the permanent state of warfare left to us by the Bush and Cheney regime. It would have taken real courage for the commander in chief to stop feeding our young troops into the relentless meat grinder of Afghanistan, to face up to the terrible toll the war is taking—on the troops themselves and in very insidious ways on the nation as a whole.
>
> More soldiers committed suicide this year than in any year for which we have complete records. But the military is now able to meet its recruitment goals because the young men and women who are signing up can't find jobs in civilian life. The United States is broken—school systems are deteriorating, the economy is in shambles, homelessness and poverty rates are expanding—yet we're nation-building in Afghanistan, sending economically distressed young people over there by the tens of thousands at an annual cost of a million dollars each.[78]

It was Empire and Inequality,[79] combined and interrelated, mutually reinforcing, caught up in a dialectically inseparable duet of viciously circular destruction, and rebranded.

A Little Historical Revisionism

Obama's Afghan "surge" address was unsurprising, given that, as Cockburn noted, "Obama has . . . surrounded himself with the same breed of intellectuals who persuaded Lyndon Johnson to escalate the [Vietnam] war." As Engelhardt pointed out, Obama's "civilian advisors" on Afghanistan in the fall of 2009 included a large number of military men, all predisposed by career background and philosophy to advocate increased force levels. Did it really make sense to be surprised, Engelhardt wondered, that Obama would opt for more troops, money, and war when the president had "turn[ed] crucial war decisions over to the military . . . functionally turn[ing] our foreign policy over to them as well?"[80]

If there was anything surprising about Obama's December 1st address, it was the extent to which he was willing to distort history on behalf of his militaristic policy:

Just days after 9/11, [Obama said] Congress authorized the use of force against al Qaeda and those who harbored them—an authorization that continues to this day. . . . For the first time in its history, the North Atlantic Treaty Organization [NATO] invoked Article 5—the commitment that says an attack on one member nation is an attack on all. And the United Nations Security Council endorsed the use of all necessary steps to respond to the 9/11 attacks. America, our allies and the world were acting as one to destroy al Qaeda's terrorist network and to protect our common security.[81]

Obama clearly meant here to create the false impression that the UN Security Council authorized the Bush administration's attack on Afghanistan in October 2001. But, of course, the council did no such thing because the attack met none of the UN's criteria for legitimate self-defense. After 9/11, the council passed two resolutions, neither of which authorized the use of military force in Afghanistan.[82] The suggestion that human civilization ("the world") was united in support of Washington's attack on Afghanistan was completely incorrect, as we have already seen.[83]

"Under the banner of this domestic unity and international legitimacy—and only after the Taliban refused to turn over Osama bin Laden—we sent our troops into Afghanistan," Obama said, adding that "we did not ask for this fight."[84] This was completely false and as such completely worthy of Bush and Cheney. In fact, the United States refused to respond to the Taliban government's offer to turn Osama bin Laden over to a foreign government for a trial once evidence pointing to his guilt had been presented. The United States made sure that bin Laden would not be turned over through legal and diplomatic channels because, quite frankly, the Bush administration wanted war and did not wish to follow the UN Charter's requirement that nations pursue all means of resolution short of force before taking military action.[85] "President George Bush rejected as 'non-negotiable' an offer by the Taliban to discuss turning over Osama bin Laden if the United States ended the bombing in Afghanistan," the *Guardian* reported on October 14, 2001.[86]

The speech was marred by broader historical deceptions that seemed to have been pasted almost without revision from the war speeches of George W. Bush. Just like his predecessor, Obama peered straight into the camera to address the people of a nation he was about to inflict more terror on and said, "I want the Afghan people to understand—America seeks an end to this war and suffering." Like the much-bemoaned messianic militarist "Dubya," the new war president claimed that "we have no interest in occupying your country." He even claimed—quite preposterously—that he wanted "to forge a lasting friendship in which America is your partner, and never your patron." Also like Bush, Obama

- exaggerated the "contributions from our allies" in the "war" effort, which is overwhelmingly American.
- cited al Qaeda's "attacks against London and Amman and Bali" as a justification for imperial interventions in distant Muslim lands.
- promised a long war against terrorism: "The struggle against violent extremism will not be finished quickly, and it extends well beyond Afghanistan and Pakistan. . . . It will be an enduring test of our free society, and our leadership in the world."
- went to remarkable rhetorical lengths to whitewash the supposed benevolent historical record of that great global "leadership," claiming that
  o "more than any other nation, the United States of America has underwritten global security for over six decades."
  o "unlike the great powers of old, we have not sought world domination."
  o "we do not seek to occupy other nations."
  o "we are still heirs to a moral struggle for freedom. And now we must summon all of our might and moral suasion to meet the challenges of a new age."

These last claims were too much for Matthew Rothschild, editor of the monthly left-liberal magazine *The Progressive*. In an essay titled "Obama Steals Bush's Speechwriters," Rothschild offered a historically informed response:

Well, let's see: The United States led the world to the cliffs of nuclear annihilation during the Cold War. The United States invaded one Latin American country after another, and subverted other governments there covertly. The United States helped overthrow governments in Ghana and the Congo, and supported racist forces in southern Africa. The United States plunged into the Korean War, and then supported one dictator after another in South Korea. The United States killed between two and three million people in Indochina. And the United States supported Suharto in

Indonesia, who killed nearly a million people, some at the behest of the CIA, after taking power in 1965. The U.S. also supported Suharto's invasion of East Timor ten years later, which took another 200,000 lives.

Obama can call that "global security," if he wants to, but it's dripping red.

... What does having almost 1,000 military bases in more than 100 countries mean, then?

... The United States has invaded or overthrown dozens of countries in the last six decades, and it doesn't need to occupy them if it can install a puppet regime instead.

"If you closed your eyes during much of the President's speech on Afghanistan Tuesday night and just listened to the words," Rothschild added, "you easily could have concluded that George W. Bush was still in the Oval Office. ... And that he didn't choke on these words tells you all you need to know about Obama."[87]

Demonstration Elections
amid More Civilian Death

The decision to further escalate in Af-Pak was made roughly three months after a highly rigged demonstration election was held on August 20 to reinstall U.S.-backed Afghan president Karzai and to thereby increase the perceived legitimacy of the U.S. occupation. Charges of corruption and vote tampering forced a highly staged runoff election in October that was canceled at the last minute, with Karzai's opponent reasonably observing that no serious contest was possible.[88] Obama, who had been delaying his "strategy review" until the election, declared himself satisfied with the "democratic" outcome of the second staged exercise in, supposed popular governance and then proceeded down the deadly road of escalation.

During the delay, a UN report released in the last week of September noted that roughly 1,500 civilians had died in Afghanistan from the beginning of the year to August. Civilian deaths had jumped more than 20 percent in 2009 compared with previous year. Most of the deaths were blamed on insurgent roadside bombs and suicide attacks. But a significant number of civilians were killed by airstrikes conducted by U.S. and NATO forces, the report said.[89] Consistent with that finding, NATO reported on October 1, 2009, that eleven civilians, including women and children, had been killed in an airstrike by coalition forces in Helmand Province. CNN calmly and banally reported that "civilian deaths have risen in recent months as the war intensifies and the country deals with the recent disputed presidential election"[90]—more interesting developments for the president's speechwriters to ponder as they drafted Obama's oration thanking the Nobel Peace Prize committee for granting him its annual award in Oslo, Norway, on December 10, 2009.

"A Replay of Baghdad"

Obama means for the American Empire to stay in Af-Pak for a long time. He has announced the building of gargantuan U.S. "superembassies"—modeled on the gigantic "city within a city" that is the U.S. Embassy in American-occupied Baghdad—in Kabul and Islamabad, along with massive new consulates in Peshawar and Lahore. According to McClatchy Newspapers in May 2009, "The scale of the projects rivals the giant U.S. Embassy in Baghdad, which was completed last year after construction delays at a cost of $740 million." State Department officials claimed that the huge building projects were required to support a "surge" of civilian officials into Afghanistan and Pakistan ordered by Obama and Hillary Clinton. "This is a replay of Baghdad," said Khurshid Ahmad, a member of Pakistan's upper house of Parliament. "This [Islamabad embassy] is . . . for the micro and macro management of Pakistan, and using Pakistan for pushing the American agenda in Central Asia."[91]

In an effort to mollify his fading liberal base as he tacked further right and into alliance with the Republicans on "Af-Pak," Obama made reference in his West Point speech to a timetable for the beginning of withdrawal in July 2011. This should not be even remotely confused with a schedule for actual withdrawal, however. Just in case anyone thought otherwise, the White House public relations machine went into hyperdrive the weekend after the speech, sending out what the *New York Times* called a "forceful public message . . . that American military forces could remain in Afghanistan for a long time. . . . In a flurry of coordinated television interviews," the *Times* reported, "Defense Secretary Robert M. Gates, Secretary of State Hillary Rodham Clinton and other top administration officials said that any troop pullout beginning in July 2011 would be slow and that the Americans would only then be starting to transfer security responsibilities to Afghan forces under Mr. Obama's new plan."

In his West Point War Speech, Obama naturally failed to note that his drone war and Washington's murderous presence in South Asia were fueling the very destabilization and terrorism he purported to oppose and wanted Americans to fear in Afghanistan and Pakistan. He did not note that the United States intended to remain in the region for a very long time, something that powerfully validated Osama bin Laden's longstanding narrative on how the American Empire had dug in for a long occupation of the Muslim world.

Punishing Iran

"Lying Through [His] Teeth" on the Iranian Nuclear Threat

Meanwhile, as Obama prepared to reescalate in Afghanistan in the late summer and early fall of 2009, the new, soon-to-be designated Nobel Peace Prize–winning president took another script from George W. Bush's playbook by helping to build a false "weapons of mass destruction" case for a future attack on Iran. In a dramatic appearance alongside French president Nikolas Sarkozy and British prime minister Gordon Brown at the G-20 economic summit in Pittsburgh on September 25, Obama announced that Iran had been caught "red-handed" with "a secret nuclear facility" designed to produce nuclear weapons that would threaten Israel, the United States, and the world. Obama took on a menacing tone as he warned Iran of dire consequences for possessing a covert, illegal "nuclear weapons program" and adding for good measure that he did not rule out a U.S. military assault on Iran.

The charges were nonsense, reminiscent of Bush's claim about weapons of mass destruction in Iraq. As former Reagan administration official Paul Craig Roberts explained in late September, Iran's nuclear energy program was open to routine and careful inspection by the International Atomic Energy Agency (IAEA), which had repeatedly announced that Iran was diverting no nuclear material to nuclear weapons production. Each of the sixteen U.S. intelligence agencies had repeatedly confirmed that Iran had discarded any interest in nuclear weapons years ago. On September 16, *Newsweek* reported these agencies' conclusion that Iran's "nuclear status" had not altered since November 2007, when the U.S. National Intelligence Estimate reported with "high confidence" that Iran had ended its alleged onetime nuclear weapons program in 2003.

Iran honored IAEA guidelines and fulfilled its responsibilities under its "safeguard agreement" with that agency by informing the IAEA on September 21 that it had a new nuclear facility under construction. Obama's hyperbolic, headline-grabbing claim that Iran was trying to deviously subvert international regulation to create a bomb that would endanger the world was, Roberts reported, "another hoax, like the non-existent 'Iraqi weapons of mass destruction.' Just as the factual reports from the weapons inspectors in Iraq were ignored by the Bush regime, the factual reports from the IAEA are ignored by the Obama Regime. Like the Bush Regime, the Middle East policy of the Obama Regime is based on lies and deception." Along with Brown and Sarkozy, Roberts noted, the president was "lying through [his] teeth."[92]

Roberts's judgment was consistent with that of IAEA director General Dr. Mohamed ElBaradei. In a September 9, 2009, report, ElBaradei expressed "dismay" at "politically motivated" and "totally baseless" accusations being made against Iran by the United States, Israel, and other IAEA member states.[93]

MOP-ping Up: Celebrating the
Nobel Peace Prize by Speeding Up
Production of "the Ultimate Bunker-Buster"

Nearly five weeks later, just days after the announcement that Obama would be awarded the Nobel Peace Prize, the British newspaper the *Daily Mail* reported that Obama was accelerating the production and delivery to the Middle East of a colossal, thirteen-ton "bunker-buster" bomb to be carried by B-52 and B-2 Stealth Bombers and designed "to destroy hidden weapons bunkers buried underground and shielded by 10,000 pounds of reinforced concrete. . . . The 13-ton behemoth—called the 'massive ordnance penetrator,' or 'MOP—will be the largest non-nuclear bomb in the U.S. arsenal and will carry 5,000 pounds of explosives." Planning for the MOP had begun in the Bush II years but had languished for "budgetary" reasons until Obama called for developing MOPs rapidly as he came into office. The Nobel-winning president decided "to bring the bomb on line more quickly," directing the Pentagon to award "a nearly $52 million contract to speed up placement of the bomb aboard the B-2 Stealth Bomber."[94] Obama's Pentagon denied that the president's "nuclear standoff" with Iran was the reason, but this was clearly a lie, as was well understood among knowledgeable observers.

The "Mafia Principle" Holds

Meanwhile, the basic premise on which Obama's weapons-developing, saber-rattling line on Iran was based was fundamentally preposterous. That premise posited a real risk that a nuclear-armed Iran might attack already heavily nuclear-armed Israel. As Noam Chomsky explained to London's School of Oriental and African Studies in early November 2009, "The chance of Iran launching a missile attack, nuclear or not [on Israel] is about at the level of an asteroid hitting the Earth—unless, of course, the ruling clerics have a fanatic death wish and want to see Iran incinerated along with them." Chomsky further explained that U.S. "anti-missile weapons" were placed in Israel in order to prepare a possible missile attack on Iran, not (as the Obama administration and the Bush White House before it claimed) to defend Israel. The "real purpose of the U.S. interceptor system . . . is to prevent any retaliation to a U.S. or Israeli attack on Iran."[95]

Under Obama as under both Bushs, Reagan, and Clinton, Chomsky noted, two fundamental principles of post–World War II U.S. foreign policy remained firmly intact in regard to the Middle East. The first principle holds that if the U.S. "can control Middle Eastern energy resources, then [it] can control the [oil-dependent] world." The second core premise—the "Mafia Principle"—maintains that "the Godfather" does not tolerate "successful defiance." Other nations standing up successfully against the one superpower is "too dangerous" . . . a "virus" that could "spread [a] contagion" of resistance to Western and U.S. domination. "It must therefore be stamped out so that others understand that disobedience is not an option." Under Obama as under previous presidents, Iran is perceived by top U.S. policymakers as insufficiently submissive to imperial masters and must therefore be punished with "sanctions and other means," including possibly military assault.[96]

As prolific left Australian author, filmmaker, and columnist John Pilger explained, "Iran's crime is its independence. Having thrown out America's favourite tyrant, Shah Reza Pahlavi, Iran remains the only resource-rich Muslim state beyond US control. As only Israel has a 'right to exist' in the Middle East, the US goal is to cripple the Islamic Republic. This will allow Israel to divide and dominate the Middle East on Washington's behalf, undeterred by a confident neighbour. If any country in the world has been handed urgent cause to develop a nuclear 'deterrence,'" Pilger added, "it is Iran." Ludicrously accused by the Obama and Bush II administrations of posing a significant danger to Europe and the United States, Iran is surrounded on its western (Iraq) and eastern (Afghanistan) boundaries by nations occupied by the U.S. military. "The threat, as ever, is one-way, with the world's superpower virtually ensconced on Iran's borders."[97]

Protecting Israel and the Middle Eastern Status Quo

Obama's approach to the broader Middle East has followed in accord with the well-worn tension between his progressive-sounding rhetoric and his "deeply conservative" substance. He has continued (beneath false and heavily advertised claims to have taken a dramatic "new departure") the long-standing U.S. policy of supporting leading American client state Israel's illegal occupation and disfigurement of Palestine in defiance of world opinion and international law. Showing himself "unable or unwilling to halt Israel settlement growth and aggressive ethnic cleansing operations in East Jerusalem," Obama has refused to pay minimally honest attention to the legitimate grievances and aspirations of the Palestinian people. He has sustained the Bush administration practice of ignoring the Palestinians' elected government and refusing to acknowledge that Israel's incursions into the West Bank and Israel's forced separation of Gaza from the West Bank and its apartheid policies make the official U.S. goal of a two-state Israel-Palestine solution impossible. This was the harsh reality beneath and beyond Obama's much-ballyhooed effort to "touch the Muslim soul" during and after his high-profile speech "to the Muslim world," delivered from Cairo in early June 2009.[98]

Obama's Cairo speech called for Arab governments to "normalize" relations with Israel in accord with the 2002 Arab Peace Initiative but ignored key Israeli actions that the plan requires before such "normalization" can occur. The plan, approved by twenty-two Arab League nations, offered normalization with Israel only in exchange for complete withdrawal of Israel to its pre-1967 borders, the sharing (between Israel and a new Palestinian state) of Jerusalem, a fair resolution of the Palestinian refugee crisis in accord with international law, and more. Obama coldly ignored Israel's obligations under the initiative, demanding that Arab governments establish normal relations with Israel without getting anything substantive in return. Obama's Cairo call for Israel to cease further "natural growth" expansion of its West Bank settlements was next to meaningless. As Phyllis Bennis of the Institute for Policy Studies noted, "The fundamental problem of the settlements is not just their creeping expansion—it's their existence," housing close to half a million Israeli occupiers in a long stretch of "Jews-only settlements across the West Bank and East Jerusalem."[99]

Four months later, after Obama was gifted with the Nobel Peace Prize (granted in part because of his supposed service to the cause of healing between Israel and Palestine), Palestinian rights activist Sonja Karkar was struck by how "hollow" Obama's campaign slogan "Yes, We Can" now seemed to the Palestinian people:

> As each day passes, Mr. President, people everywhere believe less and less that you will change the eight awful years of neoconservative rule. In fact,

they see things getting much worse. The words "yes we can" increasingly grate, as you do nothing: and you of all people could have turned the Titanic midstream. The world would have been with you, no matter how powerful the military-industrial complex that your late President Eisenhower warned Americans about, no matter how shrill the cries of some 30 million Christian Zionists salivating over End Times in Jerusalem, no matter how intimidating the Israel lobby that shamefully holds Congress in its sway to the detriment of America's own interests.

. . . Billions of people in the world are ready to carry you on the crest of a tsunami, if you would only give us more than words. Perhaps from where you stand Mr. President you don't hear how hollow they sound. . . .

Yet, it is in that very same hollow space that more and more people can hear the keening sounds of silence from Gaza and the rapidly fading echoes of your "Yes we can."[100]

A telling moment came in the aftermath of the issuance of the Goldstone Report in mid-September 2009. Led by distinguished South African judge Richard Goldstone, the UN Human Rights Council joined numerous human rights organizations, including Amnesty International and the Israeli group B'Tselem, in concluding that that Israeli government had committed outrageous human rights crimes during its savage assault on the Palestinian Gaza territory in December 2008 and January 2009. Goldstone's account showed that Israel's grossly "disproportional response" to alleged provocations by the Palestinian group Hamas included around-the-clock carpet bombing that did not spare even hospitals, schools, and UN shelters and "the shooting of civilians holding white flags, the deliberate and unjustifiable targeting of UN shelters and the killing of over 300 children whilst the Israeli Army had at their disposal the most precise weaponry in the world." Goldstone's report accurately demonstrated how the powerful, U.S.-funded, and U.S.-equipped state of Israel turned its full, lethal force against a besieged and defenseless population imprisoned on a narrow strip of the land cut off from the rest of the world. "Actions amounting to war crimes, and possibly in some respects crimes against humanity, were committed by the Israel Defence Force," Goldstone concluded.[101]

The issuance of the report was an opportunity for Obama to prove his commitment to international and human rights law over and above the U.S. longstanding blank-check defense of Israel. Instead, the "changed" White House used its power to bury the report, encouraging the UN to shelve the document by smearing it as (in the words of Obama's UN ambassador Susan Rice) "unbalanced" and "deeply flawed." It strong-armed the Palestinian Authority into withdrawing a UN resolution supporting the report.[102]

Consistent with this response, Obama made no effort to resist the U.S. Israel lobby's torpedoing of Charles Freeman's nomination as chairman of the National Intelligence Council in the spring of 2009. The veteran national security operative was brusquely dismissed because he had once dared to suggest that the Israeli apartheid and occupation state might bear some responsibility for violence and hatred in the Middle East.[103]

But Obama's pronounced "pro-Israel" (pro-Israeli occupation and apartheid) bias was less than surprising to those who had followed his behavior during the period between his election and his inauguration. The Palestinians and their many supporters across the Middle East and the world watched in dread as famously wordy President-elect Obama stood mute as Israel conducted a dreadful U.S.-approved massacre with U.S. weaponry of trapped innocents, murdering thousands of civilians in the open-air Israel-imposed prison called the Gaza Strip in December 2008 and January 2009. He claimed that "institutional constraints" prevented him from commenting on the dreadful massacre while he gave regular proto-presidential speeches on the economy and condemned an Islamic terrorist action in Mumbai, India, in late November 2008. As Noam Chomsky noted:

> To these crimes Obama's response has been silence—unlike, say, the terrorist attack in Mumbai, which he was quick to denounce, along with the "hateful ideology" that lies behind it. In the case of Gaza, his spokespersons hid behind the mantra that "there is one president at a time," and repeated his support for Israeli actions when he visited the Israeli town of Sderot in July: "If missiles were falling where my two daughters sleep, I would do everything in order to stop that." But he will do nothing, not even make a statement, when U.S. jets and helicopters with Israeli pilots are causing incomparably worse suffering to Palestinian children.[104]

Even worse, the *New Yorker*'s tireless investigative reporter Seymour Hersh disclosed that American "smart bombs" and "other high tech ordnance" used in the attack on Gaza were resupplied to Israel after "the Obama team let it be known that it would not object."[105] Obama's call during his inaugural address for Muslims to "unclench [their] fists" must have seemed darkly ironic to many who noted his cold silence on the U.S.-Israel assault on Gaza, which conveniently ended on the new president's first day in office.[106]

Orwellian Absurdities on
Nuclear Weapons in the Middle East

Meanwhile, President Obama lectured Arabs on their duty to "unclench [their] fist[s]" and warned against the danger of "nuclear weapons in the Middle East" while saying nothing about Israel's murderously employed military fist and refusing to acknowledge the well-known fact that Israel (armed with as many as two hundred active nuclear warheads) is a heavily nuclearized state in the region.[107] He has gone to remarkable lengths to "reaffirm Israel's rogue status as a nuclear weapons state beyond the reach of the Nuclear Non-Proliferation Treaty [NPT]."[108] Thus, for example, when the IAEA in October 2009 passed a resolution calling on Israel to join the NPT and open its nuclear facilities to nuclear inspection, Washington tried (without success) to block the measure.[109]

The Orwellian absurdities have been positively surreal as the Obama administration has beat its chest over the nonexistent nuclear threat from Iran. "As one of the original signatories of the Nuclear Non-Proliferation Treaty," John Pilger observed in October, "Iran has been a consistent advocate of a nuclear-free zone in the Middle East. In contrast, Israel has never agreed to an IAEA inspection, and its nuclear weapons plant at Dimona remains an open secret."[110] Passed unanimously in the same month, UN Security Council Resolution 1887 called for the end of threats of force and for all nations to join the NPT. "The NPT non-signers," Chomsky noted in November, "are India, Israel, and Pakistan, all of which developed nuclear weapons with U.S help, in violation of the NPT. Iran hasn't invaded another country for hundreds of years—unlike the United States, Israel and India (which occupies Kashmir, brutally)." Chomsky added that "both India and Pakistan are expanding their nuclear weapons programs. They have twice come dangerously close to nuclear war, and the problems that almost ignited this catastrophe are very much alive."[111]

On October 2, 2009, a remarkable article in the *Washington Times* reported that Obama had agreed to follow a forty-year-old White House policy of openly pretending that Israel is not a nuclear-armed state. Three officials familiar with the longstanding secret U.S.-Israel pact on the official nonexistence of Israel's daunting nuclear arsenal told *Post* reporter Eli Lake that "President Obama has reaffirmed a 4-decade-old secret understanding that has allowed Israel to keep a nuclear arsenal without opening it to international inspection." By Lake's account, "the officials, who spoke on the condition that they not be named because they were discussing private conversations, said Mr. Obama pledged to maintain the agreement when he first hosted Israeli Prime Minister Benjamin Netanyahu at the White House in May." In late September 2009, Netanyahu let news of continued "agreement" slip on Israeli television when asked if he was worried that Obama's recent call for "a world without nuclear weapons" might apply to Israel. "It was utterly clear from the context of the speech that he was speaking about North Korea and Iran," Netanyahu told Israel's Channel 2, "But I want to remind you that in my first meeting with President Obama in Washington I received from him, and I asked to receive from him, an itemized list of the strategic understandings that have existed for many years between Israel and the United States on that issue."[112]

Moderate Allies

Meanwhile, Obama has continued the basic Bush policy of encouraging an anti-Iran alliance between the Israeli occupation state and so-called moderate Arab states. These moderate states include Egypt's atrocious police-state dictatorship and Saudi Arabia's misogynist theocracy, which is perhaps the most reactionary government on earth. All of these states continue to be lavishly funded by the United States under Obama—ironically enough given Obama's following comment in his anti-Iraq war speech in Chicago in the fall of 2002: "You want a fight, President Bush? Let's fight to make sure our so-called allies in the Middle East, the Saudis and the Egyptians, stop oppressing their own people, and suppressing dissent, and tolerating corruption and inequality and mismanaging their economies so that their youth grow up without education, without prospects, without hope, the ready recruits of terrorist cells." Six and a half years later, Obama as president refused to call Egypt's dictator Hosni Mubarak "authoritarian." He praised the Egyptian government as "a force for stability and good in the region." He claimed to have been "struck" by the "wisdom and graciousness" of Saudi king Abdullah, the head of state in a nation that regular practiced public beheadings. These comments amounted to a clear endorsement of torture, martial law, secret police, and worse in the Middle East.[113]

As feared and predicted by many Middle Eastern democracy activists, Obama's trip to the Middle East in early June 2009 ended up blessing repression in the Middle East. Obama used his high-profile diplomatic visit to the heart of the Arab world to call for a cooperative era of ambitious regional diplomacy. He made no far-reaching calls for political reform, reflecting the administration's decision to tolerate repression on the part of Middle East allies willing to assist the U.S. on "regional issues" (the U.S. occupations of Iraq and Afghanistan, the general U.S. support for Israel and its occupation and apartheid policies, and the U.S. campaign against Iran). President Mubarak and other Middle Eastern authorities naturally interpreted Obama's reluctance to raise questions of democracy as a green light to crack down on regime critics.

(In a similar vein, Obama followed in Bush's footsteps by privileging the country's perceived global economic interests over human rights in relation to totalitarian, state-capitalist China. The Dalai Lama, leader of the China-oppressed Buddhist state of Tibet, was unsuccessful in his attempts to meet with Obama during the late summer and early fall of 2009. Obama refused to confer with Tibet's spiritual leader until after visiting China in November. This reflected a policy that the Obama administration called in good Orwellian terms "strategic reassurance." The policy involved "softening criticism of China's [atrocious] human rights record and financial policies," *New York Times* columnist Maureen Dowd noted, "to calm its fears that America is trying to contain it (not to mention our own fears that the Chinese will quit bankrolling our debt").[114]

It was depressing for many who sought peace in the Middle East to hear Obama's Cairo speech buy heavily into the language of an epic global conflict between the Judeo-Christian world and the Muslim world. As brilliant left Middle East scholar Gilbert Achcar noted the day after the address:

> [Obama's] speech was lamentably constrained within the parameters of the "clash of civilizations" paradigm—whose main theoretician, the late Samuel Huntington, did not advocate the clash, as his non-readers believe, but warned of it. The paradigm was one of a world divided into blocs, the majority of which are constituted around a single religious criterion. Thus, Obama in Cairo exclusively addressed the "Muslims," scattering his speech with quotes from the Koran, expressing a view of the world dominated by religion—and only Abrahamic religions at that, forgetting that in his own country there are millions who do not belong to any [sects] of Christianity, Judaism or Islam, not to mention those who refuse to belong to any religion at all. In doing so, he paid an unintended tribute to the man whom he mentioned at the beginning of his speech and built up as its main target: Osama bin Laden.[115]

Jon Alterman, a State Department Middle East advisor under George W. Bush, offered an interesting perspective on the unchanged bipartisan and imperial continuities beneath and beyond Obama's much-ballyhooed trip to the Arab world. "Our policies," Alterman explained at a forum in Washington, "are a reflection of our interests and our alliances and while they may change moderately from administration to administration, the underlying interests are simply not allied with the policies that many Muslims around the world would like to see the United States pursue. We're going to have to agree to disagree, and that's the first task for the President—*to frame U.S. policy in a way that takes some of the passion out of the widespread hostility for the United States* [emphasis added]."[116] Obama's real task, Alterman felt, wasn't to change actual U.S. policy in the Middle East; it was rather to take the dangerous sting out of how those policies were perceived across the predominantly Muslim and Arab region. It was about *public relations and rebranding.*

Snubbing Durban II

Consistent with the general continuity between the foreign policies of Bush and Obama, the new president followed in his predecessor's footsteps by boycotting the second international UN conference on racism, the so-called Durban II gathering in Switzerland in April 2009. He did so for the same two basic reasons that had led Bush to steer clear of Durban I (in Durban, South Africa in 2001). First, the conference dared to raise the issue of slavery reparations. Second, the conference discussed the heavily racialized oppression experienced by Arab Palestinians under the apartheid-like system in the Israel-occupied territories. And so the new White House, with its first black president, its first black attorney general, and its first black ambassador to the United Nations decided not to be present at the world's leading forum to address international race relations.

Military Spending:
"No Stomach for Major Departures from Conventional Wisdom . . . on Questions of National Defense"

It is unlikely the many of Obama's "progressive," "liberal" and "left" fans (abroad as well as at home) know that the "not-Bush" peace president increased "defense" (empire and military) spending in his opening year.[117] In mid-June 2009, venerable Pentagon spending expert and critic Winslow T. Wheeler noted that

> if we add in the costs for the wars in Iraq and Afghanistan, the Pentagon budget for the current fiscal year—2009—exceeds any year since the end of

World War II, including the spending for the Korean and Vietnam wars. President Obama's plan is to increase that lead. Obama also will outspend Ronald Reagan on defense. Obama will outspend Reagan in his first four years by $369 billion. . . . Obama has already shown he has no stomach for major departures from conventional [Pentagon and war hawk] wisdom and the "moderate"—i.e., politically safe—thing to do on questions of national defense.[118]

In August 2009, the mainstream and nonpartisan, Washington-based budget and security monitor *Government Executive* reported that "the Obama administration's request for $538 billion for the Defense Department in fiscal 2010 and its stated intention to maintain a high level of funding in the coming years put the president on track to spend more on defense, in real dollars, than any other president has in one term of office since World War II. And that's not counting the additional $130 billion the administration is requesting to fund the wars in Iraq and Afghanistan next year, with even more war spending slated for future years."[119]

More Nuclear Hypocrisy

As the mainstream U.S. media failed to report, moreover, Obama's defense spending included $55 million for nuclear weapons production even as the White House was attacking Iran for its alleged engagement in the same behavior. In a remarkable report that was completely ignored outside marginal left U.S. media, the Inter Press Service (IPS) reported in late September 2009 that "despite statements by Barack Obama that he wants to see the world reduce and eventually eliminate nuclear weapons, the U.S. Department of Energy continues to press forward on a program called Complex Modernization, which would expand two existing nuclear plants to allow them to produce new plutonium pits and new bomb parts out of enriched uranium for use in a possible new generation of nuclear bombs." Left political scientist and media critic Anthony Dimaggio found the story's "timing" to be highly "ironic": The administration was openly funding the reconstitution of its own nuclear arsenal while denouncing a supposed Iranian nuclear weapons programs for which no direct physical evidence existed. According to IPS reporter Matthew Cardinale, "Obama has signaled his support for a significant shift toward [nuclear] disarmament as part of his upcoming Nuclear Policy Review. . . . However, so far, Obama has not taken any steps to stop Complex Modernization in its tracks and has not addressed the National Nuclear Security Administration's plans to develop new nuclear weapons or refurbish old ones."[120]

In mid-September 2009, Obama announced that the United States would be taking down "redundant" nuclear missiles positioned on Russia's border.[121] But this was meant, as John Pilger noted, "to cover the fact that the number of [U.S. nuclear missile]" sites was "actually expanding in Europe" under Obama while the supposedly "redundant" missiles were simply redeployed onto U.S. ships. The announcement was part of a public relations game meant "to mollify Russia into joining the U.S. campaign against Iran."[122]

Bullying Russia

Such mollification efforts notwithstanding, however, the Obama White House has continued the Bush administration's dangerous imperial practice of bullying Russia, still very much the world's second leading nuclear power. The administration has conducted military-training operations and supplied weapons to Georgia, site of a likely U.S.-sponsored war with Russia in August 2008. It has persisted with and possibly increased Bush's provocative efforts to incorporate Georgia and Ukraine and even formally neutral Sweden and Finland into NATO, a U.S.-dominated political and military alliance aimed at encircling Russia and rolling back Russian influence and power in Europe. And even though the administration scrapped George W. Bush's plans for "antimissile" bases near Russia's western border in Poland and Czechoslovakia, it reconfigured the anti-Russian "missile shield" with a more widely dispersed and mobile missile system that will be operational much more quickly than the previous administration promised. "With the growing threat of encirclement and aggressive militarization and technical advancement of western (mainly U.S.) weaponry proceeding apace," left researchers Edward S. Herman and David Peterson noted in November, "Russia had moved to an openly greater reliance on tactical and other nuclear weapons. On these areas, Obama once again represents *continuity rather than change*."[123] Just like Bush, Pilger added, Obama was using the ridiculous notion that Europe was threatened by Iran to "justify building a missile system aimed at Russia and China."[124]

The Counterattack on Latin America

In a late October 2009 *Salon* essay titled "Obama's Foreign Policy Report Card," left-liberal historian Juan Cole gave the president high marks: an

"A" on Iran and "B's" on Iraq and Pakistan. The "left" professor granted Obama "incompletes" on the Israeli-Palestinian conflict and Afghanistan. Herman and Peterson rightly found these mostly positive assessments "a bit shocking" given Cole's "knowledge and frequent enlightening comments" and in light of the record that I have sketched in the previous sections of this chapter. But the oddest thing about the "progressive" academician's "report card" was that it completely omitted the Western Hemisphere, where, as Herman and Peterson noted, "Obama's performance has been abysmal"[125]—abysmal, that is, from a left and democratic perspective.

"'New Beginning' on Cuba Is a Dead End"

Like his Middle Eastern policy, Obama's conduct toward Latin America has been richly consistent with that of previous U.S. presidencies, including the Bush administration. The story starts with Cuba, where Obama's slight lifting of travel restrictions—heralded by many liberals and some leftists as a sign of the administration's "progressive" intentions—has been "more than offset by [his] continuation of the notorious economic blockade." In mid-September 2009, he officially extended the crushing nearly half-century U.S. trade embargo on Cuba, rejecting broad Latin American sentiment and even the opinion of some Republicans. Introduced in 1962 to undermine the Cuban Revolution, which was widely supported by the Cuban people, the goal of the U.S. blockade on Cuba—significantly strengthened by the 1992 Cuban Democracy Act and the 1996 Helms-Burton Act—has always been simple: "to inflict pain and suffering on ordinary Cubans so as to drive them towards regime-change-type submission" to the imperial dictates of Washington. Bipartisan Beltway doctrine insists on trying to punish and collapse Cuban socialism, which can never be forgiven for daring to modernize and develop outside and against the supervision of Uncle Sam. In pursuit of this undying objective, the United States has been willing to violate international and human rights laws and conventions and to encroach on the rights of other countries to transact with Cuba as they see fit. The UN General Assembly has protested that encroachment every year since 1992.[126]

On October 28, 2009, that body voted 187 to 3 in favor of the United States lifting the blockade. The three countries that opposed the resolution were the United States, Israel, and the U.S. dependency Palau (administered by the United States until 1994). The U.S.-dependent states of Micronesia (still partly under direct U.S. control) and the Marshall Islands abstained. On the day of the vote *Guardian* correspondent Tom Fawthrop noted matter-of-factly that "Obama [has] followed in the footsteps of

George Bush by signing the annual renewal of Cuban sanctions in defiance of world opinion and intense lobbying by Latin American heads of states. By taking this step he has assumed authorship—it is now in effect Obama's trade blockade." The column in which this forthright judgment was advanced bore an appropriate title: "'New Beginning' on Cuba Is a Dead End."[127] Fawthrop's title referred to Obama's promise of "a new beginning with Cuba" during an April meeting with Latin American heads of state at the Summit of the Americas in Trinidad and Tobago. At the meeting, where Obama launched a "charm offensive" and extended a symbolic "olive branch" to increasingly leftist and independent Latin America, most of the thirty-four nations represented opposed the U.S. embargo against Cuba, "a 47-year-old policy which has become symbolic of 'Yankee' bullying."[128]

Cozying Up to Rightist Colombia

Also continuous with previous administrations, Obama has signed off on continuing expensive U.S. taxpayer and military investment in the repressive drug war efforts of Mexico and the heavily militarized right-wing U.S. client state of Colombia, whose corrupt leader, Alvaro Uribe, continues to receive a pass from Washington for his ongoing effort to undermine what remains of constitutional democracy and to make his rule permanent in his home country. The Colombian regime sponsors death squads and possesses the worst human rights record in Latin America. With guidance from Pentagon satellites, its paramilitaries conduct covert operations inside Venezuela with the aim of deposing the democratically elected left government of the self-proclaimed socialist and antineoliberal Hugo Chávez, whom the Bush administration attempted to overthrow in 2002. Valued as a bastion of U.S. power in a continent and region that has moved "dangerously" (from an imperial U.S. perspective) to the left and away from U.S supervision, Colombia continues in the Age of Obama to receive hundreds of billions of dollars in "military assistance" from Washington. As during the Bush years, it receives U.S. military support second in scale only to Israel.

On July 15, 2009, the Obama administration negotiated a deal (to be formally signed by the United States and Colombia later that year) that would grant the United States seven giant military bases. "The idea," reported the Associated Press, "is to make Colombia a regional hub for Pentagon operations. . . . Nearly half the continent can be covered by a C-17 [military transport] without refueling," which "helps achieve the regional engagement strategy." "Translated," Pilger wrote, "this means Obama is planning a 'rollback' of the independence and democracy that the people of Bolivia, Venezuela, Ecuador and Paraguay have achieved against the odds, along with a historic regional co-operation that rejects the notion of a U.S. 'sphere of influence.'"[129] Each of those countries except Paraguay was (and remains—along with Cuba and Nicaragua) a member of the anti-imperialist association ALBA (Alternativa Bolivariana para las Américas [Bolivarian Alternative for Latin America and the Caribbean]), an alternative to the U.S.-sponsored Free Trade Area of the Americas (FTAA). Formed by Venezuela and Cuba in 2004, ALBA differs from FTAA in that it advocates "a socially-oriented trade block rather than one strictly based on the logic of deregulated profit maximization." (ALBA "appeals to the egalitarian principles of justice and equality that are innate in human beings, the well-being of the most dispossessed sectors of society, and a reinvigorated sense of solidarity toward the underdeveloped countries of the western hemisphere, so that with the required assistance, they can enter into trade negotiations on more favorable terms than has been the case under the dictates of developed countries."[130])

Silence on Free-Trade Slaughter in Peru

Consistent with the notion of a U.S. "rollback" strategy, in Latin America, Obama remained silent as the government of Peru slaughtered indigenous people trying to prevent global corporations from exploiting Amazonian ecology under the terms of the U.S.-Peru Free Trade Agreement (USPFTA) in early June 2009. In the spring, the U.S.-backed Peruvian government enacted a series of laws and executive orders enabling it (in accord with USPFTA) to ease restrictions on the granting of indigenous lands to multinational oil, mining, and energy corporations. In response, the nation's Awajan and Wambis indigenous people participated in an impressive general strike for repeal. Meanwhile, hardly reluctant to voice criticism of human rights abuses in the empire's officially designated enemy states (such as North Korea, Sudan, Venezuela, and Iran), Obama had nothing to say after 650 heavily armed Peruvian National Police and Special Forces officers in full riot gear surrounded and then savagely attacked several thousand peaceful and relatively defenseless Awajun and Wambis protesters from land and air at a roadside blockade on the nation's Fernando Belaunde Terry Highway. "At about 6 am on June 5," Mexico-based journalist and author John Gilber reported on the *Huffington Post*, "the police attacked the indigenous people's highway blockade, ignoring their pleas for dialogue and opening fire with automatic weapons on two sides of the blockade and firing teargas grenades and live rounds from helicopters.

The protesters were unarmed or carrying traditional wooden spears. Many fled into the surrounding hillsides and became trapped. Many hid. And some fought back in self-defense." More than forty protesters were slaughtered by state gunfire and grenades, and hundreds were reported missing and detained by the police. Numerous observers reported that the police threw bodies into Maranon River and took other corpses to undisclosed locations to encourage underreporting of the number of indigenous people massacred.[131]

The Obama administration issued no statements of condemnation. It played along with Peruvian state propaganda linking generic, vaguely described "violence" and "rioting" in Peru to the government's longstanding conflict with violent Maoist (Shining Path) guerrillas. Interestingly enough, as no press accounts noted, USPFTA, an antilabor and antienvironmental measure, was supported by candidate Obama over and against significant criticism from John Edwards in the fall and winter of 2007.[132]

Studies in Imperial Ambiguity: A "Two-Faced" Response to a Coup in Honduras

There was what seemed like a brief shining moment at the end of June 2009 when Obama's progressive fans thought they had found evidence for their belief that the president represented a significant departure from Bush and the broader imperial habits of Washington. On June 28, 2009, right-wing generals and politicians in Honduras undertook a full-blown and highly illegal military coup against a left-leaning and democratically elected president, Manuel Zelaya. He was seized at his home in his pajamas and flown out of the country on the order of the Honduran Supreme Court for the sin of proposing a nonbinding popular vote on possible future constitutional reform.

In contrast to the Bush administration's immediate embrace of a short-lived right-wing coup against Hugo Chávez—a coup in which the CIA and U.S. military were centrally involved—in April 2002 Obama did not rush to defend this criminal action. To the delight of some of his liberal supporters, he even briefly condemned the illegal removal of Zelaya from power (and indeed from Honduras) and expressed his belief that the deposed president should be returned to power—an opinion he seemed to share with nearly every Latin American state and the UN General Assembly. On June 29, 2009, Obama said, "We believe the coup was not legal and that President Zelaya remains the president of Honduras, the democratically elected president there." Obama expressed "deep concern" regarding "the detention and expulsion of President Mel Zelaya" and called on "all political and social actors in Honduras to respect democratic norms" and the "the rule of law" so as to resolve "existing tensions and disputes . . . through dialogue free from any outside interference."

This, various liberal commentators proclaimed, was indicative of a new day in U.S. foreign policy. "Previously resigned Obamaphiles, desperate to grasp at any shred of proof suggesting that they were right to get high on hope and expect imminent change," left journalist George Ciccareillo-Maher noted on *CounterPunch*, "are closing ranks around their government and insisting that the U.S. government's response to the Honduran coup is proof positive of such change. Some even go so far as to claim that the Obama administration's support for Zelaya has been 'unambiguous,' adding that 'complaints that Washington hasn't acted fast enough to denounce the Honduran coup are silly and ignorant on the face of them.'"[133]

But progressive hopes for Obama's Honduran policy were naïve and soon betrayed. The subsequent action, or inaction by Obama and Secretary of State Hillary Clinton, sent strongly "mixed messages" on the blatantly criminal coup,[134] carried out by U.S.-trained and U.S. funded military forces and conducted with U.S.-supplied military equipment.[135] His initial rhetoric notwithstanding, Obama "stepped lightly" (as the *Washington Post* charitably put it) when it came to substantive policy response.[136] The White House possessed but refused to exercise its power to quickly restore Zelaya to his rightful office in Honduras, a nation whose government and economy had long been exceedingly dependent on the United States.[137] John Negroponte, a former U.S. ambassador to Honduras and a leading, blood-soaked figure in U.S. coordination of mass-murderous right-wing state terror across Central America under Ronald Reagan,[138] was *a leading advisor to Secretary of State Clinton on Latin American affairs*.[139] He told the *Washington Post* with approval that the Obama administration's disinclination to fully acknowledge the reality of recent events in Honduras "appeared to reflect reluctance to see Zelaya returned unconditionally to power."[140]

Would the United States work seriously for Zelaya's return to power? Secretary of State Clinton was a close associate of the Honduran coup regime's leading lobbyist in Washington—former White House counsel for Bill Clinton, Lanny Davis.[141] She refused to say whether the declared U.S. goal of "restoring constitutional order" in Honduras required Zelaya's restoration. After his initial seeming condemnation, Obama quickly ceased commenting on Honduras. Clinton *denounced* Zelaya for making what she felt was an unduly provocative and "irresponsible" effort to return to his home country in late July.[142] As the Honduran situation fell to the remote margins of corporate media coverage in mid-July (with no small help from the death of pop icon Michael Jackson and the emergence of major civil disturbances in Iran) and with the dominant U.S. media firms essentially supporting the legitimacy of the coup (falsely claiming that Zelaya had sought to unconstitutionally extend his reign beyond his elected term), the White House refused to officially classify Zelaya's ouster as a "military coup." Making such a declaration would have triggered (under the Foreign Assistance Act) a cutoff of tens of millions of dollars of U.S. aid to the Central American nation, whose budget was 65 percent dependent on foreign (very predominantly U.S.) assistance.[143] The White House made no hint of movement toward freezing the U.S. financial assets of leading Honduran coup leaders and participants—an obviously indicated action if the administration had been serious about punishing the Honduran putschists.

The White House's tepid and ambivalent response stood in sharp contrast to that of most Latin American nations and the European Union's quick and sharp call for Zelaya's rapid and unconditional return to power, raising what Latin America expert Mark Weisbrot called in early July 2009 "suspicions about what the U.S. government is really trying to accomplish in this situation."[144] More than two months later, progressive journalist Bill Conroy rightly described the Obama administration's policy toward the criminal de facto government that now ruled Honduras as "two-faced—expressing rhetorical outrage publicly while quietly continuing to prop up the coup regime economically behind the scenes." Conroy found that "nothing has changed—including the fact that the U.S. government continues to send millions of dollars in foreign aid to Honduras, which continues to be ruled by an illegal, thuggish junta." The United States had suspended a token amount of assistance, a tiny amount that suggested the disingenuous nature of the State Department's claims that the United States was "ratcheting up economic pressure" on the right-wing regime holding power in Honduras.[145]

Many mainstream U.S. media reports contrasted the Obama White House's outward rejection of the Honduran coup with the Bush administration's initial support for the 2002 coup that briefly ousted President Hugo Chávez in Venezuela. In reality, Weisbrot noted, there were "more similarities than differences" between the two administrations' responses to these two events. Within just one day, the Bush White House "reversed its official position on the Venezuelan coup, because the rest of the hemisphere had announced that it would not recognize the coup government. Similarly, in this case, the Obama administration is following the rest of the hemisphere, trying not to be the odd man out but at the same time not really sharing their commitment to democracy."[146] Worse, also continuous with the Bush-Chávez drama, there were (and remain) disturbing questions about the Obama administration's role leading up to the coup. The coup "followed conferences with U.S. officials and used a U.S. military base in that country, clearly with the tacit approval of U.S. officials."[147] As Jeremy Scahill noted one day after Zelaya's removal:

> It is impossible to imagine that the US was not aware that the coup was in the works. In fact, this was basically confirmed by the *New York Times*. . . . While the US has issued heavily-qualified statements critical of the coup—in the aftermath of the events in Honduras—the US could have flexed its tremendous economic muscle before the coup and told the military coup plotters to stand down. The US ties to the Honduran military and political establishment run far too deep for all of this to have gone down without at least tacit support or the turning of a blind eye by some US political or military official(s).
> . . . The US is the top trading partner for Honduras. The coup plotters/supporters in the Honduran Congress are supporters of the "free trade agreements" Washington has imposed on the region. The coup leaders view their actions, in part, as a rejection of Hugo Chavez's influence in Honduras and with Zelaya and an embrace of the United States and Washington's "vision" for the region. Obama and the US military could likely have halted this coup with a simple series of phone calls.[148]

The Obama administration claimed that it made its best effort to change the minds of the coup plotters in advance. But it is hard to imagine that U.S. officials were unable to succeed in that effort given the longstanding reach of U.S. power in Honduras. Of course, as Weisbrot noted, it would have been fascinating to know the exact content of these discussions: "Did administration officials say, 'You know that we will have to say that we are against such a move if you do it, because every one else will?' Or was it more like, 'Don't do it, because we will do everything in our power to reverse any such coup?'" The Obama administration's actions since the coup suggest something much closer to the former, if not something worse.[149]

The Hoax Agreement of October 30, 2009

When Zelaya audaciously returned to Honduras, speaking to the nation's people from the Brazilian Embassy in Tegucigalpa in late September of

2009, left-liberal U.S. television personality and talk-show host Amy Goodman sensed that "the Obama administration may be forced, finally, to join world opinion in decisively opposing the [Honduran] coup" and to "finally help the people of Honduras undo the coup."[150] There were indications that the White House might support Zelaya's return, *but only on a conditional basis*—with the expectation that the democratically elected president's beginning efforts to turn Honduras into a left state would be placed on hold for the remaining two months of his term. Such a policy outcome would have been very much in the imperial tradition of the Clinton administration, which reversed a coup in Haiti and returned that nation's democratically elected president, Jean-Bertrand Aristide, to power there only on the condition that he accede to the neoliberal policy agenda promoted by the United States. This would hardly be something for progressives to praise, for, as Weisbrot noted, any effort to "extract concessions from Zelaya as part of a deal for his return to office" would have violated the essence of "how democracy works."[151]

As of mid-October 2009, however, Zelaya continued to sit in the Brazilian Embassy. Since Zelaya had returned to Honduras, the coup regime had been violating human and civil rights. It surrounded the embassy with troops and cut off the embassy's power and water in a campaign to force Brazil to turn Zelaya over. The regime used tear gas on large crowds gathered outside and imposed a curfew to clear the streets, detaining violators in a football stadium where observers saw people who had been severely beaten.[152] It also cut off power to any alternative media outlets. Meanwhile, a front-page *New York Times* article calmly discussed how the right-wing coup regime was working with veteran former high-ranking officials responsible for setting U.S. Central American policy during the Reagan years (a period when the United States funded, sponsored, and directed massive state repression of leftists and civilians in El Salvador, Guatemala, and Honduras) to launch a successful high-profile lobbying and public relations campaign claiming that Zelaya was—to quote the testimony of Otto Reich (a former leading and archrepressive Central American operative in both the Reagan and Bush II administrations) to Congress in July 2009—part of "Hugo Chavez's attempt to undermine democracy in this hemisphere." According to the *Times*, the right-wing campaign involved "law firms and public relations firms with close ties to Secretary of State Hillary Rodham Clinton" and "had the effect of forcing the administration to send mixed signals" on the coup government. Chris Sabbatini, an editor of *America's Quarterly*, an academic policy journal focusing on Latin America, was less charitable. "There's been a leadership vacuum on Honduras in the administration," Sabbatini told the *Times*—a "vacuum" that was being rapidly and effectively filled by right wing neo-colonialists and the thuggish coup government itself, through its proxies in Washington.[153]

Obama had still refused to condemn the coup-makers. He had yet to recall the U.S. ambassador to the illegal Honduran government or the U.S. armed forces that trained a Honduran military acting in accord with Washington's longstanding expectation that it would repress popular resistance. Zelaya had still not been granted his request to meet with Obama, who approved an International Monetary Fund loan of $164 million to the coup regime. "The message," Pilger noted, "is clear and familiar: thugs can act with impunity on behalf of the U.S."[154]

Then, on October 30, 2009, the United States helped broker a supposed "end" to the coup and a belated, short-term "restitution" of Zelaya to office on strictly conditional and limited terms indicating Washington's continuing opposition to independent and democratic political development in Latin America. With the making of this U.S.-imposed "agreement," which was celebrated by liberals, the White House immediately removed the few and minor restrictions it had placed on the coup regime. The resolution enforced by Washington weakly called upon the Honduran Congress—"the same Congress that falsified Zelaya's resignation letter in order to justify the coup, the same Congress that that supported the illegal institution of [Roberto] Micheletti in the presidency" (in the words of progressive Latin American journalist Eva Gollinger)—to decide if it wished to reinstate Zelaya. The decision was to be made only after that Congress received a legal opinion on the matter from the Honduran Supreme Court, "the same one that said Zelaya was a traitor for calling for a non-binding vote on potential future constitutional reform, and the same one that called for his violent capture."

Even if the Congress were to agree to Zelaya's short-lived restoration (he had less than a month remaining in his term-limited time in office by early November), the deal was structured so that Zelaya would be powerless. The "agreement" required that his cabinet members would be assigned by the parties involved in the coup and the Honduran military would be under the command of the Supreme Court. It said that Zelaya could be tried for "treason" and put the "agreement's" implementation under the supervision of a "truth commission" headed by Richard Lagos, codirector of the Board of Directors of the Inter-American Dialogue, a right-wing think tank dedicated to rolling back independent development and left-wing political power in the name of "democracy." It was a foregone conclusion that the truth commission would not seriously examine the severe repression (including curfews, mass imprisonments, media shutdowns, and even murders) imposed by the coup regime on civil and democratic forces that dared to resist the coup.[155] No wonder the "agreement" struck critical observers as a "U.S.-staged hoax," a "publicity stunt" that was never intended for actual implementation.[156]

Within two weeks, the "deal" to "restore Zelaya" unraveled completely. The Honduran Congress announced that it would postpone a vote on Zelaya's return to power until after a presidential election scheduled for the end of November. Zelaya responded by refusing to submit names for a coalition government. Most of the thirty-four members of the Organization of American States (OAS) announced that they would not recognize the results of the November election unless Zelaya was first reinstated to finish his term. The White House, reversing its prior position, said that it would recognize the election's outcome—a decision that was welcomed by Republicans while it "ignited a storm of criticism from Mr. Obama's allies at home and across Latin America" (the *New York Times*). Senator John Kerry's (D-MA) office said that the senator believed that the administration's "abrupt change of policy" toward Honduras "caused the collapse of the accord it helped negotiate." Coldly rebuffing the charges of betrayal and reversal made by Latin American governments and left and liberal critics inside the United States, Obama's OAS representative, W. Lewis Amselem, argued that "the agreement signed in Honduras two weeks ago did not guarantee Mr. Zelaya's reinstatement, but put that decision in the hands of the Honduran Congress." According to the *New York Times*, Amselem "urgently pressed" the OAS to take "a more pragmatic line." Adding insult to injury, he arrogantly said the following about most Latin American states' declared refusal to recognize the forthcoming election: "What does that mean in the real world, not in the world of magical realism?" Here Amselem took a revealingly needless and sarcastic swipe at a cherished Latin American literary tradition (magical realism).[157]

It was an appropriately dismissive and disrespectful comment for Amselem to make, given his own past ugly history in Latin America, which included four years (1988–1992) as a politico-military officer at the U.S. Embassy in Guatemala City in a period when the United States was actively engaged with Guatemalan government authorities in the mass-murderous terrorization of Guatemalan peasants, workers, intellectuals, and activists. Amselem, who called Zelaya's return to Honduras in September "irresponsible" and "foolish," had been "denounced years ago for having concealed the identities of individuals, one of whom was a U.S. national, who tortured and raped a U.S. nun in Guatemala." As progressive Latin American journalist Jean Guy Allard noted, Amselem was "a diplomat from the Bush Administration, who remained in place, *just like many other ultra right-wingers in the current Obama administration* [emphasis added]."[158]

Far from a victory for the forces of progressive democracy and independence in Latin America, Gollinger pointed out, the October 30th agreement was an attempted exercise in imperial U.S. "smart power" of the sort that hoped to "disguise Washington's unilateralism as multilateralism." As Gollinger reflected on November 2, the coup's outcome combined with other less-than-portentous developments under Obama—an expanding U.S. military presence in right-wing Colombia and continuing U.S. antidemocracy efforts (potentially linked to future putsches) across the region—to raise real alarms on the part of those who supported Latin America's welcome shift toward progressive and independent development:

From day one, Washington imposed its agenda. . . .

In the end, "smart power" was sufficiently intelligent to deceive those who today celebrate an "end to the crisis" in Honduras. But for a majority of people in Latin America, the victory of Obama's "smart power" in Honduras is a dark and dangerous shadow closing in on us. Initiatives such as ALBA have just begun to achieve a level of Latin American independence from the dominant northern power. For the first time in history, the nations and peoples of Latin America have been collectively standing strong with dignity and sovereignty, building their futures. And then along came Obama with his "smart power," and ALBA was hit by the coup in Honduras, Latin American integration has been weakened by the US military expansion in Colombia, and the struggle for independence and sovereignty in Washington's backyard is being squashed by a sinister smile and insincere handshake.[159]

Four days after Gollinger penned this critique, the supposedly defeated and chastened postcoup coup government announced that it would create a new "government of reconciliation" to be headed by none other than coup leader and head of the de facto government Roberto Micheletti! Such was the glorious outcome of what Obama's secretary of state called "a tremendous achievement for the Hondurans"—the ridiculous October 30th agreement.[160]

On November 30, 2009, the Honduran coup regime held a sham demonstration election that voted into the presidency a "conservative businessman" and coup supporter ("Pepe" Lobo). The voter-abstention rate was very high, especially in poor and working-class districts, reflecting the determination of many Hondurans that the process was a laughable attempt to provide international legitimacy to the right-wing government. Except for the

U.S.-allied states of Colombia, Peru, Panama, and Costa Rica, the Latin American community of nations refused to recognize the election. In a revealing statement the Obama's State Department commended Hondurans for "peacefully exercising their democratic right to select their leaders."[161]

Advancing "Full Spectrum Operations" Throughout South America

Remarkably enough, October 30, 2009, was the same day on which the United States and Colombia signed a critical military agreement—an accord about which the White House lied and deceived in accord with long-standing imperial public relations procedure. The deal extended the U.S. military presence in Colombia by increasing U.S. access to seven military bases there for ten years. Under the agreement's terms, U.S. "anti-drug flights" that had previously originated from Ecuador (where left president Rafael Correa had suspended such operations) would now operate from the Colombian base at Palanquero, in the central Magdalena valley, and U.S. Navy port visits would be more frequent. Construction at the Palanquero base would be expanded. Under the terms of the pact, U.S. military and civilian personnel—including private military and "security" contractors—would enjoy diplomatic immunity from prosecution, exempting them from local criminal jurisdiction. The United States was authorized to utilize any installation throughout the entire country, even commercial airports, for military purposes. The accord "signifies," Eva Gollinger noted, "a complete renouncing of Colombian sovereignty and officially converts Colombia into a client-state of the US."[162]

According to the governments of both nations, the agreement related only to counternarcotics and counterterrorism operations within Colombian territory. Colombia's President Uribe repeatedly stated that it would not affect Colombia's neighbors. The leading U.S. Defense Department official for Latin America, Frank Mora, told the Associated Press in August that there would be no "U.S. offensive capacity," such as fighter jets, connected to any of the bases. He was trying to alleviate regional concerns—articulated in no uncertain terms by the left-led governments of Venezuela, Bolivia, and Ecuador—that the deal's real goal was, among other things, to enhance the Pentagon's capacity to project destabilizing force across the increasingly independent, left-leaning theater of Latin America.[163]

In fact, these nations' concerns were well founded. As Gollinger reported on November 5, 2009, a recently exposed May 2009 U.S. Air Force document showed that the real purpose of the agreement was to provide the U.S. military with an opportunity to conduct (in the document's words) "full spectrum military operations in a critical sub-region of our hemisphere where security and stability is under constant threat from narcotics funded terrorist insurgencies . . . and anti-US governments."[164]

There was little doubt as to which states in Latin America were considered by Washington to be "anti-US governments." That phrase referred to the states that had joined ALBA, into which Zelaya had brought Honduras against the wishes of his nation's capitalist oligarchy and key North American business interests, such as Dole and Chiquita, heavily invested in that country. As Gollinger noted, "The constant aggressive declarations and statements emitted by the State and Defense Departments and the US Congress against Venezuela and Bolivia, and even to some extent Ecuador, evidence that the ALBA nations are the ones perceived by Washington as a 'constant threat.'"[165]

The core continuities between the rebranding Obama White House and its predecessor on Colombia and Latin America were aptly summarized by left antiwar activist Shaun Joseph in early November 2009:

> Although the Obama presidency brings an improved rhetorical sheen to U.S. policy in Latin America, as with the Middle East wars and the economic bailouts, the new administration has mostly taken up the threads of the development initiated in the waning days of the previous administration but which that administration was too exhausted to carry out. Thus Obama has continued the imperialist counter-offensive—and proposed to bring it to an ominous new phase with the U.S. plan to gain access to seven military bases in Colombia, a move widely feared and condemned in Latin America.[166]

Against Independent Development

One day in the spring of his first term, Obama told a visiting Chilean reporter that the United States could not apologize for its critical role in the September 11, 1973, coup that overthrew Chile's then–elected president, Salvador Allende, and resulted in his assassination. That earlier coup ushered in the bloody rule of neofascist dictator Augusto Pinochet, who executed many thousands of left-wing activists and intellectuals as University of Chicago economists advised the Chilean elite on how to create a supposedly "free-market" utopia—in fact, a highly regressive and repressive experiment in the upward concentration of wealth and power. The United States could not apologize, Obama explained, because this nation is "an enormous force for good in the world," one that prefers to "look forward," not "backwards."

Obama's response to the 2009 Honduran coup fell far short of what one might expect from such an "enormous force." Nevertheless, it fit nicely into candidate Obama's support for the extension of NAFTA to Peru and with the following passage from the foreign policy chapter in *The Audacity of Hope*:

> Of course there are those who would argue with my starting premise—that any global system built in America's image can alleviate misery in poorer countries. . . . Rather than conform to America's rules, the argument goes, other countries should resist America's efforts to expand its hegemony; instead, they should follow their own path to development, taking their lead from left-leaning populists like Venezuela's Hugo Chavez, or turning to more traditional principles of social organization, like Islamic law. . . . I believe [Chávez and other] critics [of the United States and neoliberalism] are wrong. . . . The system of free markets and liberal democracy . . . offer[s] people around the world their best chance at a better life.[167]

Neoliberal global capitalism has offered "other countries" *no such thing*, especially to the nations and people of Latin America.[168] Candidate Obama's reflections ended on a profoundly false judgment, properly rejected by "Mel" Zelaya, who came into office in early 2006 as a center-right politician but who subsequently moved left and shifted his desperately impoverished country into ALBA.

An Orwellian Character and "the Best Brand in the World"

As Obama passed into his ninth month atop the American Empire, Alexander Cockburn noted:

> Many Obama dreamers hoped that their man would introduce some minimal shift for the better in America's relationship with the rest of the world. Now, all they have to look forward to is Gen. Stanley McChrystal marching up to Capitol Hill and into the Oval Office to demand more troops for Afghanistan. In relations with Russia Obama and Vice President Biden have remained substantively committed to NATO expansionism. In Latin America, the handling of the coup in Honduras and warm relations with Colombia's Uribe suggest a sinister larger strategy of counterattack on the leftist trends of the past few years.[169]

Meanwhile, Anthony Dimaggio observed that President Obama remained just as committed as his predecessors to advancing transparently hyped-up claims of alleged missile threats to the United States and its allies to advance a fantastic Star Wars program. It would make use of satellite technology to "weaponize space" and thereby achieve "full spectrum dominance" by the United States over other nations. Dimaggio noted that Obama's belligerent posturing against the alleged nuclear and missile threat posed by Iran was "a hypocritical attempt . . . to bully a non-nuclear state that resides in an oil rich region" the United States still seeks—under Obama no less than under both Bushes and Clinton—"to dominate by force."[170]

"Overall," prolific left journalist Jeremy Scahill rightly noted in mid-June 2009, "he's implementing a U.S. foreign policy that in some ways— or, I think, in many ways—advances the interest of the American empire in a way the Republicans could only have dreamed of doing." Furthermore,

what people, I think, misunderstand about Barack Obama is that this is a man who is a brilliant supporter of empire—who has figured out a way to essentially trick a lot of people into believing they're supporting radical change, when in effect what they're doing is supporting a radical expansion of the U.S. empire.

I think that Obama is showing himself to be a master of misdirection— almost like a magician. He'll say a few things in his speech that sound like they're new, like a totally different U.S. approach, but then he'll also at the same time roll out a policy that is further than even Bush took things.[171]

"Really, what we're seeing are rhetorical shifts and tactical shifts," left author and activist Anthony Arnove noted at the same time. "But the underlying ideology and the underlying substance of U.S. foreign policy remains quite consistent with the broad bipartisan consensus that's defined U.S. foreign policy for decades."[172] "Like Bush's America," Pilger noted in October, "Obama's America is run by some very dangerous people."[173]

The title of the article in which Scahill made his comments spoke a mouthful: "Rebranding War and Occupation."[174] In comments made around the same time as this article during a speech at the annual meetings of the International Socialist Organization, Scahill observed that "Obama is an incredibly Orwellian character. He can make people think that war is peace."

And not just people in the United States, Scahill might have added. Consistent with much of the U.S. foreign policy establishment's preelection calculation that Barack Hussein Obama as president could provide the badly Bush-damaged "brand USA" a dramatic and instant public relations makeover on the global stage, surveys by the Pew Research Center showed that "America's" popular standing in many parts of the world had advanced significantly since Obama's election. In Germany, for example, the percentage of people interviewed who expressed a "favorable" view of the United States rose from 31 percent in the summer of 2008 to 64 percent one year later. There were double-digit increases over the same period in Argentina, Brazil, Mexico, Spain, England, France, and Nigeria and small but significant increases in China, India, Japan, and South Korea.

Obama's popularity abroad was no small part of increased global approval of the United States. According to a German Marshall Fund of the United States survey released in September, 77 percent of Europeans interviewed supported Obama's handling of U.S. foreign affairs. Just 19 percent of Europeans had reported approving George Bush II's foreign policies the previous summer. More than 90 percent of Germans had a favorable view of Obama, 80 percent higher than the approval Germans had given to Bush the summer before. "Obama Euphoria," reflecting England and the Continent's relief at the replacement of the "boorish cowboy" Bush by the "sophisticated, urbane Obama," was still intact more than a year after Obama's triumphant campaign trip to Europe in the summer of 2008.[175]

It seemed to mark a striking confirmation of the French international relations professor Dominique Moisi's precocious reflection more than two weeks before Obama won the Iowa caucus. Moisi's thoughts certainly mirrored the hopes and dreams of Obama's early backers in the U.S. foreign policy establishment. In a December 24, 2007, *Guardian* column titled "Obama's American Revolution," Moisi argued that the global difference offered by an Obama presidency would have little to do with actual policy, which could be expected to stay much the same regardless of who won the next U.S. presidential election. The real change, quite significant in Moisi's view, would be about related matters of racial identity, style, "soft power," televised global imagery, and public "impression":

> Why is Obama so different from the other presidential candidates, and why could he make such a large difference internationally? After all, in foreign policy matters, the next president's room for maneuver will be very small. He (or she) will have to stay in Iraq, engage the Israel-Palestine conflict on the side of Israel, confront a tougher Russia, deal with an ever more ambitious China, and face the challenge of global warming.
>
> If Obama can make a difference, it is not because of his policy choices, but because of what he is. The very moment he appears on the world's television screens, victorious and smiling, America's image and soft power would experience something like a Copernican revolution.

Think of the impression his election would make not only in Africa, but in Asia, the Middle East, and even Europe. With its rise to global supremacy, America had become the incarnation of the West, and the West was seen as "white." . . . If a shift across America's racial divide is not truly revolutionary, then what is?

. . . The complexity of his identity makes him truly universal, a global candidate for a global age. By virtue of his unique personal history, he can bridge Africa, America, and even Asia—where he studied as a young boy in a Muslim school—thereby reviving the universal image and message of America.[176]

Curiously, however, Obama's marked popularity overseas and the related assistance his ascendancy gave to the U.S. image abroad often seemed to garner remarkably few tangible policy gains for the new president. As *New York Times* reporter Peter Baker explained on September 20:

As much as they may prefer to deal with Mr. Obama instead of his predecessor, George W. Bush, foreign leaders have not gone out of their way to give him what he has sought.

European allies still refuse to send significantly more troops to Afghanistan. The Saudis basically ignored Mr. Obama's request for concessions to Israel, while Israel rebuffed his demand to stop settlement expansion. North Korea defied him by testing a nuclear weapon. Japan elected a party less friendly to the United States. Cuba has done little to liberalize in response to modest relaxation of sanctions. India and China are resisting a climate change deal. And Russia rejected new sanctions against Iran's nuclear program even as Mr. Obama heads into talks with Tehran.

For an administration whose officials regularly boast of having what they call "*the best brand in the world*" [emphasis added], there is what Stephen Sestanovich calls growing "frustration with what other countries are prepared to contribute to advancing supposedly common interests." Personal relations are important, said Mr. Sestanovich, a former Clinton administration ambassador with ties to the current team, but national interests still dominate.[177]

Consistent with Baker's analysis, Obama's effort to translate his global charisma into the award of the 2016 Olympics to the president's "home city" of Chicago proved a spectacular failure in late September 2009. Obama took the remarkable step of flying personally to Copenhagen to speak (along with his wife, Michelle) on Chicago's behalf to the International Olympic Committee (IOC). He spoke "movingly" of how he "would like nothing more" than to walk with his daughters from his home on the city's South Side to the Olympic games in nearby Washington Park in the summer of 2016. Then he jetted back to Washington hours before the IOC result was announced.

Chicago didn't clear the first round of the IOC's vote. It finished dead last of the top four contestants (Tokyo, Madrid, and winner Rio de Janeiro). "Despite Obama's fabled charm and powers of persuasion," the Associated Press noted, "his in-person plea for Chicago to host the 2016 Summer Games fell flat. It was a hugely embarrassing defeat. His adopted hometown—considered a front-runner heading into Friday's voting—didn't just lose, it took last place, shocking nearly all by getting knocked out in the first round while the remaining three contenders moved on."[178]

IOC delegates may or may not have been impressed by the Obamas' presentation, but the more relevant factors were that the IOC and the U.S. Olympic Committee (USOC) were feuding over recent USOC moves and that Latin America had never once hosted an Olympics, whereas North America had been home to more than twenty Olympics.[179]

"It Is Wise to Attend to Deeds, Not Rhetoric"

Baker's finding fits the notion that the transition from Bush II to Obama was more about public relations and rebranding than about any deep or substantive change in the core, underlying U.S. structures, practices, policies, and doctrines or ideologies. As Noam Chomsky observed in London one year after Obama's election: "As Obama came into office, Condoleezza Rice predicted that he would follow the policies of Bush's second term, and that's pretty much what's happened apart from a different rhetoric and style. But it's wise to attend to deeds, not rhetoric. Deeds commonly tell a different story."[180]

Even though this statement would probably have irked most leading "mainstream" U.S. journalists and conventional academicians as an irresponsibly "ideological" comment, it was seconded by an ideologically diverse handful of British professors in a commonsense letter to left-leaning British newspaper the *Guardian* in mid-September of 2009. Their missive, asked British journalists and citizens to "grow up" about the reality of Obama in the real world of imperial power:

> Though Obama's leadership has enhanced America's image, as yet there has been no major change from the policies and outcomes of the Bush years. Yet

the Obama presidency is still reported in the mainstream media as a happy departure from the "disastrous Dubya." Though we are from opposite ends of the political spectrum, we strongly challenge this. The public, we feel, should be properly informed that the US will pursue its interests, regardless of which party holds power.

Obama presents himself as the "un-Bush." But when you look at substance, rather than style and rhetoric, and the structural constraints on presidential power, you can legitimately question the extent of his ability to change US policies. We call for a richer and better informed debate on US policy abroad. We need to end this unhealthy obsession with personalities and look properly at the issues—an admittedly difficult task given the supremely gifted and charismatic president now in office.

Journalists must be more forthright about the multibillion-dollar Pentagon budget, the massive numbers of US military bases around the world, the sheer scale of the US national security state. If, in Britain, more people knew of the 57 US bases in the UK, we might all be more realistic in our attitudes to that country.[181]

"Evil Does Exist in the World": The Nobel Gift

Such counsel and Obama's militantly imperial and militarist record notwithstanding, Barack Obama was absurdly granted the 2009 Nobel Peace Prize on the morning of Friday October 9, 2009. It was a "stunning decision" meant, Associated Press writers Karl Ritter and Matt Moore wrote, "to encourage his initiatives to reduce nuclear arms, ease tensions with the Muslim world and stress diplomacy and cooperation rather than unilateralism." But many were "shocked by the unexpected choice so early in the Obama presidency, which . . . has yet to yield concrete achievements in peacemaking" and "still oversees [colonial] wars in Iraq and Afghanistan and has launched deadly counter-strikes in Pakistan and Somalia." Ritter and Moore quoted Ahmid Shabir, an eighteen-year-old student in Kabul, who reasonably said that "I don't think Obama deserves this. I don't know who's making all these decisions. The prize should go to someone who has done something for peace and humanity." Former Polish president and Nobel Prize winner Lech Walesa was also taken aback: "So soon? Too early. He has [made] no contribution so far." The prize was offered by a five-member committee elected by the Norwegian Parliament. Like the Parliament, Ritter and Moore noted, the committee had a "leftish slant," with three of its members elected by left-of-center parties. The prize was meant in part as "a slap at [George W.] Bush from a committee that harshly criticized Obama's predecessor for his largely unilateral military action in the wake of the Sept. 11 terror attacks."[182]

Preposterous in light of the record reviewed in this chapter, the prize was *a spectacular gift to the Orwellian rebranding project*. I found it less than surprising given the exaggerated Obamania—more advanced even than what can be found in the United States—of what passes for a left in Western Europe.

Obama himself sensed the absurdity of the award. In his acceptance speech in Oslo on December 10, 2009, Obama stated, "I cannot argue with those who find [other] men and women—some known, some obscure to all but those they help—to be far more deserving of this honor than I." Obama claimed to be mindful of previous Nobel Peace Prize winner Martin Luther King Jr.'s statement "at this same ceremony years ago: 'Violence never brings permanent peace. It solves no social problem: it merely creates new and more complicated ones.'" "As someone who stands here as a direct consequence of Dr. King's life work," Obama said, "I am living testimony to the moral force of non-violence."[183]

This hardly prevented Obama from accepting the award or from using the awards ceremony as an opportunity to advance what the Associated Press rightly described as "a robust defense of war."[184] "I am the Commander-in-Chief of the military of a nation in the midst of two wars," Obama lectured the Nobel committee and the world. "I'm responsible for the deployment of thousands of young Americans to battle in a distant land. Some will kill, and some will be killed."

As "a head of state sworn to protect and defend my nation," Obama argued, "he could not be guided" by the examples of Martin Luther King and Gandhi "alone." "I face the world as it is," the president said, "and cannot stand idle in the face of threats to the American people. For make no mistake: Evil does exist in the world. A non-violent movement could not have halted Hitler's armies. Negotiations cannot convince al Qaeda's leaders to lay down their arms."[185]

"He's a Killer"

"Peace prize? He's a killer."

Thus spoke a young Pashtun man to an *Al Jazeera* English reporter on December 10, 2009—the day that Obama was given the Nobel Peace Prize.

"Obama," the man added, "has only brought war to our country."

The man spoke from the village of Armal, where a crowd of one hundred gathered around the bodies of twelve people, one family from a single home. The twelve had been killed, witnesses reported, by U.S. Special Forces during a late-night raid.

"Why are they giving Obama a peace medal?" another village resident asked. "He claims to want to bring security to us, but he brings only death. Death to him."

Al Jazeera went to the Afghan village of Bola Boluk, where a U.S. bombing had butchered dozens of civilians in the spring. "He doesn't deserve the award," a young woman said. "He bombed us and left us with nothing, not even a home."[186]

Seven days after Obama received his Nobel, Yemeni opposition forces testified that many dozens of civilians, including a large number of children, had been killed in U.S. air raids in the southeast section of their country. The fighters reported the deaths of sixty-three people, twenty-eight of whom were children, in the province of Abyan.[187] The killing command came directly from the president. As left commentator Barry Grey noted:

> US President Barack Obama personally issued the order for US air strikes in Yemen last Thursday which killed scores of civilians, including women and children.
> US warplanes used cruise missiles against alleged Al Qaeda camps in the Abyan village of al Maajala, some 480 kilometers southeast of the capital Sana'a, and in the Arhab district, 60 kilometers to the northeast of Sana'a. The US strikes were apparently coordinated with the US-backed dictatorship of Yemen President Ali Abdallah Saleh.

ABC World News reported that U.S. warplanes had been involved in the attacks. "White House officials tell ABC News," reporter Brian Rose said, "the orders for the US military to attack the suspected Al Qaeda sites in Yemen on Thursday came directly from the Oval Office." ABC also noted that Obama called Saleh after the slaughter to "congratulate" him on the attacks.[188] The Nobel-honored peacemaker Obama told Yemen's ruler that the operation "confirms Yemen's resolve in confronting the danger of terrorism represented by al Qaeda for Yemen and the world."[189]

Contrary to Obama's longstanding "American exceptionalist" belief that the U.S. has always been and remains "overwhelmingly a force for good in the world,"[190] the bloody record of U.S. imperial militarism noted by Matthew Rothschild eight days before led much of the world to think that global "evil" had long been significantly headquartered in Washington, DC. It's a record that the real-world President Obama—something very different than the mass-marketed Brand Obama sold to liberal voters at home and masses abroad—has done all too much to continue in the curious name of "change." Just ask the survivors of the January 2009 U.S. assaults on Bola Boluk or countless others who witnessed Obama's South Asian escalations firsthand in 2009.

Orwell Lives

Obama stayed in Oslo for just twenty-four hours, skipping the prize committee's traditional second day of festivities. "This miffs some in Norway," the Associated Press reported, "but reflects a White House that sees little value in extra pictures of the president, his poll numbers dropping at home, taking an overseas victory lap while thousands of U.S. troops prepare to go off to war and millions of Americans remain jobless."[191] A headline in Ohio calmly reported, "Nobel-Winning Obama Defends War in Call for Peace."[192]

It got crazier in Norway. Oslo newspaper *Aftenposten*'s chief political commentator, Harald Stanghelle, called Obama's acceptance speech "powerful." According to Stanghelle, Obama "made a clear message of faith in international order and in an ethical base for the handling of the problems of this world. Obama represents a hope for change," Stanghelle wrote. "Never before has the message of the need for war been presented with stronger conviction by a peace prize winner," wrote the *Norway Post*.

Norway's largest newspaper, *Verdens Gang*, concluded its main editorial on December 11, 2009, as follows: "Yesterday's speech will remain in history as a great Nobel Speech, possibly the greatest. A sitting US president, involved in two wars, was going to speak in favor of war and of peace. He managed to do both."[193]

As I wrote in a speech prepared for peace activists in Minneapolis on the evening of December 10: "We truly live in Orwellian times."

It wasn't only leftists like myself, however, who had detected the persistence of a militaristic and imperial agenda under the new supposedly progressive and peace-oriented new presidency. Six months before, the right-wing editors of the *Wall Street Journal* had offered a telling commentary in an editorial titled "Barack Hussein Bush": "One benefit of the Obama Presidency is that it is validating much of George W. Bush's security agenda and foreign policy *merely by dint of autobiographical rebranding* [and by] . . . artfully *repackaged* versions of themes President Bush sounded with his freedom agenda [emphasis added]. We mean that as a compliment."[194]

3

Corporate-Managed "Health Reform" (2009)

I have no interest in putting insurance companies out of business. They provide a legitimate service, and employ a lot of our friends and neighbors.
—Barack Obama, speech to a Joint Session of United States Congress, September 9, 2009

You see, he's saying he wants to continue private insurance, but then he says they're part of the problem. Well, which is it? It's just ridiculous.
—Rowena Ventura, July 23, 2009[1]

The industry has already accomplished its goal of at least curbing, and maybe blocking any new publicly administered insurance program that could grab market share from the corporations that dominate the business.
—Business Week, August 6, 2009[2]

"That's Politics"

Their Political Hats Don't "Come Out for Three Years"

In mid-August 2009, the *New York Times* ran a front-page story on the difficulty the Obama White House was experiencing in getting its supporters to fight for the president's "embattled health care plan" with anything like the passion and numbers voters and activists demonstrated in getting the president elected. The story was titled "Health Debate Fails to Ignite Obama's Grass Roots." It was sent in from the largely working-class town of Muscatine in the pivotal electoral state of Iowa, where Obama's defeat of John Edwards and Hillary Clinton on January 3, 2008, proved the viability of his not-so-"improbable quest" for the presidency.[3]

"People came out of the woodwork for Obama during the campaign," one older Obama supporter told *Times* reporter Jeff Zeleny, "but now they are hibernating. . . . Now it is hard to find enough volunteers to fight the Republicans' fire with more fire." Bonnie Adkins, a leading Obama activist in Muscatine in 2007 and 2008, was now a local "leader" in the Obama front group Organizing for America (OFA). She could induce only ten Democrats to attend a potluck dinner in support of Obama's health care "reform" effort in the summer of 2009. She told Zeleny that "the enthusiasm is not there like it was a year ago. Most people, when they get to November 5, put their political hat away and it doesn't come out for three years."[4] Understood to mean efforts to elect a presidential candidate, "politics" went out the window after the general election. It would elicit little excitement until the next big presidential spectacle rolled around.

It wasn't just ordinary Democratic citizens and voters who moved off "politics" once the election was over. Zeleny interviewed more than a dozen Iowa campaign volunteers, precinct captains, and other activists who had "dedicated a large share of their time in 2007 and 2008 to Mr. Obama." These former sparkplugs in the Obama machine told the *Times* that "they supported the president completely but were taking a break from politics." They were not active members of OFA, the permanent Obama campaign's supposedly "grassroots" pressure group that was based largely on the remarkable voter database that the Obama operation had developed during the primary and general election campaigns. OFA claimed at the time to have 13 million members and to employ forty-four state political directors across the nation.[5]

The "Election Trap"

The *Times* story was a graphic illustration of how millions of Americans have been led to misunderstand meaningful democratic politics. Many have been conditioned to see making strictly limited choices in the narrow-spectrum, mass-marketed, corporate-crafted election spectacles the power elite stages for them every four years as the only politics that matters. Real issues, public policy, and the need for regular ongoing popular movements and pressure at the day-to-day grassroots level get lost in the fog induced by hypnotic, colored-lights election dramas, focused on the competing, expertly marketed images of crafty politicians who understand very well their subordination to Edward Herman and David Peterson's "unelected dictatorship of money."[6] Having engaged in some brief popular excitement to install one of a handful of carefully elite-vetted business-sponsored candidates into nominal power, the citizenry is induced to go back to sleep and leave relevant matters of governance to the proper state-capitalist authorities—the "real players."[7] Reduced to the status of a corporate-managed electorate, it is no longer expected to participate in its "democracy" in any particularly relevant way. As Noam Chomsky wrote on the eve of the 2004 elections:

> The U.S. presidential race, impassioned almost to the point of hysteria, hardly represents healthy democratic impulses. Americans are encouraged to vote, but not to participate more meaningfully in the political arena. Essentially the election is yet another method of marginalizing the population. A huge propaganda campaign is mounted to get people to focus on these personalized quadrennial extravaganzas and to think "That's politics." But it isn't, it's only a small part of politics.
>
> In the election, sensible choices have to be made. But they are secondary to serious political action. The main task is to create a genuinely responsive political culture, and that effort goes on before and after electoral extravaganzas, whatever their outcome. . . . The urgent task for those who want to shift policy in a progressive direction—often in close conformity to majority opinion—is to grow and become strong enough so that they can't be ignored by centers of power.

The urgent ("main") task of movement-building, Chomsky noted, is "cultivated by steady, dedicated work at all levels, *every day, not just once every four years*"[8] [emphasis added].

Progressives are no less immune to movement-weakening candidate-centered politics than are other Americans. Indeed, they seem especially prone to recurrent falls into what noted left social critic Charles Derber calls "the Election Trap"—the belief that serious progressive change is mainly about voting. This a great mistake, for, as Derber notes, "the main catalysts for regime change in America have not been parties glued to the next election, but social movements that operate on the scale of decades rather than two- and four-year electoral cycles. Political parties have historically become agents of democratic change only when movements infuse the parties with their own long-term vision, moral conviction, and resources"[9]

Since at least the mid-1970s, the American right has been more astute than what passes for a left when it comes to understanding the pitfalls of the election trap and the need to organize and agitate between and across elections. The "health reform" debate of summer 2009 was an excellent case in point. The right exercised significant noxious yet effective pressure (claiming ludicrously that Obama and the Democrats were "socialists" pushing for a "government take-over of American health care") at congressional town hall meetings while liberals mustered only small gatherings for the president's health care agenda even in Obama's recent electoral strongholds.

"Well, Which Is It?"

Nevertheless, we should not go too far in presenting Obama's difficulty garnering grassroots support for his health reform package as an epitome only of the "election trap" that has so long plagued U.S. "progressives." Another problem behind the president's failure to "ignite" his "grass roots" on health care was that his health care agenda was overly complicated, uninspiring, and corporate-captive—hardly the stuff to inspire meaningful citizen engagement. If the administration had been sincerely interested in a national health care reorganization that would have cut costs, covered all Americans, and achieved mass popular support, the obvious and simple policy for it to have advanced would have been a government-managed, single-payer system. The next most straightforward and popular thing to propose would have been a genuinely robust "public option"—a government-run health insurance option modeled on Medicare (the nation's essentially single-payer government health insurance plan for Americans sixty-five and older) that would have been available to all Americans and competed effectively with private health insurance plans.

But Obama rejected both of these progressive policy solutions to the American health care crisis. Consistent with the complex and convoluted Clintonian "business liberalism" (cloaking itself as "get things done" pragmatism) that has characterized the Obama White House from the outset,[10] however, the main politically viable health reform bills that he approved and shaped in the first year of his presidency all proposed to leave the top cost-driving private insurance corporations in basic power alongside an unimpressive, watered-down, and all-too dispensable (as far as Obama and other leading corporate Democrats were concerned) "public option" for people unable to afford private insurance. What he proposed in the vacuum left by his abandonment of the clear and understandable progressive policy solutions—both enjoying widespread popular support—was overly byzantine, bewildering, and (no mere coincidence) business friendly to spark much passion on the part of the populace.

When Obama gave an uninspiring prime-time press conference in support of his health "reform" in July, much of the public didn't follow his logic on why it should embrace his corporate-captive version of "change." All too common and understandable was the reaction of Rowena Ventura, forty-four, an uninsured worker in Cleveland, Ohio, who had just moved her ailing mother into a house she shared with her disabled husband. "You see," Ventura said, gesturing at the president on her television, her comments captured on the front page of the *Times*, "you see," she said, "[the president's] saying he wants to continue private insurance, but then he says they're part of the problem. Well, which is it? It's just ridiculous."[11]

"The Manipulation of Populism by Elitism"

With President Barack Obama as with candidate Obama and former president Bill Clinton, we must always distinguish between progressive style and corporate-regime[12] substance. Like Clinton, Obama epitomizes what Christopher Hitchens once (in a book about the Clintons) called "the essence of American politics"—"the manipulation of populism by elitism."[13]

The "Speech's Seductive Nature": "Enough Rhetorical Chum to Keep the Liberals Happy"

Obama's nationally televised high-stakes health care address to a joint session of Congress in the late summer of 2009 was an excellent case in point. It aptly demonstrated the superconfident oratorical athleticism that helped Obama win voters in 2007 and 2008. Invoking the memory of the recently deceased liberal-Democratic standard-bearer Teddy Kennedy, the speech contained flashes of quasi-populist indignation crafted (with the latest polling data in mind as always) to keep his "liberal base's" lips locked on the drinking gourd of "hope." Congresspersons and citizens heard horror stories (no doubt true) about American citizens who died after being denied coverage by evil insurance corporations. "We are the only advanced democracy on Earth—the only wealthy nation—that allows such hardships for millions of its people," the president said. Obama spoke smartly about insurance companies' practices of "treat[ing] their customers badly—by cherry-picking the healthiest individuals and trying to drop the sickest, by overcharging small businesses who have no leverage, and by jacking up rates." Senators, representatives, and citizens were told that insurance premiums driven by out-of-control health-care costs were rising at three times the rate of wages. Social justice activists got some red rhetorical meat when Obama said that his reform would cost "less than the tax cuts for the wealthiest few Americans that Congress passed at the beginning of the previous administration." In a signal to his onetime "antiwar" base, Obama claimed that the price tag of his proposed health reform ($900 billion between 2013 and 2023) would be less over ten years "than we have spent on the Iraq and Afghanistan wars."

A little more than halfway through his oration, the president claimed to be committed to a "public option" to guarantee universal access and "keep the insurance companies honest." Seeking to distance himself from a "frenemy" industry that had privately lobbied him quite powerfully with no small success,* Obama added that "the insurance companies and their allies don't like this idea."

There was plenty in Obama's September health care oration to keep many of the president's liberal fans buzzed on "Barack." Enough progressive-sounding language was thrown their way by the so-called community organizer in chief to sustain their belief that Obama was "one of us." Enough seemingly populist oratory was delivered to feed the myth that his challenge was to deliver on progressive campaign promises and to obscure his real task: to tamp down popular expectations and activism in accord with the top-down imperatives of (rebranded) corporate, financial, and military rule. As I noted in an Internet commentary written one day after the speech: "All it takes is some pleasing and intelligent-sounding rhetoric (the mere fact of sounding intelligent goes incredibly far in many liberal circles) to keep them remarkably loyal to 'our guy' in the White House. Poor bamboozled subjects!—if only they would read seriously beyond and between the carefully crafted faux-gressive lines to appreciate the deeper, big-business-friendly loyalties of the violin master at the helm of 'our' corporate-managed dollar democracy."[14]

One commentator who was not fooled into thinking Obama had given a left-progressive speech was Republican *New York Times* columnist David Brooks. "On Wednesday night," Brooks wrote two days after the oration, "Barack Obama delivered the finest speech of his presidency. The exposition of his health care views was clear and lively. The invocation of Teddy Kennedy was moving and effective. . . . Best of all for those of us who admire the political craft was *the speech's seductive nature* and careful ambiguity. Obama threw out *enough rhetorical chum to keep the liberals happy*, yet he subtly staked out ground in the center on nearly every substantive issue in order to win over the moderates needed to get anything passed [emphasis added]."[15]

---

*This was the main reason that Obama unsurprisingly blew off his campaign promise to broadcast his presidential health care negotiations "on C-SPAN."

Against a "Radical Shift"

"That elite is most successful," Hitchens wrote in 1999,

which can claim the heartiest allegiance of the fickle crowd; can present it-self as most "in touch" with popular concerns; can anticipate the tides and pulses of public opinion; can, in short, be the least apparently "elitist." It's no great distance from Huey Long's robust cry of "Every man a king" to the insipid "inclusiveness" of [Bill Clinton's slogan] "Putting People First," but the smarter elite managers have learned in the interlude that solid, measur-able pledges have to be distinguished by a "reserve" tag that earmarks them for the bankrollers and backers.[16]

Consistent with Hitchens's analysis, there were at least six corporate-financial "reserve tags" attached to Obama's big health care speech in Sep-tember. The biggest and most obvious corporatist earmark came early with his rapid and short dismissal of Canadian- (and Australian- and New Zealandian-) style single-payer health insurance (widely but irrelevantly popular with a majority of Americans for some time) as "a radical shift that would disrupt the health care most people currently have." Single payer—embodied in veteran black congressman John Conyers's [D-MI] bill, HR 676, technically endorsed by more than eighty U.S. House members—would constitute a significant progressive transformation (a "radical shift" if one likes) in how America funds health care. But the claim that substi-tuting the government for parasitic, for-profit corporations—the latter committed largely to denying and limiting care—in paying for and (actu-ally) guaranteeing coverage to all would drastically "disrupt" the populace's health care experience was shameful corporatist deception worthy of George W. Bush.

A single-payer health insurance plan would cut $400 Billion in annual costs currently lost to the insurance corporations' profits and massively in-efficient duplicative bureaucracies, which are dedicated to expensive mar-keting operations and endless paperwork connected with the refusal and limitation of care and coverage. Single payer would also eliminate working people's slavish dependence on bosses for health care, reduce employers' in-centives to overwork their personnel (employment-based health care is part of why Americans have the longest working hours in the industrialized world), and potentially create millions of new jobs by socializing much of employers' massive health care compensation costs. Those costs are a major hiring "disincentive" that makes it more profitable to manufacture cars in Canada than in Michigan.[17]

"They Provide a Legitimate Service" *and Employ a Lot of People*

A second corporatist reserve tag took the form of an interesting comment in Obama's September speech. "Now," the president told Congress and the nation, "I have no interest in putting insurance companies out of business. They provide a legitimate service, and employ a lot of our friends and neighbors." Obama did not describe precisely describe or define that "service."

But then single-payer advocates do not call for the abolition of insurance companies. They advocate the eviction of insurance companies from those corporations' parasitic and cost-driving role in the provision (and denial) of health care. If that expulsion drives some insurance companies out of business, causing employment problems for many Americans, left progressives reasonably argue, then the United States faces the welcome challenge of providing workers displaced from a quintessentially parasitic industry with more socially useful employment. To justify an economic activity or institution on the grounds that it employs many people is to step onto a very slippery moral slope. The fast-food industry employs many millions of Americans; it also contributes significantly to the current epidemic of obesity and diabetes rates and numerous other related health and ecological plagues within and beyond the United States.[18] The nation's excessive, globally unmatched, and racially hyperdisparate mass arrest and incarceration system (producer and jailer of more than 2.3 million U.S. prisoners, more than 40 percent of whom are black in a nation that is just 12 percent African American) provides employment to untold millions of Americans as well, as does the deadly military-industrial complex.

Feared "Sticker Shock" *Trumps Universal Coverage*

The third great business-friendly reserve tag in Obama's September health care address came when he promised not to add "a dime" to the federal deficit with health reform and with his related pledge to fund his proposal at just $900 billion over ten years. "I will not sign a plan," Obama pledged (much to the approval of leading Republican pundit Brooks), "that adds one dime to our deficits—either now or in the future. Period."[19] As the *New York Times* noted the morning after the president's speech, this key caveat meant that Obama could not deliver on the promise of coverage for every American. "The number suggests a political calculation to avoid the sticker shock of the trillion-dollar threshold," the *Times* editors observed.

"But it probably means that Mr. Obama could fall short of his goal of providing universal coverage because the lower cost may force lawmakers to reduce the subsidies needed to help more uninsured individuals and small businesses seeking coverage for employees."[20]

Despite the president's interesting (though lowball) comment on the comparative costs of "the [U.S] Iraq and Afghanistan wars [of colonial invasion and occupation]," doctrinal rules prevented either him or the *Times* from having the elementary decency to note that the supposedly horrific ten-year health care cost of $1 trillion was roughly what the federal government spent *each year* on the American "defense" (empire) budget.[21] It was far less than what taxpayers spent (also and more clearly against their will) on bailing out Wall Street perpetrators beginning in the fall of 2008. Consistent with the harsh corporate-imperial doctrine that Dr. Martin Luther King Jr. challenged in the years prior to his violent death in April 1968, Obama's promise *not to add a dime to the deficit* applied to domestic health care needs but not to the Pentagon system and apparently endless colonial war. Obama shared the conventional power elite wisdom that it was appropriate to support indefinite military escalation, occupation, and counterinsurgency-mandated "nation-building" in "Af-Pak" with borrowed money. Massive "defense" expenditures were justified by the need to "protect American lives"—a rather curious justification for mass-murderous interventions that deepened bitter anti-Americanism in the Arab and Muslim worlds. But the deficit could not be fed by "one dime" by health reform despite the fact that—as the Harvard Medical School reported one week after Obama's speech—45,000 Americans died each year in connection with the lack of health insurance.[22]

A Stealth Form of Tax Regressivity

The fourth reserve tag was Obama's deletion of any reference to reversing the archplutocratic Bush administration tax cuts he mentioned in his address. During the campaign, Obama (following the lead of "fighting" John Edwards) repeatedly cited the reversal of Bush's tax reductions for Americans "earning" more than $250,000 a year as the funding source for his proposed health reform. Instead of resurrecting that mildly progressive pledge (deemed "contrary to recovery" in the closely linked minds of Wall Street and the White House), Obama rolled out Senator John Forbes ("I Am Not a Redistribution Democrat") Kerry's (D-MA) notion of taxing health insurance companies' most expensive policies, something that would—the Kerry (and Senator Max Baucus [D-MT]) argument went—encourage employers to purchase cheaper coverage for their workers, discouraging "excessive use of medical services." Labor and many House Democrats noted correctly that this tax would be passed on to workers in the form of higher premiums, violating the spirit, if not the exact letter, of the president's promise not to raise taxes on anyone making less than $250,000 a year.[23]

An Ersatz Public Option

A fifth and critical related plutocratic reserve tag was Obama's less-than-inspiring and far-from-unequivocal call for a (small and marginal) "public option." The president maintained his standard hypercautious ambiguity on the contentious question of whether Congress should establish a new government insurance program to compete with private insurers. He indicated that the significance of the public option had been exaggerated by left and right alike. Even though he would prefer to see such an option in the mix, he said, "it is only one part of my plan," merely a "means to the end" of affordable coverage for all.

Continuing with the "mixed signals" the White House had been sending for some time, Obama declared his openness to "alternatives" to a public option, including "nonprofit insurance cooperatives and a backup plan that could be offered by the government in certain circumstances." Obama further qualified his interest in the public option by saying that it would likely enlist "less than 5 percent" of the nation's health insurance recipients (mainly composed of people unable to obtain insurance through existing channels) once it was up and running—hardly something for the insurance CEOs to lose sleep over, especially as Obama's proposal to call for mandatory health insurance purchase promised to deliver the insurance industry/mafia tens of millions of new "customers." Obama expressed no interest in seeing a truly "robust" public option—one that would be available at affordable and competitive rates to any and all consumers who wished to sign up—that would function as an extension of Medicare and a real, viable alternative to private insurance for the populace.

Here he validated *Business Week*'s candid judgment more than a month prior to the speech: "The Health Insurers Have Already Won." "The industry," *Business Week* writers Chad Terhune and Keith Epstein matter-of-factly concluded in the first week of August 2009, "has already accomplished its goal of at least curbing, and maybe blocking any new publicly administered insurance program that could grab market share from the corporations that dominate the business." And "dominate policy," in cold defiance of public opinion, Terhune and Epstein might have added—a curious reflection on life in the "world's greatest democracy."[24]

All that was left of the notion of a public alternative to corporate managed health care by the time Obama spoke in early September was what liberal commentator and former Clinton administration labor secretary Robert Reich called an "ersatz public option." Reich later explained the historical development of Obama and the Congressional Democrats' captivity and surrender to the health industry and the Republican Party as follows:

> First there was Medicare for all 300 million of us. But that was a non-starter because private insurers and Big Pharma wouldn't hear of it, and Republicans and "centrists" thought it was too much like what they have up in Canada. . . .
>
> So the [next] compromise was to give all Americans the option of buying into a "Medicare-like plan" that competed with private insurers. Who could be against freedom of choice? . . . Open to all Americans, such a plan would have the scale and authority to negotiate low prices with drug companies and other providers, and force private insurers to provide better service at lower costs. But private insurers and Big Pharma wouldn't hear of it, and Republicans and "centrists" thought it would end up too much like what they have up in Canada.
>
> So the [next] compromise was to give the public option only to Americans who wouldn't be covered either by their employers or by Medicaid. And give them coverage pegged to Medicare rates. But private insurers and . . . you know the rest.
>
> So the compromise that ended up in the House bill is to have a mere public option, open only to the 6 million Americans not otherwise covered. The Congressional Budget Office warns this shrunken public option will have no real bargaining leverage and would attract mainly people who need lots of medical care to begin with. So it will actually cost more than it saves.
>
> But even the House's shrunken and costly little public option is too much for private insurers, Big Pharma, Republicans, and "centrists" in the Senate. So Harry Reid has proposed an even tinier public option, which states can decide not to offer their citizens. According to the CBO, it would attract no more than 4 million Americans.
>
> It's a token public option, an ersatz public option, a fleeting gesture toward the idea of a public option, so small and desiccated as to be barely worth mentioning except for the fact that it still (gasp) contains the word "public."[25]

And even this pathetic, fake, partial, weakened, and tiny public option was viewed as dispensable if necessary to mollify Republican and the corporate sector.

Undue Complexity

We can add a sixth reserve tag to Obama's speech and, more broadly, to his health reform agenda: excessive and indecipherable complexity. Related to the absurdity of leaving the private insurers in power, Obama and other corporate Democrats' plans were simply too dense and intricate for many ordinary Americans to comprehend and rally behind. Unlike the single-payer government health insurance reform that has long been supported by the majority of Americans, the evolving Obama-Baucus-Pelosi schemes were simply—very much like Hilly Clinton's complex private-public proposals during the early 1990s—"too complicated to draw a constituency."[26] Of more than 1,000 American surveyed by the *New York Times* and CBS in late September 2009, fully 55 percent reported that Obama had NOT "clearly explained" his health care plan. Sixty-two percent said the president had failed to clearly explain what his health reform program "would mean" for Americans. Fifty-nine percent reported being "confused" by the Democratic reforms being considered in Congress.[27]

Triggering Yet More Mass Confusion

In the wake of his September address, Obama synthesized reserve tags five (his weak commitment to the public option) and six (ridiculous complexity) by sending out signals that he wanted a so-called public option trigger in order to get a "bipartisan bill" passed. *Politico* correspondent Mike Allen reported that at a meeting of Senate Democratic leaders on the evening of October 22, Obama said "that his preference is for the trigger."[28] Under the frankly bizarre and mysterious trigger proposal, there would be no public option whatsoever (not even the weak and watered-down, less than robust one discussed previously) unless and until private insurers failed to meet certain unspecified targets at some future date.

The "trigger" marked a new stage in the development of the deliberate policy bewilderment of the populace. As veteran progressive, Washington-based journalist and author David Sirota noted:

> The confusion deepened over the summer health care debate, which was dominated by arcane references to vaguely defined "health insurance co-ops" and "insurance exchanges." After Obama's perplexing September speech, a supposedly "new" concept—the notion of a health care "trigger mechanism"—emerged to befuddle the popular mind. The odd proposal, pushed by Obama's chief-of-staff Rahm Emanuel and others inside the administration and Democratic Party, would have required that a national health reform legislation

permit a government-run "public option" only if certain conditions were met. "It's an obscure policy tool that isn't even written," reported the news service TalkingPointsMemo.com, "But somehow, a 'trigger-mechanism' is the talk of Washington right now. How did that happen?"

Such shock is widespread. Pundits, reporters and activists are stunned that an abstruse scheme to halt reform has become a focal point of the health care debate.

By Sirota's standpoint and experience, there was nothing mysterious about the rise of the "trigger" option. It was a form of "legislative cyanide" meant to give corporate-captive politicians fake-progressive cover as they killed and diluted legislation their corporate paymasters opposed. The "trigger," Sirota reported, is "just another version of the old Blue Ribbon Commission trick. They are designed not as good public policy, but as devious political tactics to help dishonest lawmakers look like they support popular measures—all while guaranteeing those measures never become reality."[29] As Sirota noted, "the trigger had already made a prior appearance—in bipartisan drug importation legislation passed under Bill Clinton and George W. Bush." This previous legislation contained provisions giving the U.S. secretary of health and human services the power to "trigger—or not trigger"—final implementation. Specifically, the secretary would have to first certify that imported medicines were "safe" (drug companies promote the lie that Canadian medicine is mortally dangerous). The "trigger provision," was "lobbyists' poison pill—and it worked as they planned. Importation has never been implemented, as no HHS secretary has pulled the trigger. Hence, Americans are still barred from wholesale importation of lower-priced medicine—and pharmaceutical industry profiteering continues." Sirota added an interesting footnote to the story. Rahm Emanuel, Obama's chief of staff, had once been "one of the key congresspeople who portrayed sham importation bills as real progress." Emanuel was "also—not coincidentally—a huge recipient of health industry cash."[30]

To Pass "Something, Anything That Could Be Labeled Reform": Death of the Short-Lived Medicare Buy-In

The indecipherable madness of the corporate-captive health reform process that Obama largely handed off to congressional Democrats deepened in mid-December 2009. That's when Senate Majority Leader Harry Reid (D-NV) announced that that he would drop the Senate health reform bill's recently added on "Medicare buy-in provision." Facing fierce opposition to even the pathetic "ersatz" public option from Republicans, the Independent (reactionary) senator Joe Lieberman (I-CT), and the right-wing ("Blue Dog") Democrat Ben Nelson (D-NB), Reid had offered the "buy-in"—permitting Americans between fifty-five and sixty-four to participate, for a price, in the nation's old-age insurance system—as a replacement provision to keep Democratic "progressives" on board. But this, too, was unacceptable to Lieberman, and Nelson indicated at a closed-door Democratic conference meeting that he would drop it.[31] The dropping was certainly approved by Obama.

At this point, even the former Democratic National Committee head and centrist Democrat Howard Dean proclaimed that it would be better to kill the Obama Democrats' health reform and start over from scratch. A physician who had also been Vermont governor, Dean went on national television (ABC's *Good Morning America*) to say that the legislation in the Senate would benefit the insurance industry more than it helped Americans struggling to gain health coverage or pay for it. Dean said the bill was an "insurance company's dream." On Vermont Public Radio, Dean urged senators to "kill the bill." This earned Dean, a longstanding health reform advocate, a mocking rebuke from the White House, with Obama's press secretary, Robert Gibbs, suggesting that Dean was not "rational."[32]

The deeper truth, long noted by leftists and even by some liberal representatives, including Anthony Weiner (D-NY), was that the White House was more interested in "passing something, anything, no matter how ineffectual" and corporate friendly, that could be called "reform" than in making sound and seriously progressive policy.[33] There seemed to be no limits to how low Obama and his congressional allies would go to appear to have won an historic legislative victory on health reform.

There's more that could be noted in an unpleasant light (from a left-progressive perspective) about Obama's health care reform, including his threat to impose new cost controls, his concessions to Republicans' misleading medical malpractice machinations, and his denial of the fact that we actually need to find reasonable ways to cover the medical costs of human beings who happen to be illegal immigrants.

Irrelevant Public Opinion

As of December 2009 (when I stopped researching this book in the interest of sustaining my own mental health), it was already abundantly clear that whatever health reform bill passed Congress and gained Obama's signature would be hopelessly *"manacled to private insurers."* It would be a textbook case of what Team Obama calls "pragmatism," meaning it would provide supposedly postideological "get things done" cover for standard service and surrender to corporate power.[34] By retaining for-profit insurers, it would retain the $400 billion a year in excess administrative overhead that would have been eliminated by a single-payer system. Private insurers with their vast overhead costs devoted to "denial management"—to paying as few claims as possible—would stay in business. Also still intact would be the overhead costs hospitals and doctors pay to secure payments from patients and multiple insurers with complex differences in coverage.

The plan would contain no effective measures to prevent insurers from boosting profits by continually raising premiums—something that insurers were certain to do with great frequency in response to the Obama plan's (in-itself-noble) denial of insurance corporations' right to deny coverage on the basis of preexisting conditions. Also absent would be any provision to prevent insurers from continuing their practice of improperly designating numerous kinds of administrative costs as medical expenses.

The health reform's requirement that all individuals who can "afford" to do so buy health insurance or pay a financial penalty would ignore the critical fact that private health insurance premiums are typically too high for many working people. As has been seen in the handful of states (Massachusetts, Tennessee, Minnesota, Oregon, Washington, and Vermont) with "universal plans" based on individual purchase mandates (with penalties for those who do not buy in), the outcome is often "coverage without care" and a tendency for many to tragically identify "universal coverage" not with "government help" but with "government coercion."

It would also (if it passed) likely be a pyrrhic victory. As liberal journalist John Heileman explained in early December 2009:

> The widespread sense among [Washington] Democrats is that . . . Obama and his people badly botched the job of presenting reform to the country and persuading the electorate of its necessity. . . . That Obama's above-the-fray posture over the summer allowed the Republicans to define the bill in lasting and damaging ways. That he wasted precious political capital on an issue that few voters (just 17 percent) saw as paramount at this time of economic frailty. And that he allowed the potentially transformative wave that carried him into Washington to slink back into the sea.

"We'll get a health-care bill," one Democratic senator told Heileman, "but we've squandered the ability to change America."[35]

These were interesting reflections based on the false premise that the business liberal Obama really sought to progressively "transform America."[36] Leading Washington-based progressive policy expert and activist Kevin Zeese had a very different take on Obama's "failure." "This is what Obama wanted from the beginning," Zeese wrote on December 19, 2009.

> His White House health care summit—before Congress did anything—began and ended with the insurance industry speaking. It was obvious where they were going. Look at the attempted appointment (as Health and Human Services chief) of Tom Daschle, who had his hands very deep in the corporate pocket. And the press events with the insurance industry and the pharmaceutical corporations. This is what he wanted. Lieberman and [critical "reform" architect Senator Max] Baucus were just doing his dirty work.[37]

The Democracy Deficit Lives On

Like much, if not most, of the policy developments detailed in Chapters 1 and 2 of the present study, the health care "reform" that would finally pass defied majority, progressive-leaning U.S. opinion. Majority sentiment on the health care issue had long stood well to the left of the reigning business parties and the dominant political class and media, as numerous pieces of polling data revealed:

- 64 percent of Americans would pay higher taxes to guarantee health care for all U.S. citizens (CNN Opinion Research Poll, May 2007).
- 69 percent of Americans think it is the responsibility of the federal government to provide health coverage to all U.S. citizens (Gallup Poll, 2006).
- 67 percent of Americans "think it's a good idea [for government] to guarantee health care for all U.S. citizens, as Canada and Britain do, with just 27 percent dissenting" (*Business Week*, 2005).
- 59 percent of Americans support a single-payer health insurance system (CBS/*New York Times* Poll, January 2009).
- 59 percent of doctors back a single-payer system (*Annals of Internal Medicine*, April 2008).
- 73 percent of Americans feel that U.S. health care is either in a "state of crisis" or has "major problems" (Gallup, November 2007).
- 71 percent of Americans feel that we need "fundamental changes" or to have the U.S. health system "completely re-built," compared to just

24 percent who wish only for "minor changes" (Pew Research Center, 2009).

There was a remarkable CBS/*New York Times* poll conducted in late September 2009. Sixty-five percent of more than 1,000 Americans randomly surveyed by CBS and the *Times* responded affirmatively to the following question: "Would you favor or oppose the government offering everyone a government-administered health insurance plan—something like the Medicare coverage that people 65 and over get—that would compete with private health insurance plans?"[38]

But so what? Citizen opinion and democratic theory are fine and dandy. But the real world of wealth, power, propaganda, and policy is much less pleasant under the rules in the "dollar democracy," where (to quote an old working-class aphorism) "money talks and bullshit walks" and the "real players" (Wolin) are the ones with the deep pockets. Obama's "sick corporatist" health "reform" was a highly predictable (and in fact widely predicted) outcome in the real world of power that young Barack Obama chose to climb instead of resist. That world is the producer of a chilling "democracy deficit"—a plutocratic chasm between democratic public opinion and actual authoritarian public policy—that has predated and will outlast the Obama presidency. As one symptom and cause of that deficit, the health sector poured an astonishing $178,252,901 into congressional and presidential campaigns between the beginning of the 2008 election cycle and the summer of 2009. The insurance industry invested $52,739,320 into the same outlet. For his part, Obama received more than $19 million from the health sector for the 2008 election cycle—a new record.[39]

Meanwhile, Rowena Ventura was on to something. The United States cannot have meaningful health reform in accord with the national majority's longstanding support of major progressive change without removing the for-profit insurance companies from the equation and introducing the obvious social-democratic and cost-cutting solution: single-payer government health insurance on the Canadian and Australian models.

Obama certainly knew this himself. He said as much quite explicitly late in his career as a state legislator during a speech in downtown Chicago. When Obama claimed to be the first president to have passed real health reform in the United States, he didn't say anything about the following comments he had made as a state senator in the early summer of 2003 to the Illinois AFL-CIO: "I happen to be a proponent of a single payer universal health care program. I see no reason why the United States of America, the wealthiest country in the history of the world, spending 14 percent of its Gross National Product on health care cannot provide basic health insurance to everybody. And that's what Jim is talking about when he says everybody in, nobody out. A single payer health care plan, a universal health care plan."[40] This remarkable statement was made just prior to Obama's realization that he had a serious shot at national office—a realization that sharpened his willingness to subordinate himself to the unelected dictatorship of money.

Speaking of the struggle for a single-payer option in 2003, Obama said, "We may not get there immediately. Because first we have to take back the White House, we have to take back the Senate, and we have to take back the House."[41] Five and half years later, the federal legislative and executive branches were "taken back" by the Democratic Party. Sadly, however, the nation's corporate-managed "dollar democracy" and its narrow "one-and-a-half party system" (Sheldon Wolin) had yet to be taken back from concentrated wealth and the giant military-industrial complex that Dwight Eisenhower had warned about upon leaving the White House.[42] Beneath the fake-progressive imagery at the heart of the Obama rebranding, the country's "representative democracy," crippled by "too much [corporate and military] representation and too little [actual popular] democracy" (Arundhati Roy) abounds with Orwellian and Vonneguttian absurdity under Obama no less than in the Bush-Cheney years.[43] Far from being an exception to this tragic reality, health reform under Obama is an epitome of it. I end this chapter with an eloquent letter to the editor of the *New York Times* on December 18, 2009:

> To the Editor:
> Unless something very surprising and significant happens in the next week, the Senate health care bill, and likely the entire health care reform effort, can only be termed a colossal failure. Addresses rising costs? Nope. Expands choice? Nope. Holds insurers accountable? Nope. Expands access? Yes, because more money needs to be funneled to insurance companies somehow!
> Despite holding both the White House and an overwhelming majority in both houses—a situation that comes along once every few decades—the Democrats have again failed miserably.
> Health reform turns out to be a gift for insurers and a knife in the backs of the American people. How embarrassing for President Obama and Senator Harry Reid, and how depressing for the rest of us.
>
> Chad Friesen
> Brooklyn, NY

Postscript: I will discuss the actual health "reform" bill that later passed through Congress and gained Obama's signature in mid-March 2010 in this book's Postscript (written in the first week of May 2010). Although the bill contains some admirable components of real value, the legislative outcome is, I think, consistent with the critical analysis and projections contained in this chapter, written in late December 2009 and early January 2010.

4

Barack Obama, the Myth of the Postracial Presidency, and the Politics of Identity

Today, I asked a class for which I was subbing (high-school English students, about a dozen, all-black, at one of CPS's actually nice high-school facilities) what they thought of Obama. Their initial reaction was one of, for lack of a better way to say it, pride and joy.

But upon closer inspection, this turned out to be a rather shallow sentiment. For when I asked them if they expected any real changes under Obama, they all said no.

—*Eric Patton, February 12, 2009*[1]

The "Postracial" Candidate

As I went to considerable lengths to demonstrate in *Barack Obama and the Future of American Politics* (2008),[2] presidential candidate Obama bent over backward to demonstrate his "black but not like Jesse" (Jackson) safety to white America. As part of that project, he worked very hard to distance himself as much as the potential "first black president" could from identification with the race issue and from the traditional black political charge—some (including this writer) might prefer to say "observation"— that the United States is a racist society. Expressing what *Newsweek* reporters Richard Wolffe and Darren Briscoe called in the summer of 2007 a "surprising lack of [racial] grievance,"[3] candidate Obama was less than eager to challenge reigning white wisdom on the "over"-ness of antiblack racial oppression in post–civil rights America. In the words of *Black Agenda Report* executive director Glen Ford, voiced during an important January 2008 debate with black professor and Obama supporter Michael Eric

Dyson after Obama's critical victory in the Democratic presidential caucus in the predominantly white state of Iowa, the Obama campaign "relentlessly send[s] out signals to white people that a vote for Barack Obama, an Obama presidency, would signal the beginning of the end of black-specific agitation, that it would take race discourse off of the table. Barack Obama," Ford explained, "does not carry [black peoples'] burden, in addition to other burdens. He in fact promises to lift white-people-as-a-whole's burden, the burden of having to listen to these very specific and historical black complaints, to deal with the legacies of slavery. That is his promise to them."[4]

Obama's widely lauded response to the right-wing, media, and Hillary Clinton assault on his longstanding relationship with his former pastor, the explicitly antiracist Reverend Jeremiah Wright, was consistent with that "promise." In his instantly famous and widely lauded "Philadelphia Race Speech" of March 18, 2008, Obama portrayed the racism that created the preacher's (supposedly) dysfunctional "anger" as a function mainly of *the past*. As I noted in a *ZNet* commentary that appeared two days later:

> The oppression that angers Wright and other black Americans oppose is more than an overhang from the bad old past. The humiliation and hopelessness felt by millions of those Americans are being reinforced, generated, and expanded anew on a daily basis right now . . . in the *21st century*. Black "anger and bitterness" is being generated within the U.S. by racist policies and practices in *these* "Joshua Generation" years as well as in *those* ("Moses Generation") years. New "memories" of racial tyranny are being created *right now* beneath the national self congratulation over the defeat of level-one racism.

As *Black Commentator*'s Bill Fletcher noted, Obama "attributed much of the anger of Rev. Wright to the past, as if Rev. Wright is stuck in a time warp, *rather than the fact that Rev. Wright's anger about the domestic and foreign policies of the USA are well rooted—and documented—in the current reality of the USA* [emphasis added]."[5]

But it was, of course, smart politics. Sadly enough, the majority of the white U.S. electorate in the "post–civil rights era" did in fact turn long ago against the notion that racism still poses significant barriers to black advancement and equality. Obama and his campaign team knew very well that his chances of winning over enough white voters to attain the presidency depended on biracial Obama projecting himself as "not all that black"—as someone Caucasians could trust not to push on the race issue beyond the simple fact of being technically African American. It was imperative for victory, they knew, to keep his imagery and politics strictly segregated from the "angry" black politics and horrid "racial divisions" of "the past." Obama, being "in it to win it"—the "it" being the arena of the white majority United States "winner-take-all" elections system—was not about to follow Jesse Jackson's earlier model in pursuing a cultural or policy orientation that violated predominantly white "mainstream" sentiments.

No Betrayal in Racial Cowardice: A Race-Neutral President

"The Pain of Discrimination"

The same postracial calculations have survived into the postelection and presidential phase of the Obama phenomenon. Obama, it is true, seemed to break postracial character when, during a mid-July 2009 press conference dedicated mainly to health reform, he responded angrily to a recent incident in which white Cambridge, Massachusetts, police officers had clumsily and unnecessarily arrested celebrated black Harvard literature professor Henry Louis Gates Jr. in Gates's home. But Obama quickly backed off his stance as right wing talk radio had a field day claiming that Obama had been unfair to the Caucasian cops, as the brouhaha over the Gates-Cambridge incident stole the thunder of the president's health care message, and as it became clear that Gates was not without a considerable degree of blame for the incident.

As no mainstream reporters or commentators noted, moreover, Gates (described by the president as "a personal friend" from Harvard) was a curious martyr in the struggle against racial oppression. He had made something of a career on PBS arguing (in a sophisticated, Ivy League version of the well-known black-bourgeois Bill Cosby argument) that lower- and working-class blacks needed to stop pointing to racist and other forms of oppression as an explanation for their position at the bottom of the nation's social hierarchies, arguing in a 2004 PBS special (titled "Beyond the Color Line") for blacks to "master the ABCs, stay in school, work hard, defer gratification. What's happened to these values?" asked Gates, adding that "my father always said, and it's true, if we studied calculus like we studied basketball, we'd be running MIT. It's true and there's no excuse." This was the key theme in a previous PBS special narrated by Gates. In that documentary, titled "Two Nations," Gates proclaimed that black poverty was mainly about poor decisions: "deciding to get pregnant or not to have protected sex. Deciding to do drugs. Deciding not to study. Deciding, deciding."[6]

Revealingly enough, the Gates-Cambridge-Obama episode came to a conclusion not with a presidential initiative to tackle the widespread problem of racial bias in the criminal justice system but rather with the officer who arrested Gates being invited to "have a beer" with the professor and the president in the White House's rose garden.

A second seeming exception to the postracial rule of the Obama presidency came in his mid-July address to the National Association for the Advancement of Colored People (NAACP), marking the one-hundredth anniversary of that venerable civil rights organization. In this oration, Obama said that, even though "there probably has never been less discrimination in America than there is today," Americans should still "make no mistake: The pain of discrimination is still felt in America. . . . But we also know that prejudice and discrimination—at least the most blatant types of prejudice and discrimination—are not even the steepest barriers to opportunity today." Obama added, "The most difficult barriers include structural inequalities that our nation's legacy of discrimination has left behind; inequalities still plaguing too many communities and too often the object of national neglect."[7] Obama was unusually forthright on the extent of racial inequality in the country when speaking to the NACCP:

> Even as we celebrate the remarkable achievements of the past 100 years; even as we inherit extraordinary progress that cannot be denied; even as we marvel at the courage and determination of so many plain folk—we know that too many barriers still remain.
>
> We know that even as our economic crisis batters Americans of all races, African Americans are out of work more than just about anybody else—a gap that's widening here in New York City, as a detailed report this week by Comptroller Bill Thompson laid out. (Applause.)
>
> We know that even as spiraling health care costs crush families of all races, African Americans are more likely to suffer from a host of diseases but less likely to own health insurance than just about anybody else.
>
> We know that even as we imprison more people of all races than any nation in the world, an African American child is roughly five times as likely as a white child to see the inside of a prison.[8]

Precisely the Programs That Are Missing from the Obama Administration

Nevertheless, the lion's share of Obama's speech reverted to conservative form, giving primary focus to a self-help message rallying black America to practice internal uplift through hard work and attention to the virtues and value of education. More importantly, the Obama White House had done nothing really to back up Obama's claim to the NAACP that "we are beginning to tear down" racial barriers in the United States "one by one." There were no major White House initiatives to tackle remarkably persistent and steep racial disparities in wealth and income and the shockingly durable overconcentration of poverty, unemployment, and other negative social indicators in the still highly segregated black community. There was nothing in Obama's agenda remotely related to addressing the steep "structural inequalities" that he acknowledged (when speaking to an all-black audience of civil rights activists) to be tied to "our nation's legacy of discrimination." The behavior of the Obama White House naturally had nothing to do with the preposterous charge of right-wing talk radio hosts and other Republican commentators and activists that Obama was a "leftist" reparations activist fanatically preoccupied with making white people pay for past racism.

"If Racists Can Ostensibly Lose an Election . . . "

Obama demonstrated his continuing willingness to accommodate white racist sentiments in other ways. He offered no words of defense of the largely minority-based urban activist organization ACORN when right-wing media and leading Republicans launched a neo-McCarthyite smear campaign against that group over the spring and summer of 2009. And the Obama White House asked for and received the resignation of the brilliant, highly qualified African American green jobs czar Van Jones, smeared as a communist and black nationalist reparations advocate by the ludicrous far-right FOX News television host Glenn Beck in the same season. By the perceptive account of the black, Pennsylvania death row inhabitant and political commentator Mumia Abu-Jamal, "Jones resigned, to protect a President who wouldn't protect him." Abu-Jamal was "reminded . . . of Lani Guinier, another brilliant Yale-trained Black lawyer, who got left hanging when racists dubbed her 'quota queen' when she was nominated for a post in the Clinton administration's Justice Dept."—a very apt analogy. "If racists can ostensibly lose an election, and still dictate policy," Abu-Jamal added, "then, have they really lost?"[9]

"President Says He Shouldn't Put Focus on Blacks' Troubles"

In early December 2009, as I completed this chapter, the nation's first black president received some interesting criticism from the Congressional Black

Caucus (CBC). Accusing the White House of ignoring the economic plight of minorities, ten members of the caucus boycotted a key House committee vote on financial regulations. The group expressed frustration at the White House and Congress's failure to tackle minority-specific economic problems, including an official black unemployment rate of 16 percent, higher than the national rate of 10 percent. "We can no long afford for our public policy to be defined by the world view of Wall Street," the CBC announced, adding that "policy for the least of these must be integrated into everything we do."

Obama flatly rejected the criticism in a special interview with *USA Today* and the *Detroit Free Press* prior to a White House "jobs summit" in early December. "It's a mistake," Obama told the newspapers, "to start thinking in terms of particular ethnic segments of the United States rather than to think that *we are all in this together and we are all going to get out of this together*" [emphasis added].[10] Just because he happened to be black, Obama was announcing, black Americans should have no reason to think that he would be any more willing than George W. Bush or Bill Clinton to acknowledge and act upon the distinctive oppression still experienced by many in the nation's still highly separate and unequal black population. The title of the *USA Today* article reporting Obama's response to the CBC criticism was on point: "President Says He Shouldn't Put Focus on Blacks' Troubles."

"A Nation of Cowards"

In February 2009, in a speech to his new employees at the Justice Department, the nation's first black attorney general, Eric Holder, caused a momentary media stir by saying that the United State "is a nation of cowards on race." Most Americans, Holder argued, avoid honest and serious discussion of the nation's continuing racial problems. Sadly enough, the administration in which Holder serves has done little to move itself or the nation past racial cowardice beyond the simple fact of being headed by an African American.

There is no "betrayal" on this score, however. Obama's political team has always taken an official position of cowardice on race, generally refusing to seriously engage the volatile question of racism beyond the simple and admittedly symbolically powerful fact of advancing a half-black ("but not like Jesse") candidate for the presidency. The refusal is, of course, politically astute given post–civil rights white America's majority sentiment that racism no longer poses significant obstacles to black American advancement and racial equality—a sentiment that is sadly but unavoidably furthered by Obama's historic election.

A "Summer Obsessed with Race"

But just as Obama's militantly race-neutral campaign did not prevent him from losing most white votes in the 2008 election, his racially accommodationist ("cowardly," if you prefer) presidency has not exactly succeeded in keeping race at bay as a critical factor in U.S. politics. "This summer really has been a turning point" showing "that the myth of post-racial America is definitively buried," Naomi Klein told Amy Goodman in September 2009. "After the election of Barack Obama," Klein noted, "we heard again and again that the country had entered into a post-racial era; it was no longer important to talk about race." But, Klein observed, "this whole summer . . . has been obsessed with race."

The highlights of the not-so-postracial summer of 2009 included the following:

- The Gates-Cambridge-Obama incident of mid-July, accompanied by loud right-wing commentary to the effect that the president was antiwhite.
- A highly identity-politicized national debate over Obama's appointment of a Latina, the centrist and pro–Wall Street federal judge Sonia Sotomayor, to fill the U.S. Supreme Court seat vacated by white male justice David Souter. The national discussion of Sotomayor revolved largely around her onetime statement, which she was compelled to rescind, to the effect that a "wise Latina" justice would be in a better position to rule on certain cases than would a white male justice given different life experiences and around her decision in a lawsuit by white firemen who were passed over on promotions in the name of affirmative action principles Sotomayor supported. (The right-wing media machine and many Republican politicians accused Sotamayor and her appointer of being racist.)
- The popular right-wing FOX News television personality Glenn Beck's remarkable statement that Obama was "a guy . . . who has a deep-seated hatred for white people, the white culture . . . this guy is, I believe, a racist"—a comment that led to a liberal boycott effort that caused Beck to lose more than fifty corporate sponsors by early September 2009.[11]

- Beck and other right-wing media actors' relentless assault on ACORN and on the supposedly racist and communist Van Jones, which ended in Jones resigning from his midlevel White House position and the Obama administration distancing itself from the activist organization—itself actually a moderately progressive group that had helped elect Obama through standard voter registration drives and the like.

It wasn't just the right wing that drove racialized politics in President Obama's first summer. At one point during Obama's health care address to Congress in September 2009, white and right-wing South Carolina representative Joe Wilson shouted, "You lie!" Wilson's cry came after the president commented that "illegal aliens" would be ineligible for federal subsidies to buy health insurance. The remark earned Wilson an official congressional censure. It also and importantly elicited a remarkable comment from former U.S. president Jimmy Carter. "I think it's based on racism," Carter said. "There is an inherent feeling among many in this country that *an African American should not be president*," Carter said in response to an audience question at a town hall held at his presidential center in Atlanta. The former president said that Wilson's outburst was a part of a "disturbing" trend of hatred directed at the president that included demonstrators equating Obama to Hitler. "Those kind of things are not just casual outcomes of a sincere debate on whether we should have a national program on health care," he said. "It's deeper than that. . . . I think an overwhelming portion of the intensely demonstrated animosity toward President Barack Obama is based on the fact that he is a black man," Carter told NBC News. "Racism . . . still exists and I think it has bubbled up to the surface because of a belief among many white people, not just in the south but around the country, that African-Americans are not qualified to lead this great country. It's an abominable circumstance and grieves me and concerns me very deeply," Carter added.[12]

Meanwhile, somewhat to Carter's left and at a far lower level of public exposure, professional white antiracist and "Progressives for Obama" member Tim Wise argued that the only real content behind the American right's attempt to ludicrously demonize Barack Obama as a radical leftist—a "socialist"—was racism. "It is not, and please make note of it," Wise proclaimed, "about socialism. Or capitalism. Or economics at all, per se." The people issuing the charge of "socialism" against Obama were really "using the term *as a symbol for something else entirely* [emphasis added]."[13] That "something else," Wise argued in a typical overreach, was race.[14]

Carter's statement brought forth a predictable flood of Republican and right-wing talk radio outrage. "Race," Republicans railed, "has nothing to do with" growing right-wing outrage at Obama, which came to a boil with a massive Republican march on Washington against supposed White House and Democratic Party "socialism" in September. The real basis of their anger, the right insisted, was principled opposition to the president and Democrats' supposedly "leftist" (the hard-right talk radio FOX News regularly said "socialist") and, even, at the ridiculous margins (right-wing shock jock Mark Levin) "Marxist-Leninist" policy agenda in health care and other policy areas.

Reluctant to involve himself in the nasty racial politics he claimed to have transcended, Obama did his best to stay above the fray. Carter's comment and the wrath it provoked on the right elicited a careful but sharply distanced comment from the White House. "The president," White House spokesman Robert Gibbs said, "doesn't think that criticism of his policies is based on the color of his skin."[15] The White House position was that the majority of the angry opposition he was facing from the predominantly white right was about policy and partisan identity and not about "race."

"What Matters, . . . Above All, Is the Class One Serves"

Meanwhile, behind the scenes, the "real players," the corporate elite and bankrollers, could hardly have been displeased over the unflattering spectacle of the nation's ugly racial obsessions. The racial accusations and the related preposterous charges that the corporate-imperial, center-right president was a black nationalist and/or communist helped keep the citizenry's focus off the (predominantly Caucasian) wealthy few and away from the bipartisan state-capitalist policies that serve the interests of the rich and powerful. As John Pilger noted on July 4, 2009, in San Francisco:

> The clever young man who recently made it to the White House is a very fine hypnotist, partly because it is indeed exciting to see an African American at the pinnacle of power in the land of slavery. However, this is the 21st century, and race together with gender and even class can be very seductive tools of propaganda. For what is so often overlooked and what matters, I believe, above all, *is the class one serves* [emphasis added]. George W. Bush's inner circle from the State Department to the Supreme Court was perhaps

the most multiracial in presidential history. It was PC par excellence. Think Condoleezza Rice, Colin Powell. It was also the most reactionary.[16]

While liberal Obama supporters did battle with the right over presidential skin color, *the predominantly white business elite Obama (like all presidents) served* saw its wealth and power get concentrated yet further upward and empire relegitimized and redeployed in South Asia and around the world. Meanwhile, none dared recall or consider that Obama was attractive to the establishment in part because elites sensed that all-too-widespread white American fears of the "angry black man" would make it close to impossible for a black president to conduct the "epic fight" with the wealthy few that John Edwards said would be required to attain any meaningful progressive reform in.[17]

"They All Said No"

At the same time, curiously enough, the black working and lower classes fell all too invisibly into deeper misery. Following the standard racial pattern in the history of American business cycles, the Great Recession that Obama inherited from the Bush years hit people of color harder than whites. The rising black poverty and unemployment rates continued (as usual) to hover around double that of whites. Black and Latino/a communities already struggling with poverty and a shortage of affordable housing were pushed into shocking levels of destitution, joblessness, and foreclosure, experiencing a degree of concentrated misery before which the very real economic discomfort of white communities seemed mild by comparison. In a 2009 report titled "The Silent Depression: State of the Dream 2009," progressive social research organization United for a Fair Economy noted that 10 percent of U.S. whites were living in official poverty, as compared to 24 percent of U.S. blacks and 21 percent of the nation's Latino/as. Sociologist Celine-Marie Pascale and law student Katie Beran noted that "Native Americans who live in circumstances that rival those of the poorest countries often do not even appear in government statistics."[18]

The stark racial dimension of the nation's growing poverty and unemployment problem was rarely discussed in the "mainstream" media. It didn't help, of course, that, notwithstanding Obama's anger over the arrest of "Skip" Gates and his comments to the NAACP (directed to the predominantly black membership of that organization, not to the broad public) in mid-July, the new administration stayed essentially mute on the nation's savage racial inequalities and the institutional racism that continued to feed those disparities.[19]

For what it's worth, the difference between (a) electing a bourgeois president (or mayor or governor) who happens to be black (if thoroughly enmeshed with the predominantly white corporate and imperial elite) and (b) undertaking a serious engagement with deeply entrenched social disparities when it comes to attacking the problem of racism is well understood in much of the black community. For many black Americans and for antiracists of all colors, the lesson (already clear to many beneath understandable but fading excitement over the emergence of a first black president) is that there is curiously little to be concretely gained by most black Americans, and more perhaps to be lost (mainly what's left of the white majority's willingness to acknowledge the persistent role of racism in explaining black disadvantage) from (a). Only (b) carries serious promise of advancing racial equality, something that will become more and more evident over time—with educational help from progressive antiracists—as savage racial inequality and the racist institutional forces that feed it survive the Age of Obama. Here is an interesting message I received from Eric Patton, a teacher of black students in the Cincinnati Public Schools (CPS), last February:

Today, I asked a class for which I was subbing (high-school English students, about a dozen, all-black, at one of CPS's actually nice high-school facilities) what they thought of Obama. Their initial reaction was one of, for lack of a better way to say it, pride and joy.

But upon closer inspection, this turned out to be a rather shallow sentiment. For when I asked them if they expected any real changes under Obama, they all said no.

So while they are (currently) happy he is in the White House, they know full well that he will be no different from any other president—and it's not something they only know "deep down." They know it pretty close to the surface.

Olympic Silence: "U All Think That Derrion Albert's Mother Will Be Invited to the White House for Beer?"

I was reminded of Eric Patton's message at the end of September 2009 when Michelle Obama and then the president himself flew to Copenhagen to join Oprah Winfrey in high-profile lobbying of the International

Olympic Committee (IOC) in support of Chicago's corporate-Democratic mayor Richard M. Daley's failed bid to make Chicago home for the 2016 Olympics. As progressive social justice and civil rights activists and community organizers across the city had been pointing out for years, a Chicago Olympics would have primarily benefited the city's downtown business elite at the expense of city taxpayers. The city's plans particularly targeted inner-city black residents on Chicago's South Side for clearance and removal, escalating an ongoing urban gentrification project that was pushing hundreds of thousands of impoverished African Americans out of black neighborhoods and to the margins of the metropolis and its glittering, ever-expanding corporate downtown.[20] Whose side was Obama on? As black bourgeois Chicago superstars the Obamas and Winfrey joined Daley in pitching the midwestern metropolis as a glorious global city, hundreds of South Side residents planned to attend the funeral of a young black teenager, Derrion Albert, an honor student and innocent bystander who had recently been clubbed to death in a videotaped gang melee outside his South Side high school.[21] "Chicago," the president told the IOC, "is that most American of American cities, but one where citizens from more than 130 nations inhabit a rich tapestry of distinctive neighborhoods." Furthermore,

> each one of those neighborhoods . . . has its own unique character, its own unique history, its songs, its language. But each is also part of our city—one city—a city where I finally found a home.
>
> Chicago is a place where we strive to celebrate what makes us different just as we celebrate what we have in common. . . .
>
> Chicago is a city where the practical and the inspirational exist in harmony. . . . It's a bustling metropolis with the warmth of a small town; where the world already comes together every day to live and work and reach for a dream—a dream that no matter who we are, where we come from; no matter what we look like or what hand life has dealt us; with hard work, and discipline, and dedication, we can make it if we try.
>
> That's not just the American Dream. That is the Olympic spirit.[22]

City public schools staffers noted that bloody battles were common in and around schools set in black Chicago's desperately impoverished neighborhoods, including communities where real unemployment had certainly climbed to 40 percent and higher. As the nation's first black president trumpeted his "home city" as a fit setting for the global games, the reality of black living conditions in that city's highly segregated ghetto communities spoke to the persistence and deepening of the concentrated urban misery that Dr. Martin Luther King Jr. tried without success to overcome in black Chicago in the mid-1960s.[23]

Interestingly enough, Derrion Albert's murder took place outside one of the the city's "turnaround schools." As part of the aggressive schools privatization ("reform") agenda pursued by former Chicago Public Schools CEO and current Obama education secretary Arne Duncan, Fenger High School (the scene of Albert's brutal murder) was "subjected," in the words of Chicago Teachers Union activist Deborah Lynch, "to the CPS' latest attack on struggling schools by dumping all the staff, even the engineers, and keeping the same students. The 'reform' was after probation, restructuring, reconstitution, and a host of other unsuccessful Daley-team draconian, top-down efforts"—efforts that stripped Fenger's highly troubled, poor, and black student population of connection to teachers and other staff who had known them for years. "No one at Fenger this year has known their kids for more than three weeks," Lynch noted, adding that "this is a tragedy for all the students, not to mention the effects of the staff elimination on the staff."[24]

Revealingly enough, the best that the Olympics-focused White House could do in responding to news of Albert's murder was a weak comment from Press Secretary Gibbs. The president found the video of Albert's beating "chilling," Gibbs assured the nation. This comment came only in response to a reporter's question and not as part of any formal statement.

The *chilling* insult of the first black president's relative silence on the widely watched fatal beating as he sold his ghetto-ridden "home" metropolis's "small-town" warmth to the IOC was not lost on some black Chicagoans. As liberal columnist Ruben Navarette Jr. reported on the same day the Obamas tried to wow the IOC in white Denmark:

> Back in Obama's adopted hometown of Chicago, Illinois, some members of the black community are incensed at the president for not personally speaking out about the murder of Derrion Albert. . . .
>
> What really set them off was that Obama, in an awkward case of bad timing, instead flew to Copenhagen to pitch Chicago to the International Olympics Committee as the ideal city to host the games in 2016. . . .
>
> There is plenty for Obama to say about this tragedy in the Windy City. And the longer the president waits before he starts talking, the more damage he does to his reputation, even among some of his most ardent supporters.
>
> Judging from what's being said on talk radio, Web sites and blogs frequented by residents of Chicago, the fact that Obama put the Olympics

ahead of responding to the breakdown of the social order in Chi-Town is a slap in the face.

Just yesterday, a self-identified African-American called into "The Rush Limbaugh Show" and complained about how Obama flew off to "a foreign country" while black kids in Chicago are being consumed by violence. The caller wondered when other African-Americans were going to realize that Obama wasn't like them, because he's an elitist living an extraordinary life and breathing rarified air.

That sentiment was all over black-oriented blogs. One blogger wrote: "More children died violent deaths in Chicago this year than in any other city in America. But all Obama cares about is bringing the Olympics to a city where basic services like water, sanitation and power often don't work. . . . If Chicago does win the bid there will be plenty of police and National Guard on hand to protect the international visitors. That's more than they are willing to do for their own residents."

. . . Someone compared Obama's reaction to this societal problem to how he reacted to another one a while back, racial profiling. The person wrote: "U all think that Derrion Albert's mother will be invited to the White House for beer?"[25]

"We've Got to Go Through Procedures"

I was reminded of Patton's observation again two weeks later. That's when Obama made his belated first presidential visit to New Orleans, site of tropical storm and societal disaster Katrina—the disastrous August 2005 hurricane and federal fiasco that left tens of thousands of disproportionately black and poor inner-city residents trapped in deadly floodwaters. Seeking to deflect criticism claiming that he had not paid sufficient attention to the city and the broader Mississippi Delta region, Obama appeared to overwhelming applause at a town hall meeting to claim that "progress is being made" with federal recovery efforts. But the event's happy feeling was interrupted when a local resident asked, "Why is it four years after Katrina, we're still fighting for money to repair our devastated city?" The questioner added, "I expected as much from the Bush administration. But why are still being nickeled and dimed?"

The president's response was less than inspiring. It waxed dry, wonkish, and technocratic as he referred to "complications between the state, the city, and the feds in making assessments of the damages."[26] According to the *New York Times*:

The president, in a rare moment on the defensive in a format that is usually friendly to him, said many people in New Orleans were "understandably impatient" and said he had inherited a backlog of problems.

"These things were not going to be fixed tomorrow," Mr. Obama said. "So we are working as hard as we can, as quickly as we can." He added, "I wish I could just write a check."

When some shouted, "Why not?'" Mr. Obama replied, "There's this whole thing about the Constitution."

He added that "We've got to go through procedures."[27]

Surely many in the town hall were well aware that the new president, the Democratic-majority Congress, and their constitutionally encoded "procedures" had managed to quickly grant trillions of taxpayer dollars to the nation's predominantly white financial barons and to the Pentagon and thus to the nation's powerful "defense" contractors. Some certainly reflected on the fact that Obama, the U.S. House, and the U.S. Senate were spending vast federal resources on overseas wars of occupation while black ghettos, Latino barrios, and working-class communities of all races and ethnicities deteriorated across the imperial "homeland."

Tellingly enough, Obama the U.S. senator and Obama the presidential candidate made five visits to New Orleans after Katrina—a great symbol of Republican and Bush administration incompetence and callousness toward the poor. After waiting nine months to visit the devastated majority-black city he'd found so politically useful to speak from during his campaign, President Obama now stayed for only a few hours before jetting off to a posh ruling-class fund-raiser in San Francisco. During his short stop in New Orleans, Obama did manage to promote his and Arne Duncan's corporate-neoliberal schools privatization agenda by visiting the oxymoronically named "Martin Luther King Jr. Charter School" in the city's predominantly black, flood-ravaged Lower Ninth Ward. "The school," *Times* reporters Peter Baker and Campbell Robertson noted, was "surrounded by boarded-up houses, empty lots with overgrown grass and dilapidated storefronts with for-rent signs."[28] Baker and Campbell might have noted that corporate education forces had seized on Katrina as a great opportunity, using the crisis to advance their privatization model on the reconstitution of the New Orleans school system.[29]

Activists from a group of nonprofit organizations seeking relief on the Mississippi coast held up signs outside Obama's town hall. The signs read "The Recovery Is Not Over" and "Mississippi Will Not Be Forgotten." Their holders had been unable to secure tickets to the president's public relations event.[30] As *New York Times* columnist Maureen Dowd noted three days after Obama's brief stopover, the White House Web site that had gone up during Obama's first week in office boasted of his trips to New Orleans as U.S. senator. It pledged to "keep the broken promises made by President Bush to re-build New Orleans."[31]

"The Final Piece of Evidence That America Has Reached Full Racial Equality"

In one key sense at least, it seems possible that Obama's ascendancy heralded not simply "no change" for poor blacks but perhaps even change for the worse. I am referring to the significant extent to which the election of a technically black president reinforces the longstanding conventional white illusion that racism has disappeared and that the only obstacles left to African American success and equality are internal to individual blacks and their community—the idea that, in Derrick Bell's phrase, "the indolence of blacks rather than the injustice of whites explains the socioeconomic gaps separating the races."[32] "It's hard," Leonard Steinhorn and Barbara Diggs-Brown noted in 2000, "to blame people" for believing (falsely in Steinhorn and Diggs-Brown's view) that racism is dead in America "when our public life is filled with repeated affirmations of the integration ideal and our ostensible progress towards achieving it." In a similar vein, black scholar Sheryl Cashin observed in 2004 that "there are [now] enough examples of successful middle-class African-Americans to make many whites believe that blacks have reached parity with them. The fact that some blacks now lead powerful mainstream institutions offers evidence to whites that racial barriers have been eliminated; the issue now is individual effort."[33]

And what could trump the attainment of the U.S. presidency—the most powerful office on earth—in feeding and locking in that belief? Black urban studies professor Marc Lamont Hill said it well in an important *CounterPunch* critique in early February 2008:

> After Obama's recent success with white voters, particularly his win in Iowa, many have announced America's transition into a post-racial moment. Even Obama himself has claimed that race will no longer prevent the fair-minded citizenry from supporting his bid. In reality, however, an Obama presidency is already being treated as a racial talisman that would instantly heal the scars of a nation wounded by racism.

For whites, an Obama victory would serve as the final piece of evidence that America has reached full racial equality. Such a belief allows them to sidestep mounds of evidence that shows that, despite Obama's claims that "we are 90 percent of the way to equality," black people remain consistently assaulted by the forces of white supremacy. For many black people, Obama's success would provide symbolic value by showing that the black man (not woman!) can make it to the top. Although black faces in high places may provide psychological comfort, they are often incorporated into a Cosbyesque gospel of personal responsibility ("Obama did it, so can you!") that allows dangerous public policies to go unchallenged.[34]

The white-run political culture's regular rituals of self-congratulation over the defeat of overt, level-one racism—the Martin Luther King national holiday, the playing of King's "I Have a Dream" speech over school sound systems and on television, the routine reference to integrationist ideals in political speeches, and the presidential viability and the victory of Obama, for example—have long reinforced the dominant post–civil rights white sentiment that the United States no longer has much of anything to answer for in regard to its treatment of black America and the ubiquitous white American notion that racism is something only from the now relatively irrelevant and distant "past." "Now we can finally forget about race" is the basic dangerous widespread white wish that sought fulfillment in the election of someone like Obama. As one white Obama supporter told the *Washington Post* at a campaign event, he hoped that an Obama presidency would help America "erase all this nonsense about race."[35] How nice to imagine that racial oppression is something so nonsensical and superficial that it could be expunged by the mere act of putting in the White House a technically black politician who has gone out of his way not to threaten white cultural and ideological sensibilities surrounding race.

Betrayals: Latino/a, Reproductive, and Gay Rights

"Those Who Should Be On Our Side": Latino/as and Immigration Rights

Disadvantaged black Americans aren't the only group among the nations' leading "identity politics" categories who have found that the dawning Age of Obama involves no small degree of oppressive continuity rather than liberating change in basic social and political experience beneath and beyond the great rebranding. Conscious of the pivotal role their communities' votes played in electing Obama (selected by 67 percent of the nation's Hispanic voters in November 2008), leaders of the nation's large and expanding Hispanic or Latino/a population have been displeased with Obama's failure to spark any meaningful progress toward the passage of a comprehensive immigration reform bill.

In late May 2008, Obama went on the Latino television station Univision to guarantee such legislation "during my first year" in the White House. Fifteen months later, Univision anchor Jorge Ramos found it "very disconcerting" that Obama had (quite predictably) decided to delay immigration reform until 2010. Ramos noted that many Latino/a voters had been willing to vote for Obama "in exchange for his promise of legalizing undocumented immigrants."[36]

But the Hispanic community's problems with Obama have gone far beyond what the president hasn't done. They include some of his direct initiatives. Latino/a and other U.S. ethnic spokespersons and commentators have observed with horror that the Obama administration has decided to appease right-wing nativists by expanding a federal program whereby local police can partner with the federal Immigrations and Customs Enforcement agency (known as ICE) in the enforcement of federal immigrant laws. At the same time, they have been less than delighted with the new White House's shift of ICE from high-profile workplace raids and roundups (a common Bush-era practice) to the more systematic and effective elimination of immigrant labor through the large-scale auditing of employment records to force employers to fire "illegal" workers. An especially egregious mass firing forced by ICE audits took place at American Apparels, a giant Los Angeles clothing manufacturer that lost 1,800 workers—more than a quarter of the company's workforce—at the end of September 2009. Los Angeles mayor Antonio Villaraigosa complained bitterly that the ICE policy was economically "devastating" and suggested that the White House would do best to "focus on employers that exploit their workers." As the *New York Times* reported, American Apparel compensated workers "above the garment industry standard, offering health benefits and not long ago giving $18 million in stock to its workers."[37]

ICE started its audit of American Apparel in April 2008 under George W. Bush. In July 2009, under Obama, ICE opened similar payroll inspections at no less than 654 companies around the country—with terrible results for untold tens and hundreds of thousands of Latino/a and Asian American workers. The *Times* noted that "Obama administration officials point out that they have not followed the Bush pattern of concluding such investigations with a mass roundup of workers. Those raids drew criticism for damaging businesses and dividing immigrant families." But "the new focus on employers to not hire undocumented immigrants has," Ramos noted, "the same effect: More firings and more deportations."[38] Here Ramos captured a perfect example of the essence of the Obama rebranding: a change of style and a modulation in image combined with a persistence of the old regime in terms of core underlying policy imperative and outcome.

Another disturbing development for Latino/a leaders and activists came when Obama announced in his September 2009 health care address that "illegal immigrants" would be denied coverage under his health "reform" plan. Two days after the speech, an Obama spokesman said that the president even opposed letting undocumented immigrants buy insurance from private companies through the administration's proposed system of government-run "purchasing exchanges."[39] This chilling statement led Chicago's Luis Luis Gutierrez (D-IL), the first Latino representative to endorse Obama for president, to "blast" the (not-so-)new administration. "Those who should be our friends, on our side," Gutierrez said, "are more and more giving Rep. [Joe] Wilson exactly what he wants to continues this prejudice against our community."[40]

"Replaying the Clinton-Era Scenario": Reproductive Rights Go Undefended in the Name of Faith

Women's rights activists have also had reason to charge betrayal. Speaking to Planned Parenthood in the summer of 2007, Obama promised that passing an abortion rights/reproductive freedom bill (a "freedom of choice act" he called it) would be his first act in office. But during his third press conference, marking his first one hundred days in office, President Obama gruffly acknowledged that that bill was "not my highest legislative priority." Nearly five months later, Obama announced in his health care address that "no federal funds will be used to fund abortions," consistent with his decision to support Bush-era "federal conscience laws" permitting doctors and other health care providers to refuse requests for treatments such as prescribing contraception or performing abortions.[41]

When Obama gave a commencement address to the Catholic Notre Dame University in mid-May 2009, thousands of antiabortion activists descended upon the campus in South Bend, Indiana. Prochoice organizations made no appearance, preferring, left feminist writer Sharon Smith observed, "to let Obama represent their side of the debate." But Obama did no such thing. His speech, Smith noted,

> called for those on opposing sides of the abortion debate to find "common ground" . . . to "work together to reduce the number of women seeking abortions by reducing unintended pregnancies, and making adoption more available, and providing care and support for women who do carry their child to term." Obama's speech never articulated his own support for women who choose abortion to end an unwanted pregnancy. His speech was so conciliatory to abortion opponents that even the Pope expressed delight. The Vatican newspaper *L'Osservatore Romano* praised Obama's speech and noted that Obama had stated at a recent press conference that passing a Freedom of Choice Act, which would protect women's right to choose, was not high on his list of priorities.

Obama struck Smith as intent on "replaying the Clinton-era scenario, in which the pro-choice presidential candidate promises supporters that he will pass the Freedom of Choice Act while on the campaign trail. Once elected, his enthusiasm vanishes and, when pro-choice supporters do not protest this betrayal, the legislation never materializes."[42]

Obama didn't help his case with prochoice feminists by selecting Alexia Kelley for a senior Health and Human Services (HHS) "faith-based" position just a week after the murder of prominent abortion doctor George Tiller.[43] Kelley was a leading antiabortion activist in her role as executive director of Catholics in Alliance for the Common Good (CACG). Obama appointed her in early June 2009 to head the Center for Faith-Based and Neighborhood Partnerships at the Department of Health and Human Services. It was an alarming move for the many prochoice feminists who had supported Obama in 2008, for, as Sarah Posner explained in the weekly liberal political affairs magazine the *American Prospect*, Kelley had made clear that she hoped to reduce abortions not simply by cutting unwanted pregnancies (a major Obama theme) but also by stigmatizing and *diminishing access* to abortion. She had also refused to challenge church doctrine prohibiting abortion and birth control. Posner noted that in a 2008 press teleconference cosponsored by CACG, Kelley stated that she supported state-imposed restrictions on abortion, such as waiting periods and informed consent. In her 2008 book, *A Nation for All*, cowritten with Chris Korzen, Kelley wrote, 'Each abortion constitutes a direct attack on human life, and so we have a special moral obligation to end or reduce the practice of abortion to the greatest extent possible.'" Tellingly enough,

CACG issued no public statements about the Tiller assassination, "though it signed one by Faith in Public Life condemning the murder. But the statement did not condemn the inciting rhetoric of the anti-choice movement. Rather, it made a kumbaya plea for common ground (which as we have seen, is not so common after all)."

Under Bush, Posner added, the faith-based centers were given no policy role at HHS. But Obama has "expanded the faith-based project to include a policy side, and one of its chief goals is to reduce the need for abortion." Beneath progressive imagery and rhetoric, the Obama administration determined to go further to the right in policy substance than Bush had.[44] During the 2008 campaign, Obama said he would expand George W. Bush's "faith-based initiatives" because "the challenges we face are too big for government to solve alone." Here he replicated earlier neoliberal doctrine from previous administrations on the supposed inherent limits of government's capacity and legitimate role in solving poverty and other social problems, creating space for religiously based institutions to fill the gap. At the same time, however, Obama pledged to end the Bush administration's unconstitutional practice of letting churches, temples, synagogues, and mosques use federal dollars for other than secular purposes. He said he would reverse Bush policy by forbidding "faith-based programs" that accepted federal money from proselytizing or discriminating against people in hiring on the basis of religion, gender, and sexual orientation (many faith-based organizations funded under Bush insisted that hiring gays violated their religious beliefs).

By the later summer of 2009, however, Obama had "backtracked or stalled on all these promises." His sprawling new Office of Faith-Based and Neighborhood Partnerships—manager of a faith-based network spread across eleven federal agencies—had already been used to reward religious supporters with federal employment on the model of Bush's "faith-based initiative." Among secularists, feminists, and religious progressives, Posner found in August, "the dissatisfaction runs deep," leading many to "question not only the constitutionality but the entire purpose of the office." According to Reverend Tony Campolo, a religious progressive who served on the Democratic National Committee's platform committee in 2008, the Obama campaign had sought to "still the anxieties" of the nation's largest religious organizations so that "if no fuss was made, the policies that were in place on these matters during the Bush administration"—discriminatory hiring and proselytizing at faith-based initiatives getting federal dollars— "during the Bush Administration would be continued."

According to Reverend Irene Monroe, a lesbian, gay, bisexual, and transgender rights activist and doctoral candidate at Harvard Divinity School, Obama was "pandering to a very conservative base that raised its horrible head during the Bush administration. He can't find a way to undo that but thinks he can refashion that. But he's actually just re-inscribing the problem."[45]

"I Wouldn't Be Surprised If I Heard Booing Next Summer": Failing to Defend Gay Rights

Gay activists have had special reason to charge unfaithfulness on Obama's part. In a 2008 interview with MSNBC's popular progressive and gay political talk-show host Rachel Maddow, Obama described himself as a "fierce advocate" of the nation's gay, lesbian, and transgender community. But despite this and other repeated campaign pledges to defend and advance gay rights, the Obama administration infuriated gay rights organizations in June 2009 when its Justice Department filed a motion to uphold the 1996 Defense of Marriage Act (DOMA) The legislation declared that same-sex marriages should not be recognized in states where gay marriage is prohibited and explicitly defined legal marriage as between "one man and one woman." In its brief on behalf of DOMA, the Justice Department called the legislation a "valid exercise of Congress' power" and said it was "reasonable and rational for Congress to maintain its longstanding policy of fostering this traditional and universally-recognized form of marriage."[46]

Administration spokespersons claimed that the Justice Department had "no choice" but to defend an existing piece of legislation. But Justice had chosen not to defend laws in the past. As John Cloud noted in *Time* in August, "The Administration could easily decline to defend the anti-gay law on discrimination grounds, just as the Administration of George H. W. Bush declined to defend federal laws setting a preference for awarding broadcast licenses to minority-owned businesses in 1990. . . . There is nothing in the constitution or the law that would have prevented the Department of Justice from sitting on the sidelines in the DOMA case. Nothing except politics. Obama's triangulation between left and right has become excruciatingly obvious on this issue."[47]

To make matters worse, Obama has made no serious effort to push Congress to change the law. A June CBS report titled "Obama Facing Gay Groups' Growing Anger" noted that the president's fear of "opening up a fight over social issues that could endanger his ambitious agenda on health care and other issues" was discouraging him from asking Congress to act in accord with his repeatedly stated campaign pledge to work for DOMA's repeal.[48] The Obama administration also did not act to keep the president's campaign promise to reverse the U.S. military's "don't ask, don't tell" policy, which prohibits openly gay Americans from serving in the U.S. armed forces.[49]

It also refused to consider strong defenders and advocates of gay, women's, and immigrants' rights for the Supreme Court position that opened up in May 2009. The Obama White House quickly passed over such highly qualified candidates as Stanford's Pamela Karland (a celebrated and brilliant "champion of gay rights, criminal defendants' rights, and voting rights"—an "Antonin Scalia for the left") to appoint the moderate, business-friendly Sonia Sotomayor, a federal judge with an uncertain record on abortion who promised to score Obama points of symbolic ethnic representation with the nation's Latinas and Latinos.[50] Among other things, the Sotomayor appointment was a reminder that Obama was hardly above playing the race, ethnicity, and gender cards thereby advancing the very identity politics he claimed to transcend.

When Obama announced a package of domestic partnership benefits for gay federal workers in mid-June 2009, several top gay activists criticized the president for failing to extend full health benefits, adding that "the initiative was a mere token effort that included benefits that had already existed." Preferring policy substance over superficial changes merely in style and rhetoric, these activists were less than impressed by Obama's holding in late June 2009 a low-key White House reception to mark the fortieth anniversary of the Stonewall Rebellion, the 1969 Greenwich Village demonstrations that gave birth to the modern gay rights movement.[51] Journalist John Cloud gave an interesting account of how a growing number of gay activists and voters were losing faith in Obama in accord with the president's by-now-standard use of progressive symbolism to gloss over conservative policy substance:

> On a sunny Saturday last month, I crashed a fancy brunch on New York's Fire Island at the swank beachside home of Daniel Cochran and Greg Sutphin, a wealthy gay couple. They served lovely Bloody Marys and a giant spread of eggs and meats and assorted asparagus dishes prepared by a white-coated chef. The brunch was the 31st to be held in Fire Island's Pines community to raise money for Lambda Legal, the gay movement's litigation arm. At last year's brunch, cheers went up virtually every time Barack Obama's name was uttered. This time, when Lambda executive director

Kevin Cathcart began to review the President's record on gay issues, he was greeted with steely silence.

"I wouldn't be surprised," Cloud concluded, "if, next summer at the 32nd Fire Island Pines fundraiser for Lambda, I hear booing when the President's name is mentioned."[52]

It would be an understandable response to some of the many betrayals and deceptions at the heart of the Great Obama Rebranding.

5

Big Brother Lives

> Almost all of the Obama changes have been at the level of packaging, argumentation, symbol, and rhetoric. . . . The main difference between the Obama and Bush administrations concerns not the substance of terrorism policy, but rather its packaging.
>
> —*Jack Goldsmith, May 18, 2009*[1]

Some of Obama's liberal fans embraced the future president in 2007 and 2008 out of the conviction that he was a serious opponent of the assault on civil liberties undertaken by Washington in the aftermath of the 9/11 jetliner attacks. "This guy used to be a constitutional law professor," one upper-middle-class voter employed at a global high-tech engineering and consulting firm told me in Muscatine, Iowa, in November 2007. "And that means he's going to get rid of all this 'war on terror' crap like wiretapping and Guantanamo and torture and the Patriot Act," this highly educated citizen believed. He was not alone. Obama struck many of my Iowa voter contacts in 2007 as a civil libertarian who could be counted on to dismantle George W. Bush's repressive "war on terror," with its multiple chilling violations of basic human and civil rights at home and abroad—abuses that Obama, like Edwards, ran against quite heavily in Iowa.

The policy has not fit the brand. As a campaigner, Obama may have played to the Democratic Party's "progressive base" by speaking eloquently of his own commitment to "restoring the Constitution" and the Bill of Rights by rolling back the repressive policies of the Bush administration. "Closing Guantanamo" was a frequent campaign promise of his. But as a U.S. senator in July 2005, Obama angered civil liberties activists by voting to reauthorize the proto-fascistic USA Patriot Act, itself "easily the worst attack on civil liberties in the last half-century."[2] Passed with strong bipartisan support in the repressive immediate post-9/11 atmosphere, this pivotal legislation increased the ability of government to search citizens' telephone, e-mail, medical, financial, and other records; eased restrictions on foreign intelligence gathering within the United States; expanded and enhanced the discretion of law enforcement and immigration authorities in detaining and deporting immigrants; and expanded the definition of terrorism to include domestic terrorism, thus enlarging the number of activities to which the USA Patriot Act's expanded law enforcement powers could be applied. The bill authorized the indefinite detentions of suspected terrorists; government searches of homes and business without the owner's or the occupant's permission or knowledge; expanded use of National Security Letters, which allows the Federal Bureau of Investigation (FBI) to search telephone, e-mail, and financial records without a court order; and expanded access of law enforcement agencies to business records, including library and financial records. As prolific left scholar and social critic Henry A. Giroux noted in a 2004 chapter titled "Living in the Shadow of Authoritarianism":

> Under the veil of legislated secrecy, the U.S. government can now name individuals as terrorists without offering them a public hearing and break into the private homes and tap the phones of U.S. citizens. As if this was not bad enough, constitutional freedoms and civil liberties are further compromised by the power of government agents to subpoena anybody's telephone, medical, bookstore, library, or university records "simply by certifying that these records are needed for an investigation of international terrorism." The CIA [Central Intelligence Agency] and Pentagon are allowed to engage in domestic intelligence work, the USA PATRIOT ACT allows government to detain people secretly and indefinitely without access to lawyers or a jury trial.[3]

Nearly three years after he voted to reinstate the Patriot Act, Senator and presumptive Democratic Party presidential nominee Obama announced his support for a sweeping intelligence law that granted retroactive immunity to telephone corporations for collaborating with the White House in the practice of electronic surveillance against American citizens. The pledge to filibuster any such unconstitutional legislation.[4] The bill had been heavily denounced, *Washington Post* reporter Paul Kane noted, "by the liberal activists who have fueled the financial engines of his presidential campaign." Obama voted for the new spy bill in his determination to walk what Kane called "the fine political line between GOP accusations that he is weak on foreign policy and alienating his [liberal] base."[5]

Denial of Habeas Corpus
Okayed at Bagram "War Zone"

Obama has continued to walk the line with a decided rightward tilt as president. Beneath superficially progressive rhetoric and symbolism meant to mollify his "progressive base" and to advance the rebranding project that is at heart of his administration, he has perpetuated core aspects of the Cheney-Bush approach to civil liberties in the waging of the "global war on terror."

In February 2009, for example, the Obama administration filed a federal brief that embraced the Bush administration's position against habeas corpus (the right not to be detained or incarcerated without just legal cause determined in a court of law) in regard to U.S. government-identified "enemy combatants" seized abroad are flown to the U.S. Air Force's Bagram Airfield prison in Afghanistan (instead of to the U.S. Naval Station at Guantanamo Bay). Because (illegally U.S-invaded and U.S.-occupied) Afghanistan was technically a "war zone," the administration argued, detainees there could be treated as "prisoners of war" and therefore denied protection against seizure and incarceration without stated cause. It was a remarkable stretch to treat suspected terrorists seized from their homes or workplaces in London or Cairo as people engaged in a "war against the United States" in Afghanistan. The cynicism involved in the Justice Department's legal reasoning was quite extraordinary.[6]

Highly Conditional
Release of Torture Memos

The Obama administration has gone to remarkable lengths to protect CIA personnel and top Bush administration officials from investigation and prosecution for human rights crimes in connection with the torture of Arabs and Muslims caught on the wrong side of the post-9/11 U.S. terror war. In mid-April 2009, the Obama Justice Department expressed its determination to shield direct CIA torturers from prosecution, even after it won accolades from liberal commentators for releasing past White House memorandums outlining the Bush administration's extreme torture practices.

But those memos saw the light of day only because of a lawsuit by the American Civil Liberties Union. As the *New York Times* reported, citing top White House aides, moreover, Obama "opted to disclose the memos [only] because his lawyers worried that they had a weak case for withholding them and [because] much of the information had already been published in the *New York Review of Books*, in a memoir by George Tenent, the former CIA Director, and even in a 2006 speech by President George W. Bush."[7] In a speech to the CIA staff at CIA headquarters in Langley, Virginia, on April 20, 2009, Obama made sure to remind the agency that he had released only the memos "as a consequence of a court case that was pending and to which it was very difficult for us to mount an effective legal defense." He said he "acted primarily because of the exceptional circumstances that surrounded these memos; particularly the fact that so much of the information was public, had been publicly acknowledged, the covert nature of the information had been compromised."[8] This was hardly a ringing declaration of the needs for transparency and respect for international law in the conduct of U.S. foreign policy.

By announcing in advance that it would not go after direct on-the-ground conductors of torture, the Obama administration destroyed its ability to use the threat of prosecution as a way of getting CIA and military intelligence personnel to testify against the top officials who had formulated Bush's torture policy. Obama's prosecution exemption echoed the Nazis' defense of human right perpetrators on the grounds that the criminals were "just following orders."

"We're All Best Suited Looking Forward"

As his Justice Department released the memos spelling out brutal CIA interrogation methods in April 2009, Obama distanced himself from the demand for the investigation and prosecution of Bush administration violations of human rights law by saying that "nothing will be gained by spending our time and energy laying blame for the past."[9] It was a revealing comment from a former "liberal" constitutional law professor, someone who might have been expected to understand that a democratic government would investigate and punish past human rights crimes precisely to discourage and prevent their occurrence in the present and future.

Obama subsequently seemed to relent a bit in the face of a wave of civil libertarian disgust by saying that Attorney General Eric Holder might choose to investigate the Bush lawyers who had approved torture. But this was not much of a threat. Holder had backed George Bush's post-9/11 "dark side" (torture) policies, supporting Bush's denial of Geneva protections to detainees. By late April, Obama and the Democratic leadership in the Senate signaled that they would block efforts to set up an independent commission to investigate Bush's torture policy. Obama spokesperson

Robert Gibbs justified this position by saying that "this is not a time for retribution" and that "we're all best suited looking forward."[10]

Resealing Torture Photos That Might "Further Inflame Anti-American Opinion"

In May, Obama reversed his original stand on behalf of releasing photographs documenting the torture and abuse of detainees in U.S. prisons. After viewing the photographs, Obama claimed that releasing them would "further inflame anti-American opinion" and thereby "put our troops in greater danger" in the Arab and Muslim worlds.[11] It was a remarkable statement when seen alongside the routine ongoing and escalated occurrence of U.S. drone strikes and other imperial attacks (e.g., the Bola Bluk tragedy of March 2009) that—along with the Obama administration's persistent occupation of Iraq and its support for Israel's oppression of the Palestinians—generated "anti-American" bitterness across the region. At the same time, Obama's argument for resealing the terrible, truth-telling pictures ignored the possibility that the United States could actually win favor in the Middle East and Muslim worlds by showing a newfound willingness to acknowledge, denounce, and apologize for its remarkable crimes—crimes Obama refused to acknowledge (out of doctrinal faith that the United States is an inherently and exceptionally benevolent nation and "an overwhelming force for good in the world," even if it occasionally makes "mistakes," such as the mass-murderous invasions of Vietnam and Iraq and the engineering of lethal coups in Latin America).[12] As Obama the proud American exceptionalist and U.S. world supremacist would proclaim in his early November 2009 memorial in Fort Hood, Texas, before the coffins of thirteen U.S. soldiers killed by a Muslim American army psychological counselor very likely driven to madness by America's continuing criminal war on the Middle East:[13] "We are a nation of laws whose commitment to justice is so enduring that we would treat a gunman and give him due process. . . . We're a nation that guarantees the freedom to worship as one chooses. . . . We're a nation that is dedicated to the proposition that all men and women are created equal. We defend that truth at home and abroad, and we know that Americans will always be found on the side of liberty and equality."[14] Or as Obama told CIA staffers in April, "What makes the United States *special,* and what makes you *special,* is precisely the fact that we are willing to uphold our values and our ideals even when it's hard, not just when it's easy;

even when we are afraid and under threat, not just when it's expedient to do so. That's what *makes us different* [emphasis added]."[15]

Wouldn't Want to "Trigger a Culture War"

In late April 2009, Obama vetoed CIA director Leon Panetta's recommendation to set up an independent truth commission to investigate the Bush II administration's criminal torture practices. He did so on the grounds that such a commission would look vindictive and could enrage his predecessor, alienate independent voters, and "trigger a culture war." Panetta told the *New Yorker's* Jane Mayer that "it was the President who basically said, 'If I do this, *it will look like I'm trying to go after Cheney and Bush* [emphasis added].' He just didn't think it made sense. And then everybody kind of backed away from it."[16]

Threatening England with Terrorist Attack to Protect Bush-Era Crimes

The remarkable, even surreal extent to which Obama would go to hide evidence of "special" and "different" America's Bush-era crimes took astonishingly cynical form in February 2009. That's when Obama's Department of Justice threatened the national security of England if that country's courts did not dismiss Binyam Mohamed's lawsuit against a company (the Chicago-based Boeing Corporation's subsidiary Jeppesen Data) that helped the CIA "render" him to the U.S. prison on Guantanamo Bay, where Mohamed survived six years of torture and detention without due process. Released to his home country of England in February 2009, Mohamed immediately sought redress in his nation's legal system. A British High Court ruled that sufficient proof existed to show that he had been subjected to torture and was therefore entitled to obtain further evidence in the possession of the British government on the details of his treatment by the CIA. A formal police investigation was initiated to examine allegations that British agents collaborated in his torture.[17]

Then the British High Court reversed itself under a very particular and remarkable form of pressure from White House. If the British court released the facts of Mohamed's torture, the Obama administration told England's judicial officer, the United States could no longer guarantee its willingness to engage in vital intelligence sharing with Britain. In other words, the United States would no longer pass on critical information about terrorist threats targeting British citizens. As the British High Court noted in a decision annulling its original judgment to release seven key paragraphs detailing Mohamed's criminal seizure and torture:

> The United States Government's position is that, if the redacted paragraphs are made public, then the U.S. will re-evaluate its intelligence-sharing relationship with the United Kingdom with the real risk that it would reduce the intelligence it provided . . . [and] there is a real risk, if we restored the redacted paragraphs, the United States Government, by its review of the shared intelligence arrangements, could inflict on the citizens of the United Kingdom a very considerable increase in the dangers they face at a time when a serious terrorist threat still pertains.[18]

In the letter to English authorities demanding that they delete the technically criminal act of covering up torture, Obama's Justice Department said that (to quote directly from the communication itself):

> Public disclosure of this information, reasonably could be expected to cause serious damage to the United Kingdom's national security . . . It is almost certain that the United Kingdom's ability to identify and arrest suspected terrorists and to disrupt terrorist plots would be severely hampered . . . [because] foreign partners [the United States] could take steps to withhold from the United Kingdom sensitive information that could be important to its safety and security. . . . Public disclosure of the information contained in the seven paragraphs could likely result in serious damage to U.K and U.S. national security. If it is determined that HMG [Her Majesty's Government] is unable to protect information we provided it, even if that inability is caused by your judicial system, we will necessarily have to review with the greatest care the sensitivity of the information we can provide you in the future.[19]

"Obama Now Resembles Bush"

Obama, the supposed liberal, pro–civil liberties president who taught constitutional law for years, has maintained and defended in court the Bush electronic surveillance (wiretapping) program. He has made no effort to act on his campaign pledge to strengthen the Privacy and Civil Liberties Board that is supposed to oversee and protect civil liberties in intelligence gathering. According to Harvard Law professor Jack Goldsmith, a former assistant attorney general and Office of Legal Counsel lawyer in the Bush II administration, "The Obama surveillance program appears to be identical to the late Bush era program"—something that induced *McClatchy Newspapers* reporter Michael Doyle to pen the following headline: "Obama Now Resembles Bush."[20]

Obama has invoked the "state secrets" (akin to the divine right of kings) doctrine to prevent disclosure of evidence in response to lawsuits emerging from Bush-era rendition and surveillance policies.[21] He has invoked "presidential communications privilege" to block the release of notes from an interview the Federal Bureau of Investigation conducted in 2008 with Vice President Dick Cheney as part of an investigation into the Bush administration's punitive leaking of the identity of undercover CIA agent Valerie Plume.[22] He has revived military commissions, continued the practice of renditions, and maintained secret prisons for persons held on a short-term, transitory basis. He has also continued the unspeakable torture of prisoners by an "extrajudicial terror squad" (Jeremy Scahill's description of the Pentagon's sadistic "Immediate Reaction Force" in Cuba) at Guantanamo Bay and advanced the "indefinite detention" (potentially permanent incarceration) of Guantanamo prisoners for whom no legally compelling evidence can be marshaled.[23] The "new" White House has consistently justified all of this and more in the name of the frankly terrorist U.S. global war on terror that was supposedly launched in legitimate defense against the supposedly unprovoked jetliner attacks of September 11, 2001.[24]

Obama's Bad Influence

Thanks to a "liberal" president's embrace of so much of the Bush antiterror approach, brilliant left-liberal civil libertarian lawyer, political commentator, and Obama critic Glen Greenwald worried in May, much of the liberal and progressive community was falling into line behind repressive policies it would have continued to criticize under a Republican administration. "What I find most harmful about [Obama's] embrace of things like preventive detention, concealment of torture evidence, opposition to investigations and the like," Greenwald wrote in *Salon*, "is that these policies are now no longer just right-wing dogma but also [things] that many defenders of his—Democrats, liberals, progressives—will defend as well." In addition,

> the more Obama embraces core Bush terrorism policies and assumptions— *we're fighting a "war on terror"; Presidents have the power to indefinitely and "preventatively" imprison people with no charges; we can create new due-process-abridging tribunals when it suits us; the "Battlefield" is everywhere; we should conceal evidence when it will make us look bad*—the more those prem-

ises are transformed from right-wing dogma into the prongs of bipartisan consensus, no longer just advocated by Bush followers but by many Obama defenders as well. The fact that it's all wrapped up in eloquent rhetoric about the rule of law, our Constitution and our "timeless values"—and the fact that his understanding of those values is more evident than his predecessor's—only heightens the concern.

So now, we're going to have huge numbers of people who spent the last eight years vehemently opposing such ideas running around arguing that we're waging a War against Terrorism, a "War President" must have the power to indefinitely lock people away who allegedly pose a "threat to Americans" but haven't violated any laws, our normal court system can't be trusted to decide who is guilty, Terrorists don't deserve the same rights as Americans, the primary obligation of the President is to "keep us safe," and—most of all—anyone who objects to or disagrees with any of that is a leftist purist ideologue who doesn't really care about national security. In other words, arguments and rhetoric that were once confined to Fox News/Bush-following precincts will now become mainstream Democratic argumentation in service of defending what Obama is doing.[25]

Greenwald warned here, in essence, of a domestic, "homeland" version of the "bad influence" that Naomi Klein observed (from a left-progressive standpoint) on the behavior of other rich and powerful nations.[26] He saw the danger of the president's deceptive "progressive" credentials and persona encouraging people and institutions to embrace negative policies they would criticize and resist if those policies were being carried out by more self-evidently reactionary actors such as George W. Bush or John McCain.

This was and remains the essence of the rebranding that Obama was picked by the corporate-imperial establishment to embody. Policies and practices—unjust wars and occupations, megabailouts for bankers, egregious assaults on human rights and civil liberties at home and abroad, other regressive and repressive processes and procedures—that were seen as noxious under the perceived rule of a boorish white Republican from Texas (George W. Bush) become perversely acceptable for many "progressive" and other citizens when carried out by an eloquent and urbane black Democrat from Chicago (Barack Obama).

One prominent liberal and onetime Obama fan was not fooled. According to *New York Times* columnist Bob Herbert—a major admirer of the next president during the 2008 election season—"Policies that were wrong under George W. Bush are *no less wrong because Barack Obama is in the White House* [emphasis added]." "One of the most disappointing aspects of the early months of the Obama administration," Herbert added, "has been its unwillingness to end many of the mind-numbing abuses linked to the so-called war on terror and to establish a legal and moral framework designed to prevent those abuses from ever occurring again."[27]

"The Cheney Fallacy"

Speaking of *rebranding*, we might consider the judgment of the aforementioned former Bush administration attorney Jack Goldsmith. On the eve of a heavily covered battle of dueling same-day torture-policy speeches between President Obama ("antitorture") and former vice president Dick Cheney ("protorture") in May, Goldsmith, no radical, criticized what he called "the Cheney Fallacy." "The Cheney fallacy," Goldsmith argued in the centrist journal the *New Republic*, was the inaccurate belief that "the Obama administration has reversed Bush-era policies." According to Goldsmith, a Republican, "The truth is closer to the opposite: The new administration has copied most of the Bush program, has expanded some of it, and has narrowed only a bit. Almost all of the Obama *changes have been at the level of packaging, argumentation, symbol, and rhetoric*. ... The main difference between the Obama and Bush administrations concerns *not the substance* of terrorism policy, but rather *its packaging* [emphasis added]."[28]

Consistent with Goldsmith's insight, liberal pundit E. J. Dionne made an interesting comment on National Public Radio the evening after Obama and Cheney's oratorical swordfight. Dionne said that Cheney did Obama a great service by giving his far-right speech in defense of torture on the same day as Obama's address. Cheney's hard-right ranting deflected "the left's" attention away from the current chief executive's fundamental continuation of core Bush policies and to the outrageous claims of a former vice president.

"Our Nation Is at War"

Throughout his presidency, Obama has repeatedly justified his militaristic policies and his continuation of the Bush administration's assault on civil liberties with the claim that, in the words of his inaugural address, "our nation is at war, against a far-reaching network of violence and hatred." Obama's recycling of the Bush's administration's paranoid, fear-mongering "the Battlefield is everywhere" (Greenwald's excellent phrase) language was on display during his Fort Hood funeral oration, where he took the cold murder of thirteen military personnel on a U.S.-imperial military base as an opportunity to claim that "this is a time of war. Yet these Americans did not die on a foreign field of battle. They were killed here, on American soil, in the heart of this great state and the heart of this great American community."

But where has the "war" been, on the whole? It's been taking place in Iraq, Afghanistan, Gaza, and Pakistan. And it's been a very one-sided imperial and U.S.-imposed affair. Its main victims by far and away have been civilian Arabs, Pashtuns, and (more broadly) Muslims who have done nothing to the American people. It's not over here, really. "At war" Americans aren't dodging improvised explosive devices and sniper fire and F-16s and Predator drones and B2 Stealth Bombers and Blackhawk attack helicopters on their way to work, school, and shopping centers. They haven't been displaced from their homes as millions of Iraqis, Palestinians, and Pakistanis have been. They have been encouraged to carry on with private lives focused on work, family, entertainment, and mass consumerism while U.S. military masters conduct widely unpopular wars of occupation without meaningful democratic consultation of the citizenry. Just a small and disproportionately working-class share of the U.S. population provides soldiers for the nation's bloody colonial wars through the "all volunteer" armed forces. If the U.S. government tried to make military "service" mandatory for young adults across the socioeconomic spectrum, it would encounter considerable popular resistance.

The Fort Hood attack of November 2009 was conducted by an isolated Muslim American citizen and soldier on a military base that trained troops for, and shipped them out to, imperial wars in the mostly Muslim Middle East. The perpetrator had no connection to global terrorist structures.

The "far-reaching network of [Islamic] violence and hatred" is largely a U.S. creation. It is critically fueled (and was in fact originally financed) by this country's longstanding petro-imperial presence in the oil-rich Middle East—a presence that is intimately related back to a rapacious, ecologically disastrous mass consumerism that induces Americans to devour global resources on a spectacular scale. As far as much of the world—the Arab and Muslim worlds most especially—is concerned (with good reason), the U.S. military (replete with more than 800 bases located across more than 130 countries) constitutes by far and away the planet's leading "far-reaching network of violence and hatred."

Homeland Repression, September 2009

In the Age of Obama, as under the George W. Bush administration, moreover, the Empire and its terror(ist) wars rest in part on the terrorization of the domestic populace. During the 2009 G-20 Summit in Pittsburgh in September 2009, high-tech repression in the streets of that "homeland" city provided an unnerving backdrop for Obama's menacing "revelations" on the supposed Iranian nuclear "threat."[29] Highly militarized police (recruited from across national jurisdictions) attacked so-called antiglobalization (pro–global justice) protestors with batons, pepper gas, tear gas, and the LRAD (Long Range Acoustic Device). Never before deployed inside the territory of the "world's greatest democracy," the LRAD was placed atop an armored police vehicle and emitted a sharp piercing sonic noise that threatened to shatter protestors' eardrums.[30] It was just one part of a new publicly financed, privately developed arsenal of proto-totalitarian "nonlethal crowd control technologies"—a chilling new authoritarian munitions store that is highly lethal to the popular right of free assembly. The despotic new technologies of repression have been developed by the Pentagon and local "law enforcement" agencies by such "defense" contractors as Raytheon.[31]

In the aftermath of the G-20 protests, Obama's FBI arrested a New York City–based activist named Elliot Madison for an interesting reason. Madison was seized for using the popular social networking site Twitter to help protestors avoid arrest while engaging in their right to protest corporate globalization in the streets of Pittsburgh.

It was a fascinating transgression. Twitter was hailed by corporate U.S. media and politicians for its role in helping expose state repression and organize citizen action in Iran after contested elections in that country in July 2009. When used as a tool of democratic social protest within the shores of the United States, curiously enough, Twitter elicited a reactionary response from the "progressive" Obama government. Madison's apartment was ransacked by federal "counterterrorism" agents, who confiscated "anarchist books and pictures of Marx and Lenin."[32] It was an interesting episode in light of Obama's claims that "different" and "special" America is exceptional because "we are a nation of laws whose commitment to justice is so enduring" that even "a gunman" receives due process.[33]

Secret and Hypocritical Lobbying on Behalf of Unconstitutional Search and Seizure

As I completed this chapter in late November 2009, more than a year after Obama's election had warmed civil libertarian hearts across the country, dominant "mainstream" media failed to give significant coverage to the remarkable fact that the "liberal" administration was quietly backing the renewal of three key oppressive provisions of the Bush-era Patriot Act. With the approval of the Obama White House and a number of top Republicans and against the opposition of leading liberal Senate Democrats, including Dick Durbin (D-IL) and Russ Feingold (D-WI), the Senate Judiciary Committee voted to extend the provisions (with only minor changes) beyond their original expiration date of December 31, 2009. The three provisions left unaltered were the federal government's power to force Internet service providers, libraries, banks, and credit report agencies to hand over sensitive information about their customers and patrons; to criminalize a wide variety of activities said to provide "material support to terrorists" regardless of whether the activities in question actually or intentionally assist terrorist institutions or aims; and to conduct "warrantless and suspicion-less dragnet collections of U.S. residents' international telephone calls and e-mails." Opponents of the soon-to-be renewed provisions pressed Congress to replace the three sections with new measures containing strengthened civil liberties projections. These efforts were unsuccessful thanks in no small part to what one leading civil liberties activist—Chip Pitts, president of the Bill of Rights Defense Committee (BRDC)—called "secret and hypocritical lobbying by the Obama administration." While publicly "stating receptiveness" to the reforms proposed by the BRDC, the American Civil Liberties Union, and other civil liberties defenders, the Obama administration actually worked behind the scenes against the reforms. White House duplicity, Pitts told the Inter Press Service, was "undoubtedly a huge if lamentable factor" in the defeat of efforts to provide protections to citizen rights from unconstitutional search, seizure, and surveillance.[34]

Obama's stealth collaboration with the Republicans on the three Patriot Act provisions mirrored his fascinating partnership with the right-wing party on military escalation in Afghanistan.[35] On civil liberties as well as on so many other core issues, Obama the supposed "liberal Democrat" was governing like a center Republican, sometimes in actual alliance with the GOP.

It was all very interesting and (for many progressives) depressing in light of Brand Obama's comments upon receiving the Nobel Peace Prize in Oslo, Norway, on December 10, 2009. The United States, Obama explained to an audience of 1,000 in Oslo, had a "moral and strategic interest" in abiding by a code of conduct when waging war—even one that pitted the United States against a "vicious adversary that abides by no rules."

"That is what makes us different from those whom we fight," Obama said. "That is a source of our strength. That is why I prohibited torture.

That is why I ordered the prison at Guantanamo Bay closed.[36] And that is why I have reaffirmed America's commitment to abide by the Geneva Conventions. We lose ourselves when we compromise the very ideals that we fight to defend. And we honor those ideals by upholding them not just when it is easy, but when it is hard."[37]

6

We Were Warned

Those who bought into the slogans "Hope" and "Change" last fall should have read the fine print. We were warned.

—*Scott Horton, March 4, 2009*[1]

By the end of 2009, President Barack Obama seemed to be facing something of a mini-rebellion in the nation's progressive ranks, much of which had gone to remarkable, sometime even absurd, lengths to support and defend him and his administration against any and all critics, right and left. Some left and liberal types who had taken seriously and embraced Obama's campaign promises to fight for and deliver progressive health reform, to lead substantive reductions in carbon emissions (and thus in the rate of global warming), to restore civil liberties, and to move the nation's foreign policy from militarism to diplomacy seemed aghast at the political and policy developments of December 2009. Many progressives expressed disappointment, disgust, and depression as Obama's "health reform" was stripped not merely of its weak public option but even of the last-minute effort to allow a "Medicaid buy in" for fifty-five to sixty-four-year-olds. They cringed as Obama mimicked George W. Bush in announcing the escalation of Washington's war in/on Afghanistan and Pakistan, and as Obama returned home from the Copenhagen climate meetings of December 2009 with no binding global climate control regulations. The signs of progressive anger and resistance were hard to miss as the charismatic and stirring (for many) president of "Yes, we can" had more and more undeniably emerged as a pallid symbol of "No, we can't"—as another seemingly idealistic Democratic president whose inspiring campaign promises of change had translated into more of the corporate and imperial same in the real world of power:

- Former 1960s radical and Progressives for Obama (PFO) cofounder Tom Hayden announced that he was "stripping the Obama sticker off my car" after the president gave his West Point war speech at the beginning of December 2009.[2]
- Progressives for Obama (PFO) decided to drop the president's name from the organization (renamed as "Progressive America Rising").[3]
- The editor of the liberal-left magazine *The Progressive* noted ironically that Obama's West Point speech read as if had been penned by "Bush's speechwriters."[4]
- The majority of people identified as liberals by pollsters expressed opposition to Obama's Af-Pak "surge" (which barely won majority support in early surveys only because of Republican support) and to his health care "reform."
- The conclusion of many "left-liberal" activists, bloggers, politicians, and organizations—including even the often pathetically Obama-obedient MoveOn.org.—that (as centrist Democrat Howard Dean claimed) no bill was preferable to the weak, stripped-down, and corporate-captive "health reform" pushed by Obama and other top Democrats.[5]
- Widespread liberal and progressive criticism of the weak, corporate-captive climate "deal" that Obama came back from Copenhagen with in mid-December.
- The American Civil Liberties Union issued a blistering indictment of the Obama's refusal to prosecute Bush administration war crimes and the extraordinary lengths the White House was going to, to cover up these crimes.[6]
- The Congressional Black Caucus had a measured confrontation with of the first black president for placing Wall Street's agenda above the needs of black and other minority citizens.[7]

Living in a notoriously Obama-mad campus town (Iowa City) in the pivotal political state of Iowa, I personally heard and saw what struck me as a significant number of Democratic "progressives" seem to lose faith and "hope" in their president around this time. These somewhat less enthusiastic Obamanists expressed "surprise" and "disappointment" about one or two aspects of the Obama policy record, noting contradictions between what they thought the candidate had pledged and what he delivered. Some locals who reported shedding tears of relief and inspiration on the days that Obama was elected and/or inaugurated now sounded depressed and even a little angered by The One's centrism and service to wealth and power.

"Should Have Read the Fine Print"

Left-liberals were right to be angry at Obama's centrist big business- and military-friendly presidential record and his civil liberties and civil right betrayals nearly two years after tens of thousands of liberal Iowa City residents had trudged through the snow to demonstrate their readiness to support a "progressive" black president. They were justified (in my opinion) in reflecting in "cynical" and/or outraged terms on the chasm between Obama's peaceful- and populist-sounding campaign rhetoric and the corporate and imperial substance of Obama's governance. Their pique at the Obama rebranding project—the persistence of old ruling policies, practices, and structures under the deceptive guise of progressive "change"—was understandable, and (from my perspective) welcome.

Nevertheless, they had little business being surprised or disappointed about it all. As lawyer and activist Scott Horton noted in March 2009 on Antiwar.com, "Those who bought into the slogans 'Hope' and 'Change' last fall should have read the fine print. We were warned."[8] Looking back at Obama's history up to and including his inauguration, minimally attentive observers were given a large number of detectable alarms, some admittedly more immediate and obvious than others to people who do not make a business out of carefully scrutinizing politicians.

Obama's "Good War"
As we have already seen, candidate Obama made no effort at all to hide his determination as president to escalate the U.S. assault on Afghanistan and Pakistan in what he considered George Bush's "good" and "proper war."

Race Neutralist from the Start
Given his desire to win the presidency in a "post–civil rights" America where most whites deny that racism causes significant barriers anymore to black Americans, the "black but not like Jesse" candidate Obama quite naturally bent over backward to distance himself from his technical blackness and from any connection to the fact that deeply embedded white-supremacist racial oppression continues to play a powerful role in American or global life and society.[9]

"Deeply Conservative" from the Beginning
As my previous book on the Obama phenomenon went to great pains to demonstrate, candidate and President-elect Obama made his unadventurous, conciliatory, centrist, corporatist, militarist, imperial, "American

exceptionalist," and even—according to the *New Yorker's* Larissa MacFar-quhar in the spring of 2007—"deeply conservative" worldview as clear as day to those willing and able to undertake elementary investigations of his political and ideological record beneath his carefully crafted imagery. Obama's centrist presidential path has been consistent with numerous deeply conservative campaign statements he made to reassure corporate and military authorities that he posed no danger to existing ruling institutions and ideologies. Obama's speeches to establishment bodies such as the Council on Foreign Relations and his presentations to institutions such as NASDAQ, to wealthy fundraisers, and to newspaper editorial boards sent strong signals of his basic underlying allegiance to—and belief in—dominant domestic and global hierarchies and doctrines. But that allegiance was also very clear in his militantly corporate-centrist (even as its author repeatedly identified himself with "progressive" values) and badly mistitled campaign book, *The Audacity of Hope* (2006), intended for a general audience. Those statements were detectable by those willing to look beyond his fake-progressive vote-seeking rhetoric.

And they were not only detected by "hard leftists" like me. MacFarquhar, no radical, made her observations in the centrist *New Yorker.* Many of candidate Obama's conservative standpoints on domestic social and economic issues were noticed and criticized by establishment center-left economist and *New York Times* columnist Paul Krugman. Along with John Edwards (a major party candidate, after all) and others, Krugman repeatedly disparaged Obama's "big table fantasy" (mocked by Edwards as "singing Kumbaya") that meaningful progressive transformation could be achieved by negotiating with, instead of engaging in a historic conflict with, concentrated economic power and the Republicans. In a July 2008 issue of the *New Yorker*, centrist journalist Ryan Lizza noted almost casually that Obama's political career had been "marked at every stage" by "an eagerness to accommodate himself to existing institutions rather than tear them down or replace them."[10]

In mid-October 2009, as the political air was increasingly filled with liberal complaints that Obama had been "too cautious" in numerous policy areas (health care and financial regulation in particular), *New York Times* columnist Maureen Dowd noted that "Obama's legislative career offers cautionary tales about the toll of constant consensus-building. . . . In Springfield, he compromised so much on a health care reform bill that in the end, it merely led to a study. In Washington, he compromised so much with Senate Republicans on a bill to require all nuclear plant operators to notify state and local authorities about radioactive leaks that it simply devolved into a bill offering guidance to regulators, and even that ultimately died."[11]

MacFarquhar's observations in the May 7, 2007, issue of the *New Yorker* merit revisiting in the wake of Obama's hypercautious, conservative, and corporate-friendly performance in relation to his so-called health reform. In a carefully researched portrait of Obama based on extensive interviews, MacFarquhar found that Obama was about as far from being a radical reformer as one could imagine. "In his view of history, in his respect for tradition, in his skepticism that the world can be changed any way but very, very slowly, Obama," MacFarquhar determined, "is deeply conservative. . . . It's not just that he thinks revolutions are unlikely: he values continuity and stability for their own sake, sometimes even more than he values change for the good. Take health care, for example," MacFarquhar noted, quoting Obama on how this country's for-profit health insurance companies were too deeply entrenched for policy makers to evict them from their Mafia-like control of America's health care future.[12]

Praise from (and for) Republicans

It should have sent off signals of alarm to progressives that candidate and President-elect Obama's pronouncements and tone won him approval from a significant number of reactionary pundits and politicos. Obama's more-than-occasional admirers included leading Republican columnist David Brooks, aggressively militaristic foreign policy advisor Robert Kagan, and right Republican writer Christopher Buckley (the last one of these actually endorsed Obama in the 2008 election).[13] Even frothing archconservative writer and activist William Kristol saw fit to praise President-elect Obama for appointing militantly pro-Israel Rahm Emanuel as White House chief of staff—something Kristol took to show that "Obama's not going to be mindlessly leftist."[14] Genuine left progressives don't win praise from the likes of Brooks, Kagan, Kristol, and Buckley—to name just four leading Republicans who had nice things to say about Obama during the last election season. They also don't go to the extent that Obama did to praise past far-right Republican politicians such as Ronald Reagan, whom candidate Obama (and author Obama) applauded for helping pull America back from the supposed radical excesses of the 1960s.

"Personnel Is Policy"

From the start of his campaign and through his cabinet selections and appointments, Obama consistently surrounded himself with elite agents of corporate and imperial power, people such as James Jones (Obama's national security advisor, a high-ranking Pentagon official rumored to be a Republican), Robert Gates (a Republican carried over from the Bush II–Cheney) administration, Rahm Emanuel (a fiercely corporate-militarist center-Democratic party operative known for fierce attachment to Israel and ruthless disciplining of antiwar, left-leaning Democrats in the name of party unity), Lawrence Summers (a veteran Goldman Sachs–minted neoliberal operative from the Clinton administration who helped design and implement critical aspects of the very financial deregulation that blew up Wall Street in the late summer and fall of 2008), and Timothy Geithner (a veteran Wall Street bailout apparatchik and, like Summers, an acolyte of former Goldman Sachs chief and Clinton Treasury secretary Robert Rubin). Obama's claim in the wake of his election that he would provide the "vision" to move such corporate and imperial operatives in a "progressive" direction was like a baseball manager claiming that he's going to build a team based on speed and defense with a roster full of clumsy, slow-footed, 280-pound power hitters. Conventional Washington wisdom has long held with good reason that "personnel is policy."[15]

Big Money Sponsorship

Obama's presidential record matches the record-setting corporate campaign funding he garnered during the presidential race.[16] As is well known, big money election sponsors are not in the business of handing over the White House to progressive enemies of Empire and Inequality, Incorporated. Obama's strong connection to wealth patrons like Goldman Sachs has always been predicated on his leading funders' calculation that the Obama phenomenon offered no significant left or democratic threat to elite financial interests and that its central figure was someone with whom concentrated wealth could productively work in securing its interests and advancing its authoritarian agenda. As Ken Silverstein noted in an important 2006 *Harper's* article that told the story of Obama's early vetting by the money and politics class in 2003 and 2004, early in his national political career Obama was found to be a safe candidate for concentrated wealth. "On condition of anonymity," Silverstein reported, "one Washington lobbyist I spoke with was willing to point out the obvious: that big donors would not be helping out Obama if they didn't see him as a 'player.' The lobbyist added: 'What's the dollar value of a starry-eyed idealist?'" Silverstein's article was titled "Obama, Inc."[17]

"Our Greatest Asset"

Consistent with the lobbyist's judgment, Obama the candidate made recurrent statements of his faith in and attachment to so-called free-market capitalism. Those on the "left" who have wanted to find evidence that the president is a populist opponent of the profits system would do well to review an interesting passage from *The Audacity of Hope*. One key question addressed in *Audacity* came straight out of the neoconservative worldview: What makes the United States so exceptionally wonderful? To a remarkable extent, Obama found the answer to this nationally narcissistic question in the wise and benevolent leadership of the nation's great white Founders and subsequent honored policymakers, such as Franklin Delano Roosevelt, Harry Truman, and John Fitzgerald Kennedy. But Obama also grounded the nation's distinctive supposed greatness in its free-market capitalist system and "business culture." The American overclass should have been gratified by Obama's paean to this system of state and corporate capitalism:

> Calvin Coolidge once said that "the chief business of the American people is business," and indeed, it would be hard to find a country on earth that's been more consistently hospitable to the logic of the marketplace. . . .
> The result of this business culture has been a prosperity that's unmatched in human history. It takes a trip overseas to fully appreciate just how good Americans have it; even our poor take for granted goods and services—electricity, clean water, indoor plumbing, telephones, televisions, and household appliances—that are still unattainable for most of the world. America may have been blessed with some of the planet's best real estate, but clearly it's not just our natural resources that account for our economic success. *Our greatest asset has been our system of social organization, a system that for generations has encouraged constant innovation, individual initiative and efficient allocation of resources . . . our free market system* [emphasis added].[18]

Audacity's glowing paean to American capitalism was consistent with Obama's famous 2004 keynote address reference to the United States as "a magical place" that serves as "a beacon of freedom and opportunity" to those who exhibit "hard work and perseverance." His address also praised the United States for introducing to the world what he called a democratic "miracle"—*"that* we can say what we think, write what we think, without hearing a sudden knock on the door" and that "we can participate in the political process without fear of retribution, and that our votes will be counted—or at least, most of the time."

These were remarkably conservative, even reactionary reflections. *Audacity* and the keynote speech left it to genuinely radical left progressives—characterized by Obama and many of his elite supporters as insufficiently "realistic" and excessively "moral absolutist" carpers, "cranks," "zealots," and "gadflies" (Obama's insulting description of revered populist U.S. senator Paul Wellstone[19])—to observe some of the undesirable and less-than-"efficient" outcomes of America's heavily state-protected "free-market" system and "business culture." Those results include the climate-warming contributions of a nation that constitutes 5 percent of the world's population but contributes more than 25 percent of the planet's carbon emissions. Other notable effects include the generation of poverty for tens of millions of U.S. children while executives atop "defense" firms like Boeing, Lockheed-Martin, and Raytheon rake in billions of taxpayer dollars for helping the United States maintain the deadly occupations of Iraq and Afghanistan.[20]

It was left to insufficiently "pragmatic" left thinkers and activists to note the American System's monumentally wasteful and dangerous allocation of more than a third of the nation's wealth to the top 1 percent of the U.S. population and its systematic subordination of the common good to private profit.

"Unreasonable" "radicals" were left to observe that business-ruled workplaces and labor markets steal "individual initiative" from millions of American workers subjected to the monotonous repetition of often imbecilic and soul-crushing operations often conducted for such unbearable stretches of time—at stagnating levels of material reward and security—that many working people are increasingly unable to participate meaningfully in the great "democracy" Obama trumpets as the Founders' great legacy.[21] They were left also to "complain" about the fact that U.S. social mobility rates are actually quite low in comparison to other leading industrialized states (indicating a relatively fixed class structure in "magical" America) and to observe that Obama's keynote speech advanced a shockingly truncated and negative concept of democracy—one in which Americans are supposed to be grateful simply because they don't live under the iron heel of openly authoritarian state dictatorship.[22] (Obama's ode to the absence of pure repression in the United States deleted the profound weakness of substantive positive democracy here. It evaded the unpleasant fact that much of ordinary U.S. citizens' freedom to "say," "write," and "think" whatever they wish generally amounts to the liberty to whisper to one's immediate neighbor in the front row of a crowded movie theater with a blaring sound track: Our free speech is all too commonly drowned out by giant, concentrated corporate media and the special megaphones possessed by private and state power. In a similar vein, many campaign finance reformers note, ordinary working Americans—even when counted [as they usually are]—are mere political half-pennies compared to the structurally empowered supercitizenship bestowed upon great "moneyed interests" and corporations that exercise such well-known disproportionate influence on U.S. "market democracy."[23])

Some "unreasonable" thinkers have darkly noted that the country's free speech and civil libertarian traditions are an invitation to thought control and propaganda when they exist side by side with the nation's stark socio-economic inequalities. Precisely because Americans can't be dominated in purely coercive ways, they must be controlled in more subtle and less overtly oppressive fashion. Because they are "free to speak their minds," their minds must be influenced by those who wish to maintain existing extreme disparities of wealth and power. Thus, there is a huge investment in the United States in what Noam Chomsky and Edward S. Herman called "manufacturing consent" and what Alex Carey called "Taking the Risk Out of Democracy."[24]

"No One Has Asked You to Build a More Just America"

Another key expression of Obama's desire not to offend the country's real power centers is found in his efforts to appeal, à la Charles Dickens, to their supposed underlying and farseeing benevolence. In the late summer of 2007, Obama made a revealing statement at the end of a speech that purported to lecture Wall Street's leaders on their "Common Stake in America's Prosperity." Speaking at NASDAQ's headquarters, he told the nation's financial elite that "I believe all of you are as open and willing to listen as anyone else in America. I believe you care about this country and the future we are leaving to the next generation. I believe your work to be a part of building a stronger, more vibrant, and more just America. I think the problem is that no one has asked you to play a part in the project of American renewal."[25]

These were strange beliefs to (claim to) hold in light of the actual historical pattern of business behavior that naturally results from the purpose and structure of the system of private profit. A vast army of nonprofit charities and social service providers, citizens, environmental and community activists, trade union negotiators, and policymakers has spent decades asking (often enough begging) the "American" corporate and financial capitalist overclass to contribute to the domestic social good. The positive results of all these institutional efforts and moral haranguing have been (as many advocates and activists know quite well) generally marginal and fleeting as the "business community" works with structurally superempowered effectiveness to distribute wealth and power ever more upward and to serve the needs of private investors and capital accumulation over and above any considerations of social and environmental health and the common good at home or abroad. Holding no special allegiance to the American people in an age of corporate globalization, the economic elite is more than willing to significantly abandon domestic U.S. society and its workers and communities in service to the ultimate business priority: enhancing its bottom line.[26]

The Invisible Poor: All About the "Middle Class"

Obama's campaign showed a distinctive reluctance to confront the interrelated issues of poverty and inequality—issues insistently raised by John Edwards. Even as it became clear that the country was mired in a major recession, both of the two business party candidates (Obama and John McCain) followed the standard U.S. election pattern of pushing those issues to the margins of political discourse. Days before the 2008 election, liberal *New York Times* columnist Bob Herbert noted the shocking absence of the rising number of truly disadvantaged Americans from the electoral extravaganza. "The focus in the presidential campaign," Herbert noted, "*has been almost entirely on the struggles faced by the middle class* [emphasis added]—on families worried about their jobs, their mortgages, their retirement accounts and how to pay for college for their kids. . . . No one is even talking about the poor. . . . But if we are indeed caught up in the most severe economic crisis since the Great Depression," Herbert added, "the ones who will fare the worst are those who are already poor or near poor. There are millions of them, and yet they remain essentially invisible. A step down for them is a step into destitution."[27]

With the rapid dismissal of Edwards and Dennis Kucinich from the presidential campaign before the end of January 2008, there were no serious presidential candidates left willing to tackle this major problem during the last election cycle. After Obama's election, the new administration in writing set up a tepid and widely ignored "Middle Class Task Force" under the legendary "blowhard" Joe Biden (a man made of truly *vice-presidential* material), but no "Poverty Task Force" to seriously investigate and undertake the rising problem of economic destitution inside the United States.[28] The significant deepening of economic destitution among a large and growing section of the U.S. populace went strikingly unaddressed in Obama's inaugural address (to be discussed in some detail later in this chapter)

Insistent Left Warnings

A large number of radical voices have tried to warn other lefties and serious liberals off "the Obama Kool-Aid" since at least 2005. Those voices included John Pilger, Adolph Reed Jr., Glen Ford, Bruce Dixon, Michael Hureaux, Margaret Kimberly, Juan Santos, Greg Guma, Marc Lamont Hill, Pam Martens, Alexander Cockburn, Jeffrey St. Clair, Kim Peterson, David Peterson, Chris Hedges, Lance Selfa, Joshua Frank, Jeremy Scahill, John

MacArthur, David Sirota, Ken Silverstein, and Noam Chomsky in such journals *as Black Agenda Report, Z Magazine, ZNet, Dissident Voice, Harper's,* the *Progressive, Truthdig, AlterNet,* and *SocialistWorker.org.*[29] My own voluminous warnings from the left on and against the Obama phenomenon date from late July 2004—just two days after Obama's pivotal, career-making keynote address to the 2004 Democratic National Convention.[30]

My book *Barack Obama and the Future of American Politics* was the most ambitious and comprehensive effort before the 2008 election to rigorously demystify the Obama phenomenon—and to warn about the Obama re-branding project—from a left perspective. Along with Selfa's study *The Democrats: A Critical History* (2008), Wolin's chilling book *Democracy Incorporated: Managed Democracy and the Specter of Inverted Totalitarianism* (2008),[31] and the essays of a large number of left political writers (just some of whom are mentioned here), my book can reasonably be said to have essentially "predicted" the Obama administration's betrayal of the Obama campaign's liberal and progressive base. It did so through a simple insistence on rigorously (some might say "ruthlessly") situating Obama in the world of what prolific left author and filmmaker John Pilger called "power as it is, not as many of us wish it to be."[32]*

"You Haven't Been Listening to Me"

Consistent with Pilger's analysis and prediction at the end of May 2008,[33] candidate Obama lurched somewhat to the right in June 2008, well before the formal beginning of the general election campaign. His move was misleadingly reported in mainstream news media as a change from "the left to the center." As reported by the *Los Angeles Times,* the *Wall Street Journal,* and the *New York Times,*[34] the leading facts that indicated his alleged shift from the portside to the "middle" of the political spectrum were as follows:

- Obama's apparent embrace of the Supreme Court ruling invalidating a Washington, DC, ban on personal handguns and his claim that the Second Amendment of the Constitution pertains to private citizens, not just to organized state "militias."

---

*Many readers will be surprised to learn that so many left voices warned against Obama before his election. One of the many services dominant media have granted to Obama has been to consistently make serious left criticism of his campaign and administration close to invisible. Along the way, of course, powerful right-wing media voices have falsely claimed that all of "the left" has been strongly on board with Obama.

- His declaration of his belief in the state's right to kill certain criminals, including child rapists.
- His decision to become the first major party presidential candidate to bypass the public presidential financing system and to reject accompanying spending limits. (This violated his earlier pledge to work through the public system and accept those limits.)
- His support for a refurbished spy bill that would grant retroactive immunity to telephone corporations for collaborating with the White House in the practice of electronic surveillance against American citizens. (This violated his earlier pledge to filibuster any surveillance legislation containing such immunity.)
- His appointment of corporate-friendly Wal-Mart apologist and Hamilton Project economist Jason Furman as his economic policy director—something that stood in curious relation to his earlier bashing ("I won't shop there") of Wal-Mart's low-wage practices.[35]
- His increased emphasis on himself as a supporter of free trade, something that seemed to contradict his campaign-trail criticism of the North American Free Trade Agreement.
- His "tweaking" of his claim that he would meet with Iran's president (he added new and more restrictive conditions).
- His embrace (in a speech to the powerful pro-Israel lobby American Israel Public Affairs Committee [AIPAC]) of Bush-McCain rhetoric on the supposed Iranian nuclear threat and his related promise to do "anything" to protect the militarist occupation, apartheid, and nuclear state of Israel from Iran (a nation previously attacked by Israel).
- His call (in his AIPAC speech) for an "undivided" Israel-run Jerusalem despite the fact that no government on the planet (and not even the Bush administration) supports Israeli's right to annex that UN-designated international city.[36]
- Highly qualified Obama statements on "combat troop" withdrawal from Iraq, indicating that an Obama White House would maintain the openly criminal U.S. occupation of that country for an indefinite period.

In addition, there were reports (later verified) that Obama had asked Robert Gates, the hard-right, hawkish, Bush defense secretary, to stay on into an Obama administration.[37] Obama also came out in a major speech in support of a significant part of the Republican agenda: the granting of public money to private religious organizations to provide basic social services for disadvantaged Americans.[38] And Obama endorsed conservative white male Blue Dog Democratic representative John Barrow (D-GA) over progressive black female challenger Regina Thomas in a July 15 primary.[39]

There was a whopping difficulty with the dominant media's "shift-to-the-center" narrative: *Obama was already positioned well to the corporate- and Empire-friendly "middle" well before all of these developments.* And some of the supposed moves "to the center" were continuous with earlier parts of Obama's career. He was a defender of the death penalty during his career in the Illinois State Assembly (1997–2004). He had never been a strong gun control advocate and stayed noticeably mute on guns and the gun lobby after the horrific Virginia Tech gun killings (April 2007) and the terrible Northern Illinois University gun killings (February 2008). Consistent with his "categorical" March 2008 denunciation of "any statement that disparages our great country," former "civil rights lawyer" Obama voted in July 2005 to reauthorize the Patriot Act—a notable assault on civil liberties. Obama's "undivided Jerusalem" comment was over the top and had to be partly rescinded, but there was nothing new in his conservative and imperial positions on Iraq, Iran, or Israel or in his tendency to work with foreign policy hawks and interventionists.

Nonetheless, Obama's more explicitly centrist positioning in pursuit of moderate and independent voters for the general election elicited consternation and complaint on and somewhat to the left of the Democratic Party. The middle-class U.S. liberal-left's standard-bearing magazine, *The Nation*, published an Open Letter to Obama titled "Change We Can Believe In." Claiming that Obama stood "today at the head of a movement that believes deeply" in profound social and political social change, *The Nation* worried that Obama might be preparing to betray his progressive supporters in the change he had claimed as the mantle of his campaign:

> Since your historic victory in the primary, there have been troubling signs that you are moving away from the core commitments shared by many who have supported your campaign, toward a more cautious and centrist stance. . . .
>
> We recognize that compromise is necessary in any democracy. We understand that the pressures brought to bear on those seeking the highest office are intense. But retreating from the stands that have been the signature of your campaign will weaken the movement whose vigorous backing you need in order to win and then deliver the change you have promised.[40]

Obama's response to such grumbling and appeals to his supposed true-progressive, left-leaning ideals was to remind "my friends on the left" that people claiming to detect a shift to the center *"haven't been listening to me* [emphasis added]." Speaking from a conservative Atlanta suburb, Obama countered his left-liberal critics and "friends" by trumpeting his longstanding "centrist" faith in "personal responsibility," "faith," and "the individual right to bear arms."[41]

Obama had a point. Many leftish Obamanists were woefully derelict when it came to investigating the rich historical record that showed him to be a cunning, conservative, and corporate-friendly conciliator and compromiser from whom traditional economic and political elites had little to fear.[42] Many dreamy liberals and progressives wishfully projected their own values onto their charismatic candidate. Some joined Obama's right-wing critics in embracing the silly idea that the real Obama beneath that record was a stealth "true progressive"—a covert leftist pretending to be a centrist in order to win the presidency. Many liberals and even some leftists had possibly fallen prey to the belief that Obama had to be such a person in part because of the color of his skin.[43]

"I Love Reinhold Niebuhr"

Obama made clear the high likelihood that he would betray his "antiwar" campaign imagery when in spring 2007 he professed his "love" for vapid American philosopher Reinhold Niebuhr. Here is a significant passage from David Brooks in April of that year:

> Sometimes you take a shot.
>
> Yesterday evening I was interviewing Barack Obama and we were talking about effective foreign aid programs in Africa. His voice was measured and fatigued, and he was taking those little pauses candidates take when they're afraid of saying something that might hurt them later on.
>
> Out of the blue I asked, "Have you ever read Reinhold Niebuhr?"
>
> Obama's tone changed. "I love him. He's one of my favorite philosophers."
>
> So I asked, "What do you take from him?"
>
> "I take away," Obama answered in a rush of words, "the compelling idea that there's serious evil in the world, and hardship and pain. And we should be humble and modest in our belief that we can eliminate those things. But we shouldn't use that as an excuse for cynicism and inaction. I take away . . . the sense that we have to make these efforts knowing they are hard, and not swinging from naïve idealism to bitter realism."[44]

In a interview with conservative journalist Jeffrey Goldberg, Brooks recalled that "for the next 20 minutes, [Obama] gave me a perfect descrip-

tion of Reinhold Niebuhr's thought, which is a very subtle thought process based on the idea that you have to use power while it corrupts you. And I was dazzled, I felt the tingle up my knee as Chris Matthews would say."[45]
From a left perspective, there would have been more reason to feel a twinge of nausea. Niebuhr became the "theologian of the [U.S.] establishment" in the post–World War II era of American ascendancy because of the elegant-sounding ease with which he granted imperial policymakers what leading left intellectual Noam Chomsky called "a divine license to kill."[46] Niebuhr granted this moral and intellectual indulgence with his fundamentally idiotic concept of "the paradox of grace." This idea held that all great "historical achievements" were unavoidably scarred by the "taint of sin" and that great imperial policymakers must not let fear of "sinning" prevent them from acting on their "obligation to realize truth and goodness in history."[47] As Chomsky once noted:

> [Niebuhr] was revered by the Kennedy liberal types, by people [such as leading cold war architect] George Kennan. He was considered a moral teacher of the [post-WWII U.S. power elite] generation. It's interesting to look at why. I actually went through his writings once. The intellectual level is depressingly low. But there's something in there that made him appealing. It was what he called the "paradox of grace." What it comes down to is, no matter how much you try to do good, you're always going to do harm. . . .
> That's very appealing advice for people who are planning to enter into a life of crime. To say, "no matter how much I try to do good I'm always going to harm people. That's the paradox of grace. You can't get out if it." A wonderful idea for a Mafia don. Then he can go ahead and do whatever he feels like, and if he harms people, "Oh my God, the paradox of grace." That explains why he was so appealing [to U.S. elites] in the post–World War II period. They were going to be the managers or else the commissars for a period of global conquest, running the world, which is obviously going to entail enormous crimes. Isn't it nice to have this doctrine before us? Of course, we're superbenevolent and humane, but the paradox of grace![48]

Niebuhr provided a childishly simple, if superficially erudite rationalization—heralded by Brooks and other intellectual authorities as nonideological "pragmatism" (a key purported attribute of Obama and his role model, John Fitzgerald Kennedy)[49]—for U.S. war crimes in the post–World War II era. This was the basic reason that he came to be "regarded with respect approaching reverence" (Chomsky) by leading U.S. intellectuals and state managers.

(That respect, bordering on "awe," could hardly be traced to any serious cerebral accomplishment. As Niebuhr's able biographer Richard Fox observed, the venerated philosopher was a casual thinker who commonly reduced his opponents' theories to simplistic caricature. Chomsky noted in 1987 that Niebuhr's "books and papers on historical topics and contemporary affairs are . . . sparing in factual reference. . . . Evidently, many found his intellectual contributions to be compelling, but this effect cannot be traced to their factual content, documentation, or enlightening selection of factual materials; or to sustained rational argument, which is rarely to be discerned. It must lie somewhere else."[50])

Another one of Niebuhr's influential formulations should send a shudder down the spine rather than "a tingle up the knee" of those who believe in democracy instead of top-down corporate-imperial rule. Niebuhr preached that adult rationality is the property of the "cool observers"—the privileged few in the educated establishment. Ordinary working people and mere citizens, by contrast, are guided by blind faith and momentary impulse. According to Niebuhr, the "cool observers" must manage the stupidity of "the average man" by crafting and disseminating "necessary illusions" and "emotionally potent oversimplifications" to keep the ignorant and dangerous rabble in line and under the proper control of their masters.[51] There has been no small measure of illusion (necessary or not) and "emotionally potent oversimplification" at the heart and soul of "the Obama phenomenon" in both its campaign and presidential phases.

"I Don't Believe in the U.S. Apologizing"

Consistent with numerous national-narcissistic, "American exceptionalist" messages in *The Audacity of Hope* and in various foreign policy speeches he gave to establishment U.S. foreign policy bodies as a U.S. senator and presidential candidate, Obama spoke in latter-day Niebuhrian accord with the Mafia-like "paradox of grace" concept in an interview with CNN correspondent Candy Crowley during his triumphant, proto-presidential campaign trip to Europe in July 2008. When Crowley asked Obama if "there's anything that's happened in the past 7 1/2 years that the U.S. needs to apologize for in terms of foreign policy," Obama responded by saying, "No, I don't believe in the U.S. apologizing. As I said I think the war in Iraq was a *mistake*. We didn't keep our eye on the ball in Afghanistan. But, you know, hindsight is 20/20, and I'm much more interested in looking forward rather than looking backwards." For good measure, Obama added that "the U.S. remains overwhelmingly a force of good in the world"—a standard doctrinal line that is intimately related to his and the rest of the establishment's dogged refusal to remotely acknowledge that such atrocities as the wars on Vietnam and Iraq were and are actually monumentally immoral *crimes* rooted in the structure and practice of Empire.[52]

Perhaps the strong Afghan "war"[53] enthusiast[54] candidate Obama should have followed his interview with Candy Crowley by writing a Letter of No Apology to the survivors of the more than 2 million Iraqis the United States killed (through invasion and embargo) between 1990 and 2008 and/or to Orifa Ahmed. On October 7, 2001, Orifa's small house in the Afghan village of Bibi Mahru was destroyed and turned into a fifty-foot crater by a 500-pound bomb dropped by an American F-16 plane. The explosion killed her husband (a carpet weaver), six of her children, and two children who lived (and died) next door. Away visiting relatives when the bombing occurred, Orifa returned to find pieces of her children's flesh scattered around the killing site. She received $400 from U.S. authorities to compensate her for her losses.[55] Another letter could have gone to Gulam Rasul, a school headmaster in the Afghan town of Khair Khana. On the morning of October 21, 2001, the U.S. military dropped a 500-pound bomb on his house, killing his wife, three of his sons, his sister and her husband, his brother, and his sister-in-law.[56]

Yet another Letter of No Apology could have gone to Sher Kahn, an old man who lost seven relatives when the U.S. military assaulted the Afghan village of Niazi Qala on December 29, 2001. Here is how Pilger described the attack:

> The roar of the planes had started at three in the morning, long after everybody had retired for the night. Then the bombs began to fall—500-pounders leading the way, scooping out the earth and felling a row of houses. According to neighbors watching from a distance, the planes flew three sorties over the village and a helicopter hovered close to the ground, firing flares, then rockets. Women and children were seen running from the houses towards a dried pond, perhaps in search of protection from the gunfire, but were shot as they ran.[57]

Additional Letters of No Apology could have gone out from the "antiwar" Obama campaign to civilians and noncombatants facing torture and humiliation at the U.S. Air Force's Bagram Airfield (near Kabul); the survivors of the U.S. bombing of a wedding party in eastern Afghanistan in early July 2008, not long before Obama's trip to Europe (the fourth wedding party the U.S.-led "coalition" had blown up in Afghanistan since the beginning of its invasion of that country);[58] and the countless other U.S.

attacks on Afghan villages that added to a civilian death toll that certainly went well into the thousands since the United States initiated its so-called liberation of Afghanistan from a Taliban government the United States had itself largely put into place.

In all of these letters, Obama could have expounded on the logic of his "loved" philosopher Reinhold Niebuhr. He could have explained how the inherently graced duty of the United States to act in accord with its benevolent historical mission of "goodness" required it not to shrink from its paradoxical duty to sin against humanity by slaughtering the occasional village, family, or nation.

Against Independent Development in Latin America

As we have already seen, Obama declared his opposition to left and independent development in Latin America—an opposition that bore fruit in his policy regarding that region—in the foreign policy chapter of *The Audacity of Hope*.

Support for the Bush-Paulsen-McCain-Reid-Pelosi Bailout

The first version of the Bush administration's proposed bailout of Goldman Sachs and other leading Wall Street firms in September 2008 sparked a major populist rebellion throughout the country. A wave of mass citizen disgust arose in response to the White House's effort to frighten the populace into handing over $700 billion to cover the toxic assets created by financial perpetrators and at the remarkable attempt to place the bailout and Bush's Treasury secretary above the rule of law, codified in Section 8 of the original bailout package, which read as follows: "Decisions by the Secretary pursuant to the authority of this Act are non-reviewable and committed to agency discretion, and may not be reviewed by any court of law or any administrative agency." The Bush–Paulsen–Wall Street money and power grab struck many observers and citizens as nothing less than an attempted financial "coup." As Jason Linkins noted on the *Huffington Post*, "Section 8 is a singularly transformative sentence of economic policy. It transfers a significant amount of power to the Executive Branch, while walling off any avenue for oversight, and offering no guarantees in return. If the Democrats end up content with winning a few slight concessions," Linkins concluded, "they risk not putting a stop-payment on the real 'blank check'—the one in which they allow the erosion of their own powers."[59]

In his first public remarks about the Bush-Paulsen proposal, candidate and soon-to-be president-elect Obama offered what the *New York Times* called "qualified support." "This initial outlay of up to $700 billion is sober-ing," Obama said. "In return for their support, the American people must be assured that the deal reflects the basic principles of transparency, fairness, and reform." In an interview aboard his campaign plane, Obama "offered guarded praise of how Treasury Secretary Henry M. Paulson Jr. is managing the crisis. . . . While he is critical of how the crisis began," *Times* reporter Jeff Zeleny noted, "Mr. Obama offered kind words for the instincts and judgment exercised by Mr. Paulson in recent weeks. The two have spoken on the phone nearly every day for the past week about the problem.' He has been put in a situation where there are no great options,' Mr. Obama said. 'I think he's a serious person. I think he is not an ideologue. I think he's very practical-minded and he wants to solve the problem.'"[60]

Obama came to reject the remarkable extrajudicial powers proposed in Section 8, but he counseled Democratic congresspersons to vote for both versions of the historic fall 2008 bailout packages, including the second one that passed with a majority of Democratic votes in the House and Senate. Ralph Nader didn't win many votes, but honest progressives had to agree that Nader—a horrid "ideologue" of the obsolete left as far as Obama was concerned (Paulsen was, by contrast, "serious" and "practical-minded")—had got it right even as most of them prepared to block Mc-Cain with the junior U.S. senator from Illinois:

> In late September [Nader noted], Senator Obama said to the Democrats—vote for the bailout. Senator McCain said to the Republicans—vote for the bailout. President Bush said to the Congress—vote for the bailout.
>
> But the American people were fed up. They told their members of Congress—if you vote for the bailout, we will vote against you.[61]

> . . . Bush, McCain, and Obama want Congress to co-sign off on the mother of all blank checks, paving the way for a sinking dollar and higher interest rates.
>
> By bumping the FDIC's line of credit at the Treasury from $30 billion to infinity, the FDIC assumes fiat powers to bailout to its heart content, leaving the taxpayer to pay the bill. This unacceptable unlimited right to ransack taxpayers would last until 2010.[62]

"There Is No Peace Dividend"

Here are fifty-four words that have might helped us situate President-elect Barack Obama in "the world of power as it is, not as many of us wish it to be": "As we understand it, Obama has been advised and agrees that there is no peace dividend. . . . In addition, we believe, based on discussions with industry sources, that Obama has agreed not to cut the defense budget at least until the first 18 months of his term as the national security situation becomes better understood." These two sentences came from a report issued by leading Wall Street investment firm and Bush-Obama bailout recipient Morgan Stanley one day after Obama's presidential election victory.[63]

The company probably understated matters. There was no reason to anticipate significant Pentagon expenditure reductions at any point under the new administration unless forced by popular pressure that the American power elite expected Obama to preempt. "The Democrats," Morgan Stanley's researchers noted, "are sensitive about appearing weak on defense, and we don't expect strong cuts."

"Defense" was an interesting label for a giant military budget that paid for two mass-murderous occupations (in Iraq and Afghanistan) and 800-plus military bases located in more than 130 countries. The United States accounts for nearly half (48 percent) of the military spending on the planet. Coming in at $1 trillion (by the measure of the U.S. Office of Management and Budget's National Income and Product Accounts) in 2007, American "defense" (empire) spending outweighed domestic U.S. federal expenditure on education by more than 8 to 1; income security by more than 4.5 to 1; nutrition by more than 11 to 1; housing by 14 to 1; and job training by 32 to 1. The military accounted for more than 50 percent of all discretionary federal spending.

The peace dividend referred to the notion of reversing these "perverted national priorities" (Martin Luther King's phrase) by taking money spent on war and the preparation for war and using it to address such pressing social problems as poverty, ecological crisis, crumbling infrastructure, joblessness, and inadequate education, health, housing, and schooling.

The idea of a peace dividend received some attention in the United States around the end of the Cold War, when many progressives hoped that the collapse of the Soviet Union would encourage a shift in public resources from militarism to social health. For nearly half a century, the alleged (mythical) threat posed by Russian "communism" provided the core propagandistic justification for the existence and use of the extraordinary military power of the United States. With the Soviet specter eliminated, many progressives dreamed, the United States could now be realistically pressured to transfer significant new public resources to the meeting of social needs and away from the maintenance of the most spectacular and deadly military-imperial system in history.

The dream was strangled in its cradle by the presidential administrations of George H. W. Bush (two wars of invasion—Panama [1989] and Iraq [1990–1991]) and Bill Clinton (an air war on Serbia in 1999) and by dominant U.S. war media. The "military-industrial-media triangle" (John Bellamy Foster, Hannah Holeman, and Robert W. McChesney's term) and its many enablers and allies in church, school, academia, and other wings of so-called civil society rapidly substituted new rationalizations and pretexts for the persistence of a permanently militarized U.S. economy and culture: purported protection and advance of "free markets" and "democracy" (falsely conflated), the U.S. right of "humanitarian intervention," and the grave dangers posed by terrorists, drug-traffickers, and "weapons of mass destruction."

Nevertheless, a 2004 poll by the Chicago Council of Foreign Relations found that just 29 percent of Americans supported the expansion of government spending on "defense." By contrast, 79 percent supported increased spending on health care, 69 percent supported increased spending on education, and 69 percent supported increased spending on Social Security. There would appear to be a wide base of public support for a *peace dividend* if anyone in a position of power—a new president perhaps—would advance it in a meaningful way. Morgan Stanley, a leading Obama sponsor that most certainly had high-level contacts with the Obama campaign from the start, had reason to believe and reassure its investors that the new "peace president" (in the minds of millions of deluded and hopeful progressive voters) was not interested in doing any such thing.

"One President at a Time"

The Plaestinians and their many supporters across the Middle East and the world listened in terror as the famous orator Obama said nothing in defense of Arab victims while Israel executed a terrible Washington-authorized slaughter with American military hardware, butchering masses of Palestinian innocents stuck in the Gaza Strip during the 2008–2009 Christmas season. The next president claimed that harsh institutional and political realities prevented him from speaking on this horrific carnage, but he had no problem clearly denouncing Muslim terror in Mumbai, India, just weeks before. As Noam Chomsky noted:

> To these crimes Obama's response has been silence—unlike, say, the terrorist attack in Mumbai, which he was quick to denounce, along with the "hateful ideology" that lies behind it. In the case of Gaza, his spokespersons hid behind the mantra that "there is one president at a time," and repeated his

support for Israeli actions when he visited the Israeli town of Sderot in July: "If missiles were falling where my two daughters sleep, I would do everything in order to stop that." But he will do nothing, not even make a statement, when U.S. jets and helicopters with Israeli pilots are causing incomparably worse suffering to Palestinian children.[64]

Obama's later calls for Muslims to take the path of peace seemed coldly Orwellian to many who noted his cold deafening silence on the U.S.-Israel assault on Gaza, which conveniently ended on the new president's first day in office.[65] That silence darkly presaged the Obama White House's chilling and shameful response (detailed in Chapter 2) in the fall of 2009 to the UN Human Rights Council's Gladstone Report on Israelis war crimes in and against Gaza.

Election Night Comments

Obama's comments on the night of his election were loaded with warnings of progressive betrayals to come.

"Anyone Out There Who Still Doubts the Power of Our Democracy"

Citizens were given warning of audacious, privilege-, and power-friendly deception and policy to come by Obama's interesting election-night speech.[66] The first public words out of President-elect Obama's mouth on the evening of his election were revealing. "If there is anyone out there who still doubts that America is a place where all things are possible . . . who still questions the power of our democracy," Obama intoned, "tonight is your answer." The supposed "left" president-elect's first statement was NOT a call for peace, justice, and equality. It was a declaration bolstering the American plutocracy's claim that the United States—the industrialized world's most unequal and wealth-top-heavy society by far—is home to a great democracy and limitless opportunity for all.

The use (twice) of the word "still" in Obama's assertion was strange. It's not like the case for the United States being a great popular democracy had been made with special, self-evident strength in recent times. The three and a half decades prior to Obama's election had brought the deepening top-down infliction of sharply regressive corporate-neoliberal policies that were widely (but irrelevantly) repudiated by the majority of U.S.

citizens. The current century had witnessed the execution of a monumentally criminal petro-imperialist Iraq invasion sold to the U.S. populace by a spectacular state-media propaganda campaign (including preposterous claims of democratic intent Obama embraced) that mocked and subverted the nation's democratic ideals. The dominant U.S. media's role in the invasion of Iraq marked perhaps the all-time low point of the "free press" in this country.

The "democracy disconnect"—the gap (chasm really) between majority public opinion (which supports policies such as national universal health care, significant reductions in military expenditure and imperial commitment, massive public works, and reduced corporate power) and "public" policy—is a core problem in American political life.[67] The "specter" of U.S. totalitarianism, detailed in Sheldon Wolin's *Democracy Incorporated,* has never loomed larger than in the opening decade of the twenty-first century.

"Because of What We Did on This Day"

"In all of the post-election noise," a student wrote me after the election, "I think one thing Obama said in his acceptance speech was completely right on: the election itself is not the 'change' but simply the chance to make the changes we have to make. I know, I know, Obama was the ruling class candidate, but you have to admit that this represents at least symbolically a very good (first) step."

In the fifth paragraph of his acceptance oration, however, the president-elect said that "because of what we did on this day, in this election, at this defining moment, change has come to America." That line (anyway) made the election itself change.

Later in the speech Obama said that his election "proved that . . . a government of the people, by the people and for the people has not perished from this Earth." That was very premature. Whether or not that judgment proves accurate remains to be seen, and the answer is up to citizens, not politicians. I remain unwilling to consign Wolin's dark volume to the basement because of neoliberal "conciliator" Barack Obama's election.[68]

"I'll Be In Touch Soon About What Comes Next"

The real, less than radical-egalitarian nature of the next president's take on his "progressive base " was suggested in the following comment contained in a mass e-mail he sent to out to his supporters before speaking to the jubilant masses in Chicago's downtown Grant Park on November 4, the evening of his election:

> I'm about to head to Grant Park to talk to everyone gathered there, but I wanted to write to you first.
>
> We just made history.
>
> And I don't want you to forget how we did it.
>
> You made history every single day during this campaign—every day you knocked on doors, made a donation, or talked to your family, friends, and neighbors about why you believe it's time for change.
>
> I want to thank all of you who gave your time, talent, and passion to this campaign.
>
> We have a lot of work to do to get our country back on track, *and I'll be in touch soon about what comes next* [emphasis added].[69]

"I'll be in touch soon about what comes next"—a revealingly top-down sentiment for someone who won the election on the basis of his call for "change from the bottom up." Of course, during the presidential campaign, commonly described in dominant media as a great popular upsurge, Obama's "grassroots army of millions" (*Boston Globe*) "took instructions, but contributed essentially nothing," Chomsky noted in February, "to formulating his program."[70]

"Our Campaign Was Not Hatched in the Halls of Washington"

"Our campaign," Obama announced on election night, "was not hatched in the halls of Washington." That last statement was flatly false. "One evening in February 2005, in a four-hour meeting stoked by pepperoni pizza and great ambition," the *Chicago Tribune* reported in the spring of 2007, "Senator Barack Obama and his senior advisors crafted a strategy to fit the Obama 'brand.'" The meeting took place just weeks after Obama had been sworn into the upper representative chamber of the U.S. government. According to *Tribune* Washington Bureau reporters Mike Dorning and Christi Parsons, in an article titled "Carefully Crafting the Obama Brand":[71]

> The charismatic celebrity-politician had rocketed from the Illinois state legislature to the U.S. Senate, stirring national interest. The challenge was to maintain altitude despite the limited tools available to a freshman senator whose party was in a minority.

Yet even in those early days, Obama and his advisors were thinking ahead. Some called it the "2010–2012–2016" plan: a potential bid for governor or re-election to the Senate in 2010, followed by a bid for the White House as soon as 2012, not 2016. The way to get there, they decided, was by carefully building a record that matched the *brand identity*: Obama as a unifier and consensus builder, and almost postpolitical leader.

The staffers in that after-hours session, convened by Obama's Senate staff and including Chicago political advisor David Axelrod, planned a low-profile strategy that would emphasize workhorse results over headlines. Obama would invest in the long-term profile by not seeming too eager for the bright lights.

This *Tribune* story was disturbing on numerous levels. It suggested a degree of cynicism, manipulation, and ambition that did not fit very well with the progressive and hopeful likeness that the Obama campaign projected. It called to mind a tension between virtuous claims in public and selfish goals behind the scenes. The politician being sold would make sure to seem nonambitious—"not seeming too eager for the bright lights" and privileging hard work over "headlines"—and respectful toward fellow members of the political class ("establishing good relationships with my colleagues"). But by Dorning and Parsons's account, Obama and his team were actually and quite eagerly all about "the bright lights" and "the headlines" in a "long-term" sense. They were already scheming for the presidency less than a month into Obama's Senate seat. The image of Obama as a humble and hardworking rookie who got along with his colleagues across partisan lines was part of a marketing strategy on the path to higher—the highest—office. The great "reformer" Obama may have just become only the third black to sit in the august U.S. Senate since Reconstruction, but for Obama and his team the Senate was largely a marketing platform for the Next Big Thing—a place to build his image as a "unifier" and "consensus builder." They seemed unconcerned about the authoritarian implications of the concept of a "postpolitical leader," a commercialized trademark who would rise above democratic and ideological contestation on the path to power atop "the most powerful nation in history."

At the same, the term "Obama brand" suggested the commodified nature of a political culture that tends to reduce elections to corporate-crafted *marketing* contests revolving around candidate images and characters packaged and sold by corporate consultants and public relations experts. It implied an officeholder politician *for sale* and more immersed in the world of of commerce and capitalism than the realm of public service.

The Inaugural Address

And then there was Obama's *deeply conservative* inaugural address, which can reasonably be seen as a forewarning of progressive betrayals to come. Like his previous famous speeches and like his 2006 book *The Audacity of Hope* and contrary to his claim to stand above ideology, this somewhat leaden oration was chock-full of bourgeois, nationalist, and imperial doctrine and related bad and reactionary history.[72]

"Our Collective Failure"

"Our economy is badly weakened," Obama said, "a consequence of greed and irresponsibility on the part of some, but also our collective failure to make hard choices and prepare the nation for a new age." This statement evaded the special agency and culpability of Wall Street and government elites, which systematically undermined government's capacity to regulate the financial industry's dangerous speculative machinations under presidents Bill Clinton and George W. Bush. It shaded into vicious victim-blaming by preposterously saying that the country's broad populace shared equal responsibility with the investor and political class for the nation's dire economic straits. The U.S. working- and lower-class majority possesses negligible power when it comes to the direction, of "our [corporate-managed state-capitalist] economy," in which the top 1 percent owns 40 percent of the wealth and 57 percent of all claims on wealth.

"Unity of Purpose over Conflict and Discord"

"On this day," the new president proclaimed, "we gather because we have chosen hope over fear, unity of purpose over conflict and discord." "We come," Obama elaborated, "to proclaim an end to the petty grievances and false promises, the recriminations and worn out dogmas, that for far too long have strangled our politics."

These statements were fraught with threats to the notion of popular governance. The elevation of "unity" over "conflict and discord" was rife with authoritarian meaning. Democracy brings "conflict and discord." Those who believe in popular and participatory governance should hardly welcome neo-Bonapartist rulers who claim to rise above supposedly harmful "ideological" and partisan divisions to abolish "discord and conflict," inducing (ex-)citizens to close their mouths and minds.

Obama did not specify precisely what he meant by "recriminations" and "worn out dogmas." We can safely conclude from his past rhetorical record that he included "radical," "populist," and "Marxist" notions of a core conflict between the working and lower-class many, on one hand, and the rich and powerful few (his leading sponsors), on the other. And that was a problem for those committed to popular governance, for democracy disappears when that supposedly "worn out" conflict is placed outside the margins of acceptable debate.

"For Us, They Fought and Died, in . . . Khe Sanh"

Midway through his inaugural address, Obama announced an interesting perspective on the great prior sacrifices that had created what he called "the greatness of our nation." According to the brand-new president, "Our journey has never been one of shortcuts or settling for less. . . . It has been as the risk-takers, the doers, the makers of things—some celebrated but more often men and women obscure in their labor, who have carried us up the long, rugged path towards prosperity and freedom."

> For us, they packed up their few worldly possessions and traveled across oceans in search of a new life.
>
> For us, they toiled in sweatshops and settled the West; endured the lash of the whip and plowed the hard earth.
>
> For us, they fought and died, in places like Concord and Gettysburg; Normandy and Khe Sanh.
>
> Time and again these men and women struggled and sacrificed and worked till their hands were raw so that we might live a better life. They saw America as bigger than the sum of our individual ambitions; greater than all the differences of birth or wealth or faction.

Here Obama strangely wove the savage racial oppression of slavery ("endured the lash of the whip") together with European immigration, American frontier settlement (involving the genocidal removal and slaughter of millions of indigenous people—a detail he omitted), industrial labor exploitation ("toiled in the sweatshops"), the American Revolution ("Concord"), the Civil War ("Gettysburg"), World War II ("Normandy"), and the U.S-colonial war on Vietnam (the battle of Khe Sanh took place in illegally invaded South Vietnam in 1968) as part of a patriotic storyline wherein hardworking patriots pulled together across divisions of race, class, and party to selflessly create liberty and abundance for future generations of Americans.

Like his effort to make all Americans responsible for the financial meltdown, this was *sheer Orwellian nonsense.* It imposed a retrospectively virtuous tale of shared national "service" and commonality back on the pervasive possessive-individualist selfishness, rampant imperial hubris, and savage racism and classism behind the founding and often murderous settlement (conquest) of the country, the brutal exploitation of slaves and garment workers, and the rapacious execution of a bloody and expansionist foreign policy. Were we really supposed to honor the ferocious high-tech superpower assault on the peasant nation of Vietnam—an imperial onslaught that significantly undermined U.S. economic strength by the way—as some sort of noble moment (along with two and half centuries of black chattel slavery) in the selfless creation of contemporary "prosperity" through the ruggedly righteous labor of anonymous toilers embodying the spirit of the Protestant work ethic?[73]

An Issue NOT "Before Us": "Whether the Market Is a Force for Good or Ill"

"Nor is the question before us whether the market is a force for good or ill," Obama proclaimed. It was an interesting claim. Left U.S. economist and visionary Mike Albert spoke for many American progressives when he notes that

> markets are a no-confidence vote on the social capacities of the human species.... Markets mobilize our creative capacities largely by arranging for other people to threaten our livelihoods and by bribing us with the lure of luxury beyond what others have and beyond what we know we deserve. They feed the worst forms of individualism and egoism. And to top off their anti-social agenda, markets munificently reward those who are the most cut-throat and adept at taking advantage of their fellow citizens, and penalize those who insist on pursuing the golden rule.... Mutual concern, empathy, and solidarity have little or no usefulness in market economies, so they atrophy.[74]

I and many others on the left also agreed with Laurence Shoup, who observed in the summer of 2008 that the Obama campaign's trail of declarations of "love" for the market "failed to note that the market loves and rewards those who already have money and power, not those lacking these advantages." Furthermore,

> to say that you "love the market" is akin to saying that you love the ruling class (the top 1 percent of the population that controls 20 percent of the country's income and nearly 40 percent of the country's wealth) and do not

care about the great majority (the 60 percent of the population that controls only 25 percent of the income and 5 percent of the wealth). To say "I love the market"—at a time when the financial system is deflating because of decades of lies about how great unregulated markets are which fueled rampant speculation, phony valuations, and deceitful assurances—is to be deaf to the reality of how powerful interests are protected by the government while everyone gets a lecture on personal responsibility. "Change we could believe in," would involve confronting the perversity of market-driven capitalism.[75]

The market's "goodness"—along with the alleged virtues of the market's tyrannical Frankenstein creation The Corporation—*must be "the question before us."*

Evading the Root Cause of Health Care Costs

"Our health care," Obama added, "is too costly." But whose health care, exactly, was too dear? America's 2.5 million millionaires and the rest of the nation's rich easily afforded the best medical services ever, while more than 47 million Americans lacked basic medical coverage and hundreds of millions struggled with overly expensive and often inadequate care. The deeper problems are that "our health care" was too corporate, too private, too commodified, and too unequal. It was absurdly allotted primarily through the job market, making it a major contributor to both unemployment and overwork. It was placed under the cost-fueling control of bloated private insurance companies to which Obama has pledged a powerful "seat at the table" of "health care reform" and that work so effectively to undermine meaningful health reform in the summer and fall of 2009. As Obama naturally failed to mention in his inaugural address, most Americans believed that quality health care should be provided for free to all on an equal basis by the government.

"We Are Ready to Lead Once More"

"As for our common defense" the brand-new head of the American Empire proclaimed in his opening address, "our founding fathers' ideals still light the world, and we will not give them up for expedience's sake. And so to all the other people and governments who are watching today, from the grandest capitals to the small village where my father was born, know that America is a friend of each nation and every man, woman, and child who seeks a future of peace and dignity, and that we are ready to lead once more." Obama left it to "ideological" others to point out that America follows in the footsteps of past "great" global powers by covering its imperial ambitions and agendas with flowery claims of special benevolent and idealistic credentials and intent. At the same time, the avowed Christian Obama (who said in his inaugural address that the United States must "lead" through "the force of our example") might have wanted to take a closer look at the imperial "homeland." Reflecting on rising and endemic U.S. unemployment, poverty (destitution for many), homelessness, incarceration, madness, and inequality, he could consult "Scripture's" (his term) call to "Set thine house in order" (2 Kings 20:1) before talking so boldly about America "leading" others. The repair of broken societies (and the fixing of "failed states") begins at home.

"We Will Not Apologize for Our Way of Life"

Claiming that "we are the keepers" of earlier U.S. policymakers' "legacy" of "prudent" "humility and restraint," Obama said that "we will begin to responsibly leave Iraq to its people, and forge a hard-earned peace in Afghanistan. . . . We will not apologize for our way of life, nor will we waver in its defense, and for those who seek to advance their aims by inducing terror and slaughtering innocents, we say to you now that our spirit is stronger and cannot be broken; you cannot outlast us, and we will defeat you."

Here Obama proclaimed his buy-in with the false and bankrupt notion that Islamic terrorists assaulted the United States because of their hatred for "America's" supposedly democratic "way of life," NOT because of this country's provocative imperial conduct in the Middle East.[76]

The phrase "inducing terror and slaughtering innocents" referred to 9/11 and other moments of extremist Islamic terror against the West. It made no intended reference to leading U.S. client state Israel's "mass slaughter of defenseless civilians trapped in a tiny cage [Gaza] with nowhere to flee" (Noam Chomsky).[77] A good "friend of Israel['s brutal policies]," Obama had been (and has remained) shockingly but predictably silent on that horrific crime, conducted with U.S. military technology and under U.S. "diplomatic" cover. "We" were apparently not determined to "outlast" and "defeat" the apartheid and occupation state of our close ally Israel.

"Humility and restraint" were curious reflections on the Sand Creek and Wounded Knee massacres; the bloody occupation of the Philippines; the unspeakable crimes of Hiroshima and (even worse) Nagasaki; the overthrows of Jacobo Arbenz, Mohammad Mossadegh, and Salvador Allende; the U.S. "crucifixion of Southeast Asia" (Chomsky's phrase at the height of the U.S. attack) during the 1960s and 1970s; and the killing of more than half a million Iraqi children (a "price worth paying" in the famous words of President Clinton's former secretary of state Madeline Albright) through U.S.-led "economic sanctions," not to mention the more than 1 million killed and the related devastation caused by the current invasion of Iraq (March 2003 to at least 2010).

"Apologize" or not, as Obama spoke much of the world believed that the United States should drastically change its corporate-coordinated mass-consumerist "way of life" both for the sake of creating a livable ecology and for the sake of reducing its deadly, oil-related entanglement in the Middle East. As I asked in an Internet commentary on Obama's inaugural oration, moreover, "what in the name of 'God' (a frequent Obama reference) would be so bad about, *well, apologizing* to the world for the damage our interrelated consumerist and imperial ways have done to life on the planet." [78]

"If You Are Willing to Unclench Your Fist"

"To the Muslim world," Obama said, "we seek a new way forward, based on mutual interest and mutual respect. To those leaders around the globe who seek to sow conflict, or blame their society's ills on the West—know that your people will judge you on what you can build, not what you destroy. To those who cling to power through corruption and deceit and the silencing of dissent, know that you are on the wrong side of history; but that we will extend a hand if you are willing to unclench your fist."

How bitterly these words must have fallen on the ears of many Palestinians who heard them! Why, many Arabs and Muslims must have surely asked, should they receive such a lecture on the virtues of peace from a president who had promised to escalate war on Muslims in South Asia and could not muster such disingenuous counsel for Israel, on whose recent Gaza crimes Obama had stayed so damningly silent—this even as he denounced the Mumbai attacks (by Muslims) in clear terms.

Did Obama really think all of humanity would soon forget his silence of complicity regarding Israel's clenched fist as his handlers prepared to try making him look like a great new Middle Eastern peacemaker? Surely his team (loaded from the top down with militant "friends of Israel") was consulted on the terrible attack and approved of it on the condition that it would be "wrapped up"—like the murdered corpses of Gazan children—by his inauguration. Another glorious chapter in "the West's" noble record of "build[ing]," not "destroy[ing]," within and beyond the Middle East.

Obama did not comment on the critical roles that "corruption and deceit and the silencing of dissent" play in sustaining ruling-class power in this nation's "dollar democracy." Or on the credibility of the United States admonishing Muslims and others to "unclench their fist[s]" in the wake of the U.S.-Israel assault on Gaza and during an ongoing bloody multiyear U.S. invasion that had killed more than 1 million Iraqis.

According to respected journalist Nir Rosen in the December 2007 edition of the mainstream journal *Current History,* "Iraq has been killed, never to rise again. The American occupation has been more disastrous than that of the Mongols who sacked Baghdad in the thirteenth century. Only fools talk of solutions now. There is no solution. The only hope is that perhaps the damage can be contained."

"Those Brave Americans Who . . . Patrol Far-Off Deserts and Distant Mountains"

"As we consider the road that unfolds before us," Obama said in his inaugural address, "we remember with humble gratitude those brave Americans who, at this very hour, patrol far-off deserts and distant mountains." My response to this brazenly imperial comment did not fit very well with mainstream and right-wing media claims that "the left" was uniformly devoted to Obama: "No, Mr. President, no. Bring the troops home from the criminally and provocatively occupied hinterland. We have no business— zero legitimate role—patrolling (and testing the latest high-tech mass-murderous military technologies in and on) distant others' deserts, forests, cities, villages, hills, rivers, caves, rivers, seas, skies, telephone calls, and e-mails. The United States does not own the Middle East. 'We' do not own the world. And freedom, justice, and democracy at home are undermined, not protected, by Empire."

"One Common Danger"

Proclaiming a "new era of responsibility," Obama said that "God calls on us to shape an uncertain destiny." He asked Americans to remember how

in the year of America's birth, in the coldest of months, a small band of patriots huddled by dying campfires on the shores of an icy river. The capital was abandoned. The enemy was advancing. The snow was stained with blood. At a moment when the outcome of our revolution was most in doubt, the father of our nation ordered these words be read to the people: "Let it be told to the future world . . . that in the depth of winter, when nothing but hope and virtue could survive . . . that the city and the country, alarmed at one common danger, came forth to meet [it]."

For many of on the historically informed left, it was disturbing to hear the nation's first black president citing the white Founders' rebellion against England (1763–1783) as an example of how "we" Americans need to stand together "against one common enemy." Many American slaves and indigenous people found and acted on good reasons to favor the British over the colonists in the war between England and the rising new racist and settler-imperialist slave state.[79] The new republic's snows and soils and forests and tobacco, rice, and cotton killing fields had long been stained with the blood and tears of Native Americans and of a growing population of black chattel. The fate and struggle of the early republic's black and red victims foretold the future struggles of Asians, Latin Americans, and Middle Easterners caught on the wrong side of "freedom"-loving America's imperial guns, alliances, and doctrines.

Curious Deletions

There was nothing in Obama's inaugural address, really, about rising poverty and stunning socioeconomic inequality in the "homeland." Rising poverty was largely a nonissue in his speech. Obama spoke not a word about the vital need to restore union organizing and bargaining rights and to bring the labor movement—accurately described as "the leading anti-poverty program in American history" by John Edwards during the presidential primaries—back to life by passing the Employee Free Choice Act. The new "antiwar" and "progressive" president was silent about the desperate need to significantly roll back the $1 trillion annual "defense" (Empire) allotment and bring about the forgotten peace dividend that Dr. King knew to be required to fund social uplift and stave off the nation's "spiritual death."[80] Refusing to make any reference to horrific crimes against Palestinian humanity during the previous three weeks, Obama did not utter the word "Gaza" once during a speech that denounced "those who seek to advance their aims by inducing terror and slaughtering innocents."

The abundant warnings continued right up through Barack "No Apology" Obama's first day in office, two days before he ordered his first Predator drone attacks in South Asia.

Afterword
Beyond the Perverted and Deadly
Priorities of Empire and Inequality, Inc.

One year after President Barack Obama's historic election in the name of "change" and "hope," Gallup and *USA Today* reported that the U.S. citizenry's initially high expectations of the Obama presidency had fallen along with the president's popularity. In November 2008, 67 percent of the American population thought that the Obama administration would be able to reduce unemployment. By mid-October 2009, just barely more than half (51 percent) believed that. In the month of the president's election, 64 percent of Americans told Gallup and *USA Today* that the next White House would be able "to improve the health care system." Fifty-eight (58) percent thought President Obama would be able to "bring U.S. troops home from Afghanistan in a way that's not harmful to the U.S." Eleven and a half months later, just 46 percent believed that Obama could improve health care. The same percentage (46) thought the same way about Obama and Afghanistan.[1]

At one level, we might consider these reduced expectations something of a victory for the American corporate and imperial power elite. Realistically or not, much of the majority U.S. working-class populace wanted certain things from the Obama presidency. The things hoped for included increased employment opportunities and wages, a rollback of war and militarism, universal and adequate health care, rebuilt infrastructure, serious efforts to fix the environmental crisis, reduced inequality, and generally improved life circumstances for ordinary people.

The Perverted Priorities of the Elite

The corporate and imperial ruling class that backed Obama's campaign and staffed many of his key cabinet and other policymaking positions had different priorities for America. They wanted Obama to foster an illusion of democratic change that worked to prevent popular rebellion. They wanted the new administration to save and restore legitimacy to their damaged profits system and empire. Speaking to the *New York Times* in late October on why he felt the wealthy few should not be bothered by Obama's occasional, politically calculated criticism of exaggerated Wall Street compensation packages, leading Wall Street political funder and Obama backer Orin Kramer offered an interesting plutocratic perspective on the president's duty to America: "There is some failure in the finance industry," Kramer said, "to appreciate the level of public antagonism towards whatever Wall Street symbolizes. But i*n order to save the capitalist system*, the administration has to be responsive to the public mood, and that is a nuance which can get lost on Wall Street."[2]

The most interesting aspect of Orin Kramer's comment was the reason he gave that Obama had to demonstrate responsiveness to public feelings. Not because we claim to live in a democracy where the populace and the government are supposed (in theory) to be identical. Not because the popular majority is understood to be the ruling force in a nation that purports to be based on the principle of one person, one vote. No, the point, for Orin Kramer, was to "save the capitalist system," as if Obama and his team had taken an oath to honor, defend, protect, and preserve the private system of socioeconomic management, not the U.S. Constitution.

Like other rich and powerful "players," Kramer desired a public relations makeover along with improved governance for American Empire and Inequality in the wake of the grossly incompetent, unpopular, and messianic-militarist Bush-Cheney administration and the related epic financial meltdown of September–October 2008. Elite players wanted Obama's "progressive" triumph to cloak a deeper underlying triumph of conservatism. They wanted new and deceptive clothes for the persistence of the old regime. They wanted a rebranding without a restructuring—without any serious questioning of underlying institutions and ideologies.

According to the *New York Times* editorial board after Obama's election, we have seen, the new president's job was to make the "burdens yet to come" for ordinary working people seem "more bearable," holding down popular expectations and anger while funding and refashioning "a military large enough and mobile enough" to rule "a dangerous world."

Nine months after Obama's inauguration, the same perverted priorities were on display at the *Times*' corporate media cousin the *Washington Post*. In an unusual move on Saturday, October 24, 2009, the *Post*'s editorial page condescended to address a critical response from a reader who "challenged [the editors] to explain what he sees as a contradiction in our editorial positions." The reader had raised an interesting question. He had wondered how the *Post* could justify (a) demanding that Obama's health care plan not be paid for with borrowed money while at the same time (b) strongly supporting U.S. escalation in Afghanistan without specifying how to pay for it. "Why is it okay to finance wars with debt, asks our reader, but not to pay for health care that way?"[3]

The *Post*'s editors gave three answers. Their first claim was misleading and false. It held that Obama was saving money by cutting defense spending and withdrawing from Iraq. But Obama was doing none of these things. Iraq remained occupied, and Obama had actually increased the Pentagon budget. By "cutting defense," the *Post* really meant that Obama was merely decreasing the rate at which defense spending increased ("from 2008 to 2019, defense spending would increase only 17 percent"). And, of course, the president was escalating in Afghanistan and Pakistan, adding thereby to the ballooning federal deficit.

The *Post*'s second claim was also deceptive. It argued that "wars, unlike entitlement programs, eventually come to an end." But do they really? As noted U.S. military historian and former U.S. army colonel Andrew Bacevich told *Frontline* in September, dominant U.S. military doctrine did not support that argument. "Post-Vietnam," Bacevich noted, "the officer corps was committed to the proposition that wars should be infrequent, that they should be fought only for the most vital interests, and that they should be fought in a way that would produce a quick and decisive outcome. What we have today in my judgment is just the inverse of that. War has become a permanent condition."[4] Full truth told, massive and vastly expensive federal preparation for war became an undeviating aspect of U.S. government during and after World War II.

The *Post*'s third and deeper answer was darkly revealing and emblematic of the distorted priorities and perverted values of the nation's political class. It held that escalating in Afghanistan was an unqualified national obligation while providing Americans universal health coverage was basically an extra that could be put on hold. According to the *Post*'s editors:

> All this [the troubled reader's sense of contradiction between open-ended war funding and limited health care funding] assumes that defense and health care should be treated equally in the national budget. We would argue that they should not be. . . . Universal health care, however desirable, is not "fundamental to the defense of our people." Nor is it a "necessity" that it be adopted this year: Mr. Obama chose to propose a massive new entitlement at a time of historic budget deficits. In contrast, Gen. McChrystal believes that if reinforcements are not sent to Afghanistan in the next year, the

war may be lost, with catastrophic consequences for U.S. interests in South Asia. U.S. soldiers would continue to die, without the prospect of defeating the Taliban. And, as Mr. Obama put it, "if left unchecked, the Taliban insurgency will mean an even larger safe haven from which al-Qaeda would plot to kill more Americans."

This was a remarkable proclamation. Besides its abject repetition of the White House's highly problematic "safe haven" argument in defense of the occupation of Afghanistan, it was remarkably indifferent to the shocking domestic death toll imposed by the nation's corporate-ruled health insurance regime. That regime killed more Americans each month than al Qaeda did on September 11, 2001. A study released by the Harvard Medical School and Cambridge Health Alliance in September 2009 demonstrated that "nearly 45,000 annual deaths are associated with lack of health insurance" in America. According to one of the study's authors, "Deaths associated with lack of health insurance now exceed those caused by many common killers such as kidney disease. An increase in the number of uninsured and an eroding medical safety net for the disadvantaged likely explain the substantial increase in the number of deaths, as the uninsured are more likely to go without needed care."[5]

No doubt the *Post* editors who explained why the indefinite occupation of Afghanistan was a higher national priority than universal health care for Americans were all enrolled in gold-plated health insurance plans. It was all too easy for them to dismiss tens of thousands of annual deaths in the imperial "homeland" as "not fundamental"—as something that did not need to be overcome as quickly as possible.

"No matter your views on Obama's health care reform plan," incisive left-liberal writer Glen Greenwald noted, "does it really take any effort to see how warped [their] dismissive mentality is?" As Greenwald added, "It becomes . . . much worse when one considers" that the Obama administration's "venerated 'counter-insurgency' mission in Afghanistan" entailed an open-ended commitment to "securing the population" through years and perhaps decades of military, social, and political intervention guided by "an enormously ambitious project of nation-building." The cost of that project would certainly run well into the trillions of dollars.

Greenwald aptly summarized and criticized the "warped" priorities of the *Post*'s editors:

So according to *The Washington Post*, dropping bombs on, controlling and occupying Afghanistan—all while simultaneously ensuring "effective governance, economic development, education, the elimination of corruption, the protection of women's rights" to Afghan citizens in Afghanistan—is an absolutely vital necessity that must be done no matter the cost. But providing basic services (such as health care) to American citizens, in the U.S., is a secondary priority at best, something totally unnecessary that should wait for a few years or a couple decades until we can afford it and until our various wars are finished, if that ever happens. "U.S. interests in South Asia" are paramount; U.S. interests in the welfare of those in American cities, suburbs and rural areas are an afterthought.

As demented as that sounds, isn't that exactly the priority scheme we've adopted as a country? We're a nation that couldn't even manage to get clean drinking water to our own citizens who were dying in the middle of New Orleans. We have tens of thousands of people dying every year because they lack basic health care coverage. The rich-poor gap [inside the United States] continues to expand to third-world levels. And the *Post* claims that war and "nation-building" in Afghanistan are crucial while health care for Americans is not. . . .

Beltway elites have health insurance and thus the costs and suffering for those who don't are abstract, distant and irrelevant. Identically, with very rare exceptions, they and their families don't fight the wars they cheer on— and don't even pay for them—and thus get to enjoy all the pulsating benefits without any costs whatsoever.

The *Post*'s editorial reminded Greenwald of a notable passage in Adam Smith's much-misunderstood *Wealth of Nations* (1776): "In great empires the people who live in the capital, and in the provinces remote from the scene of action, feel, many of them, scarce any inconveniency from the war; but enjoy, at their ease, the amusement of reading in the newspapers the exploits of their own fleets and armies." It was as if Smith had seen into the posh corridors of the *Post* 233 years later. "Lounging around in the editorial offices in the capital of a rapidly decaying empire, urging that more Americans be sent into endless war paid for with endless debt, while yawning and lazily waving away with boredom the hordes outside dying for lack of health care coverage, is one of the most repugnant images one can imagine. It's exactly what Adam Smith denounced. And it's exactly what our political and media elite are," Greenwald wrote.[6]

Maybe It's Not About Running for President

But what to do? In the spring of 1967, after he went public with his principled opposition to the Vietnam War, Martin Luther King Jr. was approached by liberal and left politicos to consider running for the U.S. presidency. King turned the activists down, saying that he preferred to think of himself "as one trying desperately to be the conscience of all the political parties, rather being a political candidate. . . . I've just never thought of myself as a politician."[7] The minute he threw his hat into the American presidential ring, King knew, he would be encouraged to compromise his increasingly left message against what he called "the triple evils that are interrelated": racism, economic inequality, and militarism.[8]

Reflecting on his chastening confrontation with concentrated black poverty and class oppression in the "liberal" urban North and his shock at the horrors of U.S. policy in Southeast Asia,[9] King had come to radical-democratic conclusions. "For years I have labored with the idea of refining the existing institutions of the society, a little change here, a little change there," he told journalist David Halberstam that spring. "Now I feel quite differently. I think you've got to have a reconstruction of the entire society, a revolution of values." The black freedom movement, King told a crowd at the University of California–Berkeley, had shifted from civil rights to human rights, moving into "a struggle for genuine equality" that "demands a radical redistribution of economic and political power."[10] By this time, King had identified the U.S. government as "the greatest purveyor of violence in the world today," and he denounced U.S. support for U.S.-investment-friendly Third World dictatorships, all part of "the triple evils."[11]

As Dr. King knew, these were not exactly "winning" ideas in the American political system of his time. They were moral observations with radical implications that led well beyond the barriers of existing U.S. politics.

Again and again during the first year of Barack Obama's presidency, "hard-left" critiques of the Obama administration were met by a standard "left-liberal" objection. Obama, many of his so-called left apologists told me, was doing all he could for progressive values under the existing system of business and military power and in a context in which right-wing Republicans still exercised a great degree of power. Obama was imprisoned by the system he ascended in the name of democratic "change." Corporate and military Washington, the argument went, left little room for progressive maneuver. Poor "progressive" President Obama, victim of nasty plutocrats, the military-industrial complex, and terrible Republicans!

This was an unimpressive defense on two levels. First, it misses the fact that the "deeply conservative" Obama wasn't actually a progressive, something he himself had indicated to those willing to look.[12] At a certain point, one has to wonder about the intellectual and/or moral competence of those who claim to be "left" and yet continue to cling to the brand over the reality when it comes to "understanding" Obama in the world of power. The comforting, self-pacifying notion that Obama—a president who often goes farther than required to appease corporate and military masters—really wants to transform America in genuinely progressive sorts of ways is simply unsupportable in light of what can easily found and shown about his political career and worldview.

Second, although it is certainly true that Washington policymakers are captive to the interlocking directorates and revolving doors of wealth, money, power, and empire, that captivity raises an obvious point suggested in the Dr. King story I just related:[13] Even if Obama were the progressive populist and peace champion that so many of his left and liberal supporters want to believe, he would still be detained and directed by the power elite and the corporate-managed fake democracy. So *maybe it isn't about running for president and getting behind presidential candidates.* Maybe it isn't about scaling to the top of the authoritarian American system and helping that system rebrand and relegitimize itself as a "democracy" where "anything is possible."[14] Maybe citizens and activists who are serious about democracy and progressive change should heed an all-too-forgotten pearl of wisdom from the Bible: "Do not put your trust in princes."[15] Or, we might add, in this country's narrow-spectrum big-money/big-media electoral process, subjected as it is to Laurence Shoup's "hidden primary of the ruling class" and Edward S. Herman and Davis Peterson's "unelected dictatorship of money."[16]

Maybe it's really about rebuilding and expanding social movements and grassroots citizens' power and creating a more responsive political culture from the bottom up beneath and beyond the spectacular, melodramatic corporate-crafted mass-marketed, narrow-spectrum, and candidate-centered (and candidate-obsessed) "electoral extravaganzas" the power elite and its dominant media stage for us every four years.[17] And maybe it's about pursuing the radical, indeed revolutionary, change that Dr. King called for near the tragically premature end of his life.

Beyond False Pragmatism: "We Either Make the Leap or Not"

As Noam Chomsky observed four years ago, "One commonly hears that carping critics complain about what is wrong, but do not present solutions. There is an accurate translation for that charge: 'they present solutions and I don't like them.'"[18] Again and again in 2008 and 2009, I heard "liberals" and centrists accuse hard-left critics of Obama and the Democrats of being hopelessly alienated and negativistic "gripers" and "antis." We are supposedly just harsh opponents of "reality"—"cynics" and "ideologues" (our supposedly "reality-based" liberal critics purport to have transcended ideology) who are all about being "against" and are not actually "for" anything real and "pragmatic" and "practical" in *the real world.*

Consistent with Chomsky's point, however, my previous "Obama book" ended with a detailed list of action and policy proposals that are widely supported on much of the really existing hard left. The policies recommended included radical electoral reform, a socially progressive rechartering and egalitarian reconstruction of the modern corporation, checks on corporate globalization, a serious policy attack on institutional racism, substantive universal health reform on the progressive single-payer model, labor law reform, rebuilding and expansion of the union movement, removal of troops from Iraq and Afghanistan, a rollback of the Pentagon system and the global U.S. empire in connection with a major domestic and global *peace dividend*, and dismantling of the "national security" police, surveillance, and (globally unmatched) mass incarceration state built around the related official "wars on terror and drugs."[19] *Barack Obama and the Future of American Politics* was not content to call only for reforms, even radical reforms. "In trying to work creatively with the Obama moment," I insisted, "people engaged in progressive political action should not be afraid of demanding something along the lines of revolution. . . . 'Reforms will not suffice' and capitalism and democracy are two very different and indeed fundamentally opposed beasts."[20]

The demand for radical, even revolutionary change naturally strikes many, probably most, of Obama's more intellectually inclined liberal and progressive supporters as hopelessly "utopian" and "unrealistic"—as off the charts of serious consideration. The real progressive thing, the properly "practical" and "pragmatic" course, is to carefully and incrementally push for small steps on the long, slow path to a better world.[21] As Obama likes to say, we must not let "the perfect be the enemy of the good."

But for many on the actual historical left, the honest and truly informed calculation of what is realistic is profoundly different. If we leave aside the important fact that many of Obama's "reforms" are simply "just *no damn good*" (from a leftist standpoint and even just from a mildly progressive liberal perspective, such as that of, say, a John Conyers),[22] we have a very dissimilar sense of practicality and reality. As we see it, the currently reigning profits system—every bit as entrenched and intact under the "leftist" Obama and a (corporate-)Democratic congressional majority as it was with

Bush and Republicans in the saddle (possibly more entrenched now thanks in part to the superficially left cover provided by Brand Obama)—is thoroughly incompatible with basic human needs and democratic principles. The really fantastic and deadly "utopian" illusion, for us, is to believe that the United States and humanity can build a desirably democratic and sustainable future without implementing an egalitarian alternative to the capitalist order—to the so-called free market system to which Barack Obama has repeatedly pledged his allegiance and on whose financial chieftains he has so strongly relied.[23] To quote left economists Fred Magdoff and Michael Yates: "Can [democratic, socially egalitarian, and ecological] goals be achieved inside the present economic system? Perhaps some can in very limited ways, but most of them clearly cannot. The system simply will not allow it. Pragmatists say that these things are utopian, that we have to work within the system and achieve what we can, gradually and in a piecemeal fashion. It seems to us, however, that this 'pragmatic' approach is utopian."[24]

Increasingly grave ecological issues, particularly those connected with the largely profits-driven problem of global warming, call into question the "pragmatic" wisdom of pursuing nothing more than the "incremental change" that many Obama fans laud the president for embodying. As Ricardo Levins-Morales noted in an important reflection on left strategy and prospects in summer 2009, the cautious "one small step at a time" approach to progressive change loses credibility when the existing order is posing ever more imminent existential questions of—and grave threats to—survival of the species.[25] Honest appreciation of realistic imperatives calls for a more radical approach:

> If the road we are on leads to a precipice, then a shift in our strategic orientation is overdue. If the Obama administration proposes modest green-oriented initiatives and then waters them down to mollify corporate interests, we will still (it can be argued) end up further along than we were to begin with. If we envision ourselves as advancing across an expanse of open field, then we can measure our progress in terms of yardage gained and be satisfied that we are least moving in the right direction. If, instead, a chasm has opened up which we must leap across to survive, then the difference between getting twenty percent versus forty percent of the way across is meaningless. It means we have transitioned from a system of political letter grades to one of "pass/fail." We either make the leap or not.[26]

As the world enters a period of epic mass structural unemployment and (most urgently of all) related, potentially fatal ecological crisis that is directly traceable to—and fundamentally rooted in—the profits system,[27] it's long past time for millions of Americans to embrace (as some recent polling suggests many do, in fact*) the conclusion that Obama's left-liberal cheerleader Michael Moore had reached halfway into the first year of his candidate's presidency: "Folks, capitalism's got to go. Because we can't have a system where the richest 1 percent own as much as the bottom 95 percent. That just isn't democracy."[28] The last thing any administration claiming to represent "We the People" in a democracy should be doing in the name of "change" is acting on Obama's model to (following the admonitions of Wall Street moguls such as Orin Kramer[29]) sustain the capitalist system—a system that threatens to bring the human experiment to a close sooner than many of even the darkest of us had imagined.

But this is a subject for another book and, far more importantly, activism during and beyond the Age of Obama.[30]

---

*In April 2009, the national polling firm Rasmussen Reports asked 1,000 randomly selected American adults a simple question: Which is better, capitalism or socialism? Only 53 percent picked the profits system. Among younger adults (eighteen to twenty-nine), just 37 percent preferred capitalism, 33 percent chose socialism, and 30 percent were undecided (*Rasmussen Reports*, April 9, 2009). These were remarkable findings in light of decades of ongoing Red Scare propaganda in this country.

Postscript

The Sorry Surrender of the So-Called Radical Left

An Obama victory will bring intense pressure on the U.S. antiwar and social justice movements to accept a Democratic administration for all its faults. If that happens, domestic resistance to rapacious America will fall silent.
—*John Pilger, May 2008*[1]

It was a relief to complete the main intensive research for this book in the middle of December 2009. Well before the one-year anniversary of President Barack Obama's inauguration, my feeling of validation that the core argument of my 2008 book, *Barack Obama and the Future of American Politics*, had been supported by the centrist, right-leaning, and corporate-imperial "rebranding" path of the Obama presidency had given way to a sick feeling of political depression. It's one thing to predict a terrible authoritarian outcome. It is another thing altogether to live through that outcome and to see little, if any, positive and democratic popular response to it.

My previous "Obama book" advanced something of a mixed message on what the meaning of an Obama presidency might be for the left-progressive politics and movements with which I have long been identified. On the one hand, *Barack Obama and the Future* advanced dire warnings about the next president's remarkable capacity to pacify and co-opt already weakened progressive U.S. movements and politics.[2] Obama, it seemed to me and others, was potential poison for "the left," or what was left of it. On the other hand, my earlier volume held out the promise that corporate-imperial Obama might "oxygenate" (left social critic Charles Derber's term[3]) grassroots social justice and antiwar movements by provocatively raising and then betraying popular hopes for progressive change. At the same time, I hoped that Democratic Party victories at both the White House and the congressional levels in 2008 would enhance the progressive movement potential of younger citizens by giving them a graphic lesson in the bipartisan nature of American corporate-managed fake democracy and imperialism—by demonstrating that the Democrats were deeply complicit in defending and advancing the same core ruling domestic and global power structures and doctrines as the Republicans.[4]

"What Exists of a Popular Left"

Across the first sixteen months of Obama's positioning in the real world of presidential power, my warnings have proved a better guide to political reality than my hopes. It's been about suffocation, not oxygenation. The problem isn't so much that Obama has fulfilled my expectations of his service to reigning power structures and ideologies. That was as foreseen. The bigger difficulty is that Obama's (predictable and in fact predicted) progressive betrayals have transpired with only minimal opposition from what passed for a left (what we might, following George Orwell, call the so-called left[5]) in the United States. The administration and the corporate Democratic Party have faced minimal pressure from "progressive" forces, which have been predictably ignored by centers of power. Those forces (if that's really the right word) cling to the curious notion that "now"—a remarkable period of massive economic, ecological, and imperial crisis and opportunity, loaded with radical-democratic implications—"is not the time" to fight aggressively for big left ideals and radical restructuring. They hold (some out of cynicism and some out of naïveté) to the delusional belief that the self-described "New Democrat" Barack Obama is somehow their voice and "friend" in the White House on behalf of a "people's agenda."[6]

The outlines of progressive capitulation were clear to one perceptive observer less than a month after Obama's inauguration. As John Judis argued in the *New Republic* in February 2009, "There is not a popular left movement that is agitating for him to go well beyond where he would even ideally like to go. . . . *Instead, what exists of a popular left is either incapable of action or in Obama's pocket* [emphasis added]." By Judis's analysis, the U.S. labor movement and groups such as MoveOn.org were repeating the same "mistake that political groups often make: subordinating their concern about issues to their support for the [Democratic] party and its leading politicians."[7]

"The Obama Disease"

Nothing occurred in the first fourteen months of Obama's presidency to seriously question the wisdom of that judgment. For the American so-called radical left (John Pilger),[8] unjust wars and occupations, megabailouts for bankers, and other regressive policies that had been seen as intolerable under the perceived rule of a boorish white Republicans from Texas (George W. Bush) were all too acceptable when carried out by an eloquent and urbane black Democrat from Chicago (Barack Obama). The miniprogressive rebellion that I thought I was witnessing at the end of 2009 came to very little indeed. No substantive progressive and left challenges were mounted to Obama's military escalations, Obama's corporatism, and/or Obama's repressive police-statism. Antiwar activist and journalist Justin Raimondo captured the depressing reality after what was left of an antiwar "movement" held small protests marking the seventh anniversary of the ongoing U.S. occupation of Iraq in mid-March 2010. After noting that no more than a few thousand marched in Washington, along with an "altogether poor turnout" in other major cities—far less than the tens of thousands who had marched in mid-March in 2006 and 2007—Raimondo observed the paralyzing impact of "the Obama cult of personality" even on some who attended the antiwar march in Washington:

> Even among those who attended the protests, there were some whose opposition to this administration's foreign policy is squishy at best. . . . Shirley Allan of Silver Spring, Md. carried a sign that read, "President Obama We love you but we need to tell you! Your hands are getting bloody!! Stop it now."
>
> Ms. Allan's sign says more about her than it does about the issue she purports to address. To confess to loving a political leader whose hands are even a little bit bloody is quite a revealing statement to make, and it just about sums up why the crowd was smaller than on previous occasions. The hate-Bush crowd has quickly morphed into the love-Obama cult of personality, and the so-called progressives have deserted the antiwar movement in droves. Our multiple wars just aren't an issue inside the Democratic Party.
>
> On the non-Marxist left, the triumph of the Obama cult is complete. Only the old-fashioned Leninists, such as the main organizers of the ANSWER rallies, have come out in visible opposition to Obama's wars. Even the Marxist left, however, is not immune to Obama-mania: the other major antiwar coalition, United for Peace and Justice [UFPJ], led by veterans of the old Communist Party, USA, issued a euphoric statement upon Obama's election and has been essentially moribund as an active antiwar organization ever since.
>
> It was in this kind of political atmosphere, then—one of near complete political isolation—that rally attendees heard Cindy Sheehan wonder whether "the honeymoon was over with that war criminal in the White

House." Sheehan's remark was met, according to AP [Associated Press], with merely "moderate applause." Ms. Allan was not among the applauders.[9]

Reading Raimondo's essay, I flashed back to early fall 2009. In late September of that year, the progressive television show *Democracy Now* interviewed Kehban Grifter, a young activist who was among a modest number protesting the corporate-globalizationist G-20 summit in Pittsburgh. "What we're here doing this week," Grifter said, "is distributing our work and trying to talk to people about coal and climate change and globalization. And unfortunately, it seems like a lot of folks aren't turning out for these sort of mobilizations as much anymore. Maybe they're depressed, maybe they're cynical, maybe they've still got Obamaitis. We're on the outside here."[10]

Hearing Grifter's comment online, I was reminded of an e-mail exchange I had had in early 2007 with a leading left thinker, who made passing reference to what he called "the Obama disease." This point of his disparaging term was that Obama was a standard corporate and military regime Democrat, but one with an extraordinary ability to convince progressives that they would somehow be in power if he became president of the United States. I was reminded also of reports from attempted mass antiwar marches in Washington in March 2009. Led by the once-formidable UFPJ, the protest was poorly attended. It drew only a few thousand, even as Obama transparently escalated and expanded imperial violence in "AfPak," made clear his determination to increase the Pentagon budget and sustain the Iraq occupation, and went forward with a highly unpopular bailout package for Wall Street. Dejected organizers reported difficulty getting significant numbers of people to turn out against a White House that was perceived as "left" and antiwar. UFPJ's outgoing director, Leslie Cagan, reported that her "progressive" and "activist" people weren't protesting anymore because "it's enough for many of them that Obama has a plan to end the war and that things are moving in the right direction."[11]

Rebranding Bush Policy with a Pretty Progressive Face

Interest in opposing the Empire's New Clothes has not arisen to any appreciable degree across the nation's "progressive" community. It hasn't been for a lack of actionable issues, including (alongside numerous continued and terrible incidents of civilian "collateral damage" in Afghanistan and Pakistan) the following:

- Obama's escalation of the U.S. military presence in Yemen, "now" (in Glenn Greenwald's words) "another predominantly Muslim country (along with Somalia and Pakistan) in which the [U.S.] military is secretly involved to some unknown degree in combat operations without any declaration of war, without any public debate, and arguably without any Congressional authority"[12]
- Obama's explicit exclusion of Iran from his declaration that the United States would not make a nuclear first-strike attack on a non-nuclear nation—an exclusion reasonably grasped in the Muslim world and especially in Iran as a threat of a first nuclear strike on Iran
- Obama's promise in mid-March 2010 to veto any congressional legislation to enhance legislative oversight over the White House and military's unconstitutional intelligence-gathering through illegal surveillance activities, including warrantless eavesdropping[13]
- Obama's efforts (through his Department of Justice [DOJ]) to obtain from Yahoo "all e-mails" sent and received by multiple Yahoo accounts "despite the fact that the DOJ has never sought, let alone obtained a search warrant, and despite there being no notice of any kind to e-mail users"—this in bold defiance of federal law[14]
- Obama's decision to prosecute National Security Agency (NSA) whistleblower Thomas Drake, whose leaks helped the *Baltimore Sun* expose NSA efforts to discard key citizen-privacy provisions designed to ensure that the agency would not illegally eavesdrop on the domestic calls of U.S. citizens[15]
- Obama's decision to authorize the Central Intelligence Agency and military to summarily assassinate U.S. citizens "strongly" suspected of "organizing or carrying out actions against the U.S. or U.S. interests"[16]

In April 2010, Glenn Greenwald offered an eloquent reflection—richly consistent with the argument of the present volume—on the absence of any meaningful progressive resistance to Obama's assassination program:

Here again, we see one of the principal and longest-lasting effects of the Obama presidency: to put a pretty, eloquent, progressive face on what (until quite recently) was ostensibly considered by a large segment of the citizenry to be tyrannical right-wing extremism (e.g., indefinite detention, military commissions, "state secrets" used to block judicial review, an endless and always-expanding "War on Terror," immunity for war criminals, rampant corporatism—and now unchecked presidential assassinations of American citizens), and thus to transform what were once bitter, partisan controversies into harmonious, bipartisan consensus.[17]

"Ignore the Progressives":
Vindicating Rahm Emanuel

Things haven't been much better on the domestic social and economic policy front. Where has the nation's liberal and progressive political institutional infrastructure been to capture and channel what dominant U.S. media tended to arrogantly dismiss as dysfunctional "populist rage" as Obama and much of the rest of the political class act to sustain government subsidy and protection for the rich and market discipline for the poor and working class? It's been missing in action, at once bedazzled and disciplined by the nation's first black president, whose chief of staff, Rahm Emanuel, threatened egregious retaliation against those liberal Democrats and activists who dared to substantively challenge the corporate and militaristic direction of policy.[18] As left political commentator Lance Selfa noted in mid-January 2010:

> The liberal groups who could be kicking up a ruckus to push for genuine health reform or a real jobs program are instead playing the role of loyal soldiers to the White House's agenda. . . . The groups in question, led by the Democracy Alliance and the liberal think tank, the Center for American Progress . . . represent a liberal infrastructure that, in exchange for regular meetings with White House officials, has neutered itself. Meanwhile, existing right-wing networks have gone into full battle mode. That has left the field open to the conservatives. . . . Is it any wonder, then, that most of the opposition to Obama's program is coming from the right?[19]

The health "reform" legislation that finally passed Congress and gained Obama's signature into law in mid-March 2010 was a corporatist measure very much in line with the analysis presented in Chapter 3. Reflecting corrupt deals Obama had made many months earlier with the big insurance and drug companies, it contained no public insurance option, irrelevantly supported by a large majority of Americans in a *New York Times*/CBS Poll in January 2010.[20] The reform bill prohibits the government from negotiating prices with drug companies and from permitting the importation of drugs (two things that are also irrelevantly popular with most Americans). To make matter worse, the law permits the big insurance companies to retain their exemption from antitrust laws, restricts coverage for abortions, and denies coverage to "illegal" (and other) immigrants, who will continue to frequent emergency rooms and receive care.[21]

According to Emanuel, speaking on the *PBS NewsHour* just after the bill passed, "It's very similar to the bill Republicans advocated in 1993 [with its] . . . basic approach, which is a free-market, market-based-system approach."[22] This was a revealing comment on the bill's conservative essence, though Emanuel was technically incorrect to call the corporate-socialist Patient Protection and Affordable Health Care Act a "free-market" measure.

The White House and its loyal "liberal" defenders made a truly laughable and Orwellian effort to claim that the bill was some sort of bold and progressive act of "standing up to special interests."[23] But as health industry paper *Kaiser Health News* noted in a March 22 article titled "Doctors, Hospitals, Insurers, Pharma Come Out Ahead with Health Bill," "Most health industry sectors are winners—some bigger than others—under the sweeping health care legislation that will expand coverage to 32 million uninsured Americans over the next decade." The trade paper detailed the vast benefits each industry received, the slight costs all health care industries paid, and the notable success they experienced in killing the threats of real competition and serious reform—in slaying the public option, Medicare expansion, drug reimportation, bulk price negotiations, and repeal of the insurance giants' antitrust exemption. *Kaiser Health News* gave "one indication that the insurance industry is likely to do fine under the bill": Health insurers' share prices had risen by an average of 71 percent in the previous twelve months. "That's hardly surprising," Greenwald noted, observing that "a former Wellpoint executive was the principal author of the original Senate bill from which the final bill was derived."[24]

In late 2009, many members of the Democratic Party's congressional "Progressive Caucus" and leading liberal organizations such as MoveOn.org had criticized Obama's health care bill as too corporate friendly. Many of the "progressive" legislators raised political money on their pledges to refuse to vote for any legislation that lacked a public option. By the time the measure came to a vote in mid-March 2010, however, White House pressure (with Emanuel in the lead of the arm-twisting effort) elicited a total surrender of the (not-so-)left (non)opposition. Every single member of the Progressive Caucus caved in and traded his or her not so deeply held principles to help score a partisan victory for a bill that promised (in the word of principled progressive activists at the left-liberal organization Firedog Lake) "to enrich and strengthen the same industries that comprise our immoral health care system."[25] The ex-progressive, Obama-captive organization MoveOn.org actually picketed the Cleveland office of Representative Dennis Kucinch (D-OH) to pressure him (successfully) to go back on his pledge (the *Cleveland Plain Dealer* article reporting this revealing episode bore the unintentionally ironic title "Rep. Dennis Kucinch Draws Fire from the Left on Health Reform").[26] As Glenn Greenwald noted, progressive Democrats' capitulation starkly vindicated Rahm Emanuel's advice to

Obama: "Ignore the demands of progressives on the ground that they would fall into line at the end no matter what." Greenwald summed up the harsh reality of total left surrender:

> For almost a full year, scores of progressive House members vowed—publicly and unequivocally—that they would never support a health care bill without a robust public option. They collectively accepted hundreds of thousands of dollars based on this pledge. Up until a few weeks ago, many progressive opinion leaders—such as Markos Moulitsas, Howard Dean, Keith Olbermann and many others—were insisting that the Senate bill was worse than the status quo and should be defeated. But now? All of those progressives House members are doing exactly what they swore they would never do: vote for a health care bill with no public option—and virtually every progressive opinion leader is not only now supportive of the bill, but vehemently so. In other words, exactly what Rahm said would happen—ignore *the progressives, we don't need to give them anything because they'll get into line* [emphasis added]—is exactly what happened.[27]

As the bill was passed, progressive commentator Ezra Klein preposterously claimed that the bill marked the "twilight" of health and insurance industry influence,[28] which had been vanquished by the great supposed progressive president. But "to pretend that these interests were vanquished or 'neutralized'—in order to glorify the President as the Greatest Leader Since Abraham Lincoln with . . . sycophantic, Leader-worship hagiography—is," Greenwald noted, "not just deeply misleading but, worse, helps conceal what remains the greatest threat to the democratic process."[29]

"The Progressive Movement . . . Is Officially Dead"

In March 2010, Obama betrayed a campaign pledge and disregarded irrelevant progressive environmentalists by announcing that he planned to allow environmentally disastrous oil exploration and drilling in vast new offshore areas along the southeastern United States and Alaska. It was chilling news for many who remembered Obama's rejection of John McCain and Sarah Palin's eco-cidal campaign call (in the late summer of 2008) for America to "Drill, Baby, Drill" (for offshore oil). The announcement brought only minimal complaint from the nation's leading official Obama-captive environmental organizations. When a British Petroleum oil rig blew up in the Gulf of Mexico in late April, sending a "giant flaming ball of oil straight for the coasts of Alabama and Mississippi" (calling into question the ecological wisdom of the president's new drilling plans) in what could well be the worst environmental disaster in decades, leading progressive environmental organization the Sierra Club didn't mention the epic ecological debacle on the front page of its Web site for eleven days. "I know it makes the President's recent decision to allow offshore drilling look awkwardly timed," Jane Hamsher of Firedog Lake wrote to the Sierra Club, "but this is, sort of, you know, your issue, and there's no mention of it on your landing page." Reflecting also on the Progressive Caucus's recent plan to "give the coal lobby everything it wants," on the absence of any meaningful progressive response to "liberal" U.S. senator (and Obama ally) Dick Durbin's (D-IL) recent call for "bleeding heart liberals" to admit that Social Security and Medicare benefits are going to have to be cut for the economic good of the nation, and on the broader surrender of the nation's leading progressive groups to Obama's state-capitalist administration, Hamsher concluded on a cold but appropriate note: "Congratulations progressives, our already weakened institutions have finally tumbled. . . . As we watch that flaming ball of oil make its way to the coasts of Alabama and Mississippi our corrupt environmental groups do nothing about their signature issue that might make the White House uncomfortable. . . . I think it's safe to say that *the progressive movement's resistance to the agenda of corporate America is officially dead* [emphasis added]."[30]

Resentment Abhors a Vacuum

Meanwhile, a dangerous right-wing variant of elite-coordinated fake populism has arisen in the anger void left by the significantly Obama-induced slumber of "what exists of a popular left." In the absence of meaningful rage and protest on the portside, the dodgy Republican right wing and its still-potent "noise machine" have been left to soak up and express much of the legitimate "populist rage" that ordinary Americans quite naturally feel over Washington's continuing captivity to concentrated wealth, corporate direction, and the military-industrial complex in the Age of Obama. The ominous resurgence of the American right, whose leading political symbols and agents (Sean Hannity, Glenn Beck, Sarah Palin, Michelle Bachman, and Rush Limbaugh) and "movements" (including the "Tea Party") absurdly accuse the state-capitalist Obama of "socialism" and other "radical leftist" apostasies, technically contradicts a plethora of public opinion data showing that most Americans hold left-of-center attitudes on key foreign and domestic policy issues. (Massachusetts voters, among the most progressive in the nation, were hardly an exception.) But where are voters supposed to turn to act on their majority progressive opinions and on their rising populist resentment? Not to Obama and the Obama-age Democrats, who have led the record transfer of federal taxpayer dollars to Wall Street titans and funded the Pentagon at record-setting levels while largely abandoning workers and the poor and turning health reform over to the corporate insurance syndicate.[31] As Lance Selfa observed after previously unknown right-wing Republican state senator Scott Brown won a stunning victory over establishment Democrat Martha Coakley in an open seat election for the critical U.S. Senate post formerly held by leading liberal Democrat Teddy Kennedy in "archliberal" Massachusetts:

> The idea that Obama was even pursuing a liberal agenda will come as news to millions of his supporters who have become increasingly demoralized with an administration that seems more interested in helping out Wall Street bankers than "Main Street" Americans losing their jobs and houses.
> A September 2009 Economic Policy Institute [EPI] poll asked a national sample of registered voters to say who they thought had "been helped a lot or some" from the policies the administration enacted. The result: 13 percent said the "average working person," 64 percent identified "large banks," and 54 percent said "Wall Street investment companies."[32]

Consistent with the EPI's findings, Brian Mooney reported in the *Boston Globe* that Brown won mainly in the suburbs, where voter turnout was high. In less affluent and more strongly Democratic urban areas, the turnout was much lower, reflecting Obama's and the corporate Democrats' success in disillusioning and demobilizing many among the Democratic Party's working-class and minority constituents. "Many voters in traditionally Democratic cities . . . stayed home, dooming the candidacy of Democrat Martha Coakley," Mooney noted.[33]

This was hardly surprising. As the liberal Democratic *New York Times* columnist Bob Herbert observed five days after Brown's remarkable victory in a column titled "They [the Democrats] Still Don't Get It":

> The door is being slammed on the American dream and the politicians, including the president and his Democratic allies on Capitol Hill, seem not just helpless to deal with the crisis, but completely out of touch with the hardships that have fallen on so many.
> . . . While the nation was suffering through the worst economy since the Depression, the Democrats wasted a year squabbling like unruly toddlers over health insurance legislation. No one in his or her right mind could have

believed that a workable, efficient, cost-effective system could come out of the monstrously ugly plan that finally emerged from the Senate after long months of shady alliances, disgraceful back-room deals, outlandish payoffs and *abject capitulation* [emphasis added] to the insurance companies and giant pharmaceutical outfits.

The public interest? Forget about it.

The question for Democrats is whether there is anything that will wake them up to their obligation to extend a powerful hand to ordinary Americans and help them take the government, including the Supreme Court, back from the big banks, the giant corporations and the myriad other predatory interests that put the value of a dollar high above the value of human beings.[34]

A left without forthright answers for legitimately angry masses of people is a dangerous development with dark historical antecedents. As Noam Chomsky noted in an interview prior to Brown's victory:

There is a right-wing populist uprising. . . . If you look at those people and listen to them on talk radio, these are people with real grievances. . . .

For 30 years their wages have stagnated or declined. The social conditions have worsened . . . so somebody must be doing something to them, and they want to know who it is. Rush Limbaugh has answered: It's the rich liberals who own the banks and run . . . the media. They don't care about you. They just want to give everything away to illegal immigrants and gays and communists and so on.

. . . There is a whiff of early Nazi Germany. Hitler was appealing to groups with similar grievances and giving them crazy answers, but at least they were answers: that is, they blame the Jews and the Bolsheviks. . . .

Liberal Democrats aren't going to tell the average American, "yeah, you're being shafted because of the policies that we've established over the years that we're maintaining now." That's not going to be an answer. They're not getting [straight] answers from the left. [By contrast,] there's an internal coherence and logic to what they get from Limbaugh, Glenn Beck, and the rest of these guys. And they sound very convincing, they're very self-confident, and they have an answer to everything—a crazy answer, but it's an answer.[35]

Popular resentment abhors a progressive vacuum, in the Age of Obama as in numerous previous historical periods, with consequences that have often been quite unpleasant.

Notes

Notes to Preface

1. Laurence H. Shoup, "The Presidential Election 2008," *Z Magazine*, February 2008, 31.

2. The words "neoliberal" and "neoliberalism" will recur throughout this volume. A ruling corporate and political ideology in post–New Deal America (1980 to the present), neoliberalism largely recycles the classic bourgeois liberal "free-market" political-economic doctrine of the nineteenth century. It holds that the free market and possessive-individualist economic rationality are the solution to social and even personal problems. By neoliberal dictates, "The market should be allowed to make major social and political decisions. . . . The state should voluntarily reduce its role in the economy. . . . Corporations should be given total freedom. . . . Trade unions should be curbed and citizens given much less rather than more protections." I quote from Susan George, "A Short History of Neoliberalism" (Conference on Economic Sovereignty in a Globalizing World, Bangkok, Thailand, March 24–26, 1999). For useful discussions of the origins, nature, and contradictory practice of neoliberalism, see Noam Chomsky, *Profit Over People: Neoliberalism and Global Order* (New York: Seven Stories Press, 1999), 65–120; Henry A. Giroux, *The Terror of Neoliberalism: Authoritarianism and the Eclipse of Democracy* (Boulder, CO: Paradigm Publishers), xiii–xviii.

3. Richard Hofstader, *The American Political Tradition and the Men Who Made It* (New York: Vintage, Books, 1989 [1948]), xxxiii–xl.

4. Howard Zinn, *The Twentieth Century: A People's History* (New York: HarperPerennial, 1998), 328.

5. "Slaves Built the White House, Capitol," *PBS NewsHour*, January 19, 2008, at www.pbs.org/newshour/extra/video/blog/2009/01/slaves_built_the_white_house_u.html.

6. Kevin Phillips, "A Capital Offense: Reagan's America," *New York Times Magazine*, June 17, 1990, quoted in Lance Selfa, *The Democrats: A Critical History* (Chicago: Haymarket Books, 2008), 12.

7. Paul Street, "Blood on the Nobel: Reflections on Words, Deeds, and Imperial Re-Branding," *ZNet Magazine* [hereafter *ZNet*], December 15, 2009, at www.zcommunications.org/znet/viewArticle/23365.

8. George Monbiot, "Requiem for a Crowded Planet," *The Guardian*, December 21, 2009.

9. "Should Democrats Euthanize Health Reform Bill?" MSNBC *Countdown*, December 15, 2009, at http://video.aol.co.uk/video-detail/countdown-with-keith-olbermann-should-democrats-euthanize-health-reform-bill/3757912741; Jason Linkins, "Why Progressives Might Want to Kill the Health Care Bill," *Huffington Post*, December 16, 2009, at www.huffingtonpost.com/2009/12/16/why-progressives-might-wa_n_394551.html.

10. Robin Hahnel, "Economy Roundtable, Part 2," *New Left Project*, May 4, 2010, at www.newleftproject.org/index.php/site/article_comments/economy_roundtable_-_part_2/.

11. The more things change, the more they stay the same.

12. "Tea Party 48%, Obama 44%," *Rasmussen Reports*, April 5, 2010, at www.rasmussen reports.com/public_content/politics/general_politics/april_2010/tea_party_48_obama_44.

Notes to Introduction

1. Neil Postman, *Amusing Ourselves to Death: Public Discourse in the Age of Show Business* (New York: Penguin, 1985), 126–132.

2. "Obama Wins . . . Ad Age's Marketer of the Year," *Advertising Age*, October 17, 2008, at http://adage.com/print?article_id=131810.

3. "Barack Obama and the Audacity of Marketing," *Advertising Age*, November 10, 2008, at http://adage.com/print?article_id=132351.

4. "An Instant Overhaul for Tainted Brand America," *Advertising Age*, November 10, 2008, at http://adage.com/print?article_id=132352.

5. Quoted in ibid.

6. Quoted in ibid.

7. Quoted in ibid.

8. Quoted in ibid.

9. Nicholas Kristof, "Rebranding the U.S. with Obama," *New York Times*, October 23, 2008.

10. Nicholas Kristof, "The Obama Dividend," *New York Times*, November 6, 2008.

11. Gail Collins, "Thinking of Good Vibrations," *New York Times*, November 6, 2008.

12. Chris Hedges, "Buying Brand Obama," *Truthdig*, May 3, 2009, at http://www.truthdig.com/report/item/20090503_buying_brand_obama/.

13. *New York Times* Editors, "The Printing Press Cure," *New York Times*, December 22, 2008.

14. *New York Times* Editors, "A Military for a Dangerous World," *New York Times*, November 18, 2009.

Notes to Chapter One

1. William Greider, "Obama Asked Us to Speak but Is He Listening?" *Washington Post*, March 22, 2009.

2. Frank Rich, "Even Glenn Beck Is Right Twice a Day," *New York Times*, September 20, 2009.

3. Barack Obama comment to John King, *State of the Union with John King*, CNN, September 20, 2009, at http://transcripts.cnn.com/TRANSCRIPTS/0909/20/sotu .05.html.

4. Adam Smith quoted in Noam Chomsky, "Crisis and Hope: Theirs and Ours," *Boston Review* (September–October 2009), at http://bostonreview.net/BR34.5/chomsky.php.

5. David Sanger, "Obama Tilts Toward Center, Inviting a Clash of Ideas," *New York Times*, November 22, 2008.

6. As *Politico* reported, President Barack Obama firmly resists ideological labels, but at the end of a private meeting with a group of moderate Democrats on Tuesday afternoon, he offered a statement of solidarity.

"I am a New Democrat," he told the New Democrat Coalition, according to two sources at the White House session. The group is comprised of centrist Democratic members of the House, who support free trade and a muscular foreign policy but are more moderate than the conservative Blue Dog Coalition. Obama made his comment in discussing his budget priorities and broader goals, also calling himself a "pro-growth Democrat" during the course of conversation. The self-descriptions are striking given Obama's usual caution in being identified with any wing of his often-fractious party. He largely avoided the Democratic Leadership Council—the centrist group that Bill Clinton once led—and, with an eye on his national political standing, has always shied away from the liberal label, too. As recently as last week, he steadfastly refused to define his governing philosophy.

Jonathan Martin and Carol E. Lee, "Obama: 'I Am a New Democrat,'" *Politico*, March 10, 2009, at www.politico.com/news/stories/0309/19862.html.

7. James K. Galbraith, "No Return to Normal," *Washington Monthly*, March 2008.

8. *New York Times*, March 23, 2009.

9. *NewsHour*, March 23, 2009, with coin-flip comment repeated the same night on the *Charlie Rose Show*.

10. *New York Times*, March 24, 2009, A1.

11. Noam Chomsky, "Elections 2008 and Obama's 'Vision,'" *Z Magazine*, February 2009.

12. *New York Times*, March 24, 2009.

13. *Salon*, March 20, 2009.

14. James K. Galbraith, "No Return to Normal: Why the Economic Crisis and Its Solution Are Bigger Than You Think," *Washington Monthly*, March–April 2009, at www.washingtonmonthly.com/features/2009/0903.galbraith.html; *New York Times*, March 29, 2009; David Harvey, "The G20, the Financial Crisis, and Neoliberalism," *Znet*, April 3, 2009; John Burns and Landon Thomas, "English-Speaking Capitalism on Trial," *New York Times*, March 29, 2009; Paul Krugman, "The Big Dither," *New York Times*, March 6, 2009; Paul Krugman, "Behind the Curve," *New York Times*, March 9, 2009; Paul Krugman, "Financial Policy Despair," *New York Times*, March 23, 2009; Paul Krugman, "The Market Mystique," *New York Times*, March 27, 2009; Greider, "Obama

Told Us to Speak Out"; John R. MacArthur, "Obama Is Far from a Radical Reformer," *Providence Journal*, March 19, 2009, at www.projo.com/opinion/contributors/content/ CT_rick18_03-18-09_1SDM2BF_v26.3e689c2.html; Stephen Labaton and Edmund L. Andrews, "Geithner Said to Have Prevailed on the Bailout," *New York Times*, February 10, 2000.

15. Labaton and Andrews, "Geithner Said to Have Prevailed."

16. Ian Urbana, "In Cuba, Change Means More of the Same, with Control at the Top," *New York Times*, April 6, 2009.

17. Burns and Thomas, "English-Speaking Capitalism on Trial."

18. "Marxist Geographer David Harvey on the G20, the Financial Crisis, and Neo-liberalism," *Democracy Now*, April 2, 2009, at www.democracynow.org/2009/4/2/marxist _geographer_david_harvey_on_the.

19. Robert Weissman, "The Good, the Bad, the Ugly: Financial Sector Reform" *ZNet Sustainer Commentary*, June 17, 2009.

20. Michael Hudson, "Obama's (Latest) Surrender to Wall Street," *CounterPunch*, June 22, 2009, at www.counterpunch.org/hudson06222009.html.

21. Ryan Grim, "Dick Durbin: Banks 'Frankly Own the Place," *Huffington Post*, April 29, 2009, at www.huffingtonpost.com/2009/04/29/dick-durbin-banks-frankly_n_193010.html.

22. Weissman, "The Good, the Bad, the Ugly."

23. Krishna Guha, "US Seeks to Marry Dynamism and Safety," *Financial Times*, June 18, 2009, 2; Edward Luce, "White Paper Sets Out Skillful Compromises," *Financial Times*, June 18, 2008, 3; editors, "Redesigning the Financial Rulebook," *Financial Times*, June 18, 2009, 10.

24. Chomsky, "Crisis and Hope," 5.

25. "Remarks by the President on 21st Century Financial Regulatory Reform," June 17, 2009, at www.whitehouse.gov/the_press_office/Remarks-of-the-President-on-Reg-ulatory-Reform/. See Paul Street, "'We Will Not Apologize for Our Way of Life: Left Reflections on Barack Obama's Not-So-Nonideological Inaugural Address," *ZNet*, January 24, 2009, for a discussion of similar (nearly identical) language on the financial crisis in Obama's inaugural address.

26. William Greider, "Obama's False Financial Reform," *The Nation*, June 19, 2009, at www.thenation.com/doc/20090706/greider2.

27. Quoted (with approval) in Luce, "White Paper."

28. Edward S. Herman and David Peterson, "Riding the 'Green Wave' at the Campaign for Peace and Democracy and Beyond," *Electric Politics*, July 22, 2009.

29. Greider, "Obama's False Financial Reform."

30. Bruce Dixon, "Department of Broken Promises: Obama Closes Door on NAFTA Renegotiation," *Black Agenda Report*, April 22, 2009, at www.blackagendareport.com/?q =content/department-broken-promises-obama-closes-door-nafta-renegotiation; Kevin Baker, "Barack Hoover Obama: The Best and the Brightest Blow It Again," *Harper's*, July 2009, 36.

31. William Greider, "Obama's Weird Idea of Auto Industry Rescue: Use Our Money to Build Factories Abroad," *AlterNew*, May 11, 2009, at http://www.alternet.org/work-

place/139940/obama's_weird_idea_of_auto_industry_rescue:_use_our_money_to_build _car_factories_abroad.

32. Noam Chomsky, "Coups, UNASUR, and the U.S.," *Z Magazine*, October 2009, 26.

33. Greg Palast, "Grand Theft Auto: How Stevie the Rat Bankrupted GM," *GregPalast.com*, June 1, 2009, at www.gregpalast.com/grand-theft-auto-how-stevie-the -rat-bankrupted-gm/.

34. Floyd Norris, "U.S. Teaches Carmakers Capitalism," *New York Times*, November 20, 2009.

35. *New York Times*, April 19, 2009.

36. Chomsky, "Crisis and Hope." Following the militantly antiunion president Ronald Reagan's lead "with the dismantling of the air traffic controllers union," Chomsky noted, "Caterpillar managers decided to rescind their labor contract with the United Auto Workers and seriously harm the union by bringing in scabs to break a strike for the first time in generations."

37. Michael Shear, "Obama Pledges Entitlement Reform: President-Elect Says He'll Reshape Social Security, Medicare Programs," *Washington Post*, January 16, 2009, at http://www.cbsnews.com/stories/2009/01/16/politics/washingtonpost/main4727711 .shtm; Galbraith, "No Return to Normal."

38. Henry Giroux and Kenneth Saltman, "Obama's Betrayal of Public Education? Arne Duncan and the Corporate Model of Schooling," *Truthout*, December 17, 2008, at www.truthout.org/121708R.

39. Jesse Sharkey, "Arne Duncan's Privatization Agenda," *CounterPunch*, December 18, 2008, at www.counterpunch.org/sharkey12182008.html.

40. Geoff Berne, "Obama and Charter Schools: The Showdown at Schottenstein," *CounterPunch*, June 27, 2009, at www.counterpunch.org/berne06262009.html; Giroux and Saltman, "Obama's Betrayal of Public Education?"

41. Paul Street, *Segregated Schools: Educational Apartheid in Post–Civil Rights America* (New York: Routledge, 2005).

42. David Brooks, "The Quiet Revolution," *New York Times*, October 30, 2008.

43. Saltman and Giroux, "Obama's Betrayal of Public Education?"

44. *New York Times*, March 26, 2009.

45. Louise Story, "After a Pause, Wall Street Pay Is Bouncing Back," *New York Times*, April 26, 2009.

46. Jeffrey St. Clair and Joshua Frank, "How Much Has Changed? Obama Administration Deals Series of Anti-Environmental Blows," *AlterNet*, May 29, 2009, at www.alternet.org/story/140297/; Baker, "Barack Hoover Obama"; Nicole Colson, "Fresh Air or Hot Air?" *SocialistWorker.org*, April 29, 2009, at http://socialistworker .org/2009/04/28/fresh-air-or-hot-air; Johann Hari, "The Real Reason Obama Is Not Making Much Progress," *The Independent*, November 20, 2009.

47. Baker, "Barack Hoover Obama," 35–36.

48. John M. Broder, "Obama Opposes Trade Sanctions in Climate Bill," *New York Times*, June 29, 2009.

49. Paul Krugman, "Cassandras of Climate," *New York Times*, September 28, 2009, at www.nytimes.com/2009/09/28/opinion/28krugman.html.

50. Massachusetts Institute of Technology, "Climate Change Odds Much Worse Than Thought: New Analysis Shows Warming Could Be Double Previous Estimates," *MIT News*, May 19, 2009, at http://web.mit.edu/newsoffice/2009/roulette-0519.html#.

51. As Chomsky noted in "Coups, UNASUR, and the U.S."

52. Barack Obama, "A World That Stands as One," Berlin, July 24, 2008, at www .huffingtonpost.com/2008/07/24/obama-in-berlin-video-of_n_114771.html.

53. Christian Schwagerl, "Obama Has Failed the World on Climate Change," *Spiegel Online*, November 17, 2009, at www.spiegel.de/international/world/0,1518,661678,00 .html.

54. David Lindorff, "Barack Obama as the Manchurian Candidate," *CounterPunch*, November 30, 2009, at www.counterpunch.org/lindorff11302009.html.

55. Naomi Klein, "Obama's Bad Influence," *The Nation* (October 15, 2009).

56. Harri, "The Real Reason Obama Is Not Making Much Progress."

57. Schwagerl, "Obama Has Failed the World."

58. J. Broder, "Many Goals Remain Unmet in 5 Nations' Climate Deal," *New York Times*, December 18, 2009; S. Goldenburg and A. Stratton, "Barack Obama's Speech Disappoints and Fuels Frustration at Copenhagen," *The Guardian*, December 18, 2009.

59. George Monbiot, "Requiem for a Crowded Planet," *The Guardian*, December 21, 2009.

60. Peter Brown, "Obama: Washington Liberal, Copenhagen Conservative," *Wall Street Journal*, December 16, 2009.

61. Krugman, "Cassandras of Climate."

62. "Obama Nominates Pesticide Executive to Chief Agricultural Negotiator in the Office of the U.S. Trade Representative," *Democracy Now*, November 17, 2009, at www .democracynow.org/2009/11/17/obama_nominates_pesticide_executive_to_be. On CropLife's memo to the First Lady, see Bonnie McCarvel, Executive Director of the Mid-America CropLife Association and Janet Braun, CropLife Ambassador Coordinator, "MACA Letter to White House About Organic Garden," March 26, 2009, at www.croplife.com/news/?storyid=1657.

63. Catherine Mayer, "Europe's Ambassadorial Angst," *Swampland—TIME.com*, July 3, 2009, at swampland.blogs.time.com/2009/07/03/europes-ambassadorial-angst.

64. Peter Baker, "Favorites of Left Don't Make Obama's Court List," *New York Times*, May 26, 2009.

65. Steve Levine and Theo Francis, "Sotomayor: A Moderate on Business Issues," *Business Week*, May 26, 2009, at www.businessweek.com/bwdaily/dnflash/content/ may2009/db20090526_819200.htm.

66. David Sirota, "Blacklisting Progressives: The Untold Story Beneath the Daschle Headlines," *Open Left*, February 4, 2009, at www.commondreams.org/view/2009/02/04-1.

67. Consistent with the wider and powerful judgment of corporate media and big money-campaign financiers. See Paul Street, "A Very Narrow Spectrum: Even John Edwards Is Too Far Left for the U.S. Plutocracy," *ZNet Sustainer Commentary*, August 29, 2007, at www.zmag.org/sustainers/content/2007-08/29street.cfm; Paul Street, "A Message from the Corporate Plutocracy," February 5, 2008, at http://liblit.wordpress.com/ 2008/02/05/a-message-from-the-american-corporate-plutocracy-by-paul-street/.

68. See Kate Adams and Charles Derber, *The New Feminized Majority* (Boulder, CO: Paradigm Publishers, 2008), 67–75; Noam Chomsky, *Failed States: The Abuse of Power and the Assault on Democracy* (New York: Metropolitan Books, 2006), 205–250; Chicago Council on Foreign Relations, *Global Views* (Chicago: Chicago Council on Foreign Relations, 2004); and Paul Street, "Americans' Progressive Opinions v. the Shadow Cast on Society by Big Business," *ZNet Sustainer Commentary*, May 15, 2008, at www.zcommunications.org/zspace/commentaries/3491.

69. Amy Goodman, "Van Jones and the Boycott of Glenn Beck," *Truthdig*, September 8, 2001, at www.truthdig.com/report/item/20090908_van_jones_and_the_boycott_of_beck/?ln.

70. Phillip Elliot, "Obama: 'We Can't Govern Out of Anger," *Huffington Post*, March 23, 2009, at www.huffingtonpost.com/2009/03/23/obama-we-cant-govern-out_n_177 936.html.

71. Congressional Quarterly, "Economic Director Summers on 'Meet the Press,'" January 25, 2009, at www.cqpolitics.com/wmspage.cfm?docID=news-000003017643; "Obama Team Launches New Plan to Buy Bad Assets from Banks," *PBS NewsHour*, March 23, 2009, at http://webcache.googleusercontent.com/search?q=cache:L8-CQSqJ TyoJ:www.pbs.org/newshour/bb/business/jan-june09/summers_03-23.html +Lawrence +Summers+and+PBS+News+Hour+and+2009+and+can't+let+our+rage&cd=1&hl=en&c t=clnk&gl=us.

72. *New York Times*, March 26, 2009.

73. Fay Fiore and Mark Barabak, "Audacity and Ambition: Obama Begins Leading America in a New Direction," *Los Angeles Times*, April 19, 2009.

74. Greider, "Obama Told Us to Speak."

75. "Conservative Solutions to a Radical Crisis," *Real News Network*, February 13, 2009, http://therealnews.com/t/index.php?option=com_content&task=view&id=31& Itemid=74&jumival=3301.

76. MacArthur, "Obama Is Far from a Radical Reformer."

77. Simon Johnson, "The Quiet Coup," *The Atlantic*, May 2009, at www.theatlantic .com/doc/200905/imf-advice.

78. Chomsky, "Crisis and Hope."

79. Baker, "Barack Hoover Obama," 37.

80. Nomi Prins, "Obama Banking Too Much on Banks," *Mother Jones*, September 14, 2009, at www.motherjones.com/politics/2009/09/obama-banking-too-much-banks.

81. Niall Ferguson, "Wall Street's New Gilded Age," *Newsweek*, September 21, 2009, 54.

82. Rich, "Even Glenn Beck."

83. Bob Herbert, "Safety Nets for the Rich," *New York Times*, October 20, 2009.

84. Gretchen Morgenson, "Wall Street Follies: The Next Act," *New York Times*, October 25, 2009.

85. Jack Rasmus, "Financial Fragility, One Year Later," *Z Magazine*, November 2009, 18–19.

86. Robert Scheer, "Obama's Presidency Isn't Too Big to Fail," *The Nation*, September 16, 2009.

87. Mark Silva, "Only Half Now Like President," *Chicago Tribune*, August 28, 2009.

88. Maureen Dowd, "Fie, Fatal Flaw," *New York Times*, October 18, 2009.

89. Jason DeParle and Robert Gebeloff, "Food Stamp Use Soars," *New York Times*, November 28, 2009.

90. "Obama Sees Trend of Corporate Recover Without Job Growth," *USA Today*, December 4, 2009.

91. Paul Krugman, "The Jobs Imperative," *New York Times*, November 30, 2009.

92. Jackie Calmes, "Obama Turns to Job Creation but Warns of Limited Funds," *New York Times*, December 4, 2009.

93. "Obama Sees Trend."

94. Paul Krugman, "Taxing the Speculators," *New York Times*, November 27, 2009.

95. Obama to King, *State of the Union*.

96. "Barack Obama: King of Corporate Welfare," Huffington Post, April 24, 2009.

97. King, "A Time to Break the Silence."

Notes to Chapter Two

1. Jeremy Scahill, speech to "Socialism 2009," conference of the International Socialist Organization, June 20, 2009.

2. *Common Dreams*, November 9, 2009.

3. *ZNet*, October 13, 2009.

4. Matthew Rothschild, "Obama Steals Bush's Speech Writers," *The Progressive*, December 2, 2009, at www.progressive.org/wx120209.html.

5. John Pilger, "Media Lies and the War Drive Against Iran," *Pakistan Daily*, October 15, 2009, at www.daily.pk/media-lies-and-the-war-drive-against-iran-12189/.

6. www.wgal.com/politics/21917001/detail.html.

7. See Paul Street, "Imperial Temptations: John Edwards, Barack Obama, and the Myth of Post–World War II United States Benevolence," *ZNet*, May 28, 2007, at www.zmag.org/content/showarticle.cfm?ItemID=12928; Paul Street, "'We've Done More Than Talk,'" *Empire and Inequality Report*, no. 7 (January 19, 2009), at www.zmag.org/content/showarticle.cfm?ItemID=11895.

8. Stephen Zunes, "Barack Obama on the Middle East," *Foreign Policy in Focus*, January 10, 2008, at www.fpif.org/fpiftxt/4886.

9. Flyer from "Obama for America" (Des Moines, IA, November 2007).

10. See Paul Street, *Barack Obama and the Future of American Politics* (Boulder, CO: Paradigm Publishers, 2008), 136–155.

11. Anthony Arnove, "Moved On from the Struggle," *Socialist Worker*, March 13, 2009, at http://socialistworker.org/2009/03/13/moved-on-from-the-struggle.

12. Tom Curley, "Army Chief Says US Ready to Be in Iraq 10 Years," Associated Press, May 26, 2009.

13. Noam Chomsky, "Crisis and Hope: Theirs and Ours" (speech at Riverside Church, New York City, June 12, 2009), at www.democracynow.org/2009/7/3/noam_chomsky_on_crisis_and_hope; Alissa Rubin, "U.S. Moves Ahead with Vote on Security Pact," *New York Times*, June 10, 2009. As Chomsky noted, "The current U.S. efforts

to prevent the legally required referendum are extremely revealing. Sometimes they're called 'democracy promotion.'"

14. Ernesto Londono, "Iraq May Hold a Vote on U.S. Withdrawal: Troops Could Be Forced to Leave Early," *Washington Post*, August 18, 2009, at www.washingtonpost.com/wp-dyn/content/article/2009/08/17/AR2009081700949.html?sid=ST2009081701038.

15. Ibid.

16. Robert Scheer, "Obama's Presidency Isn't Too Big to Fail," *The Nation*, September 16, 2009, at www.thenation.com/doc/20090928/scheer.

17. Scahill and Arnove, "Rebranding War and Occupation."

18. Edward S. Herman and David Peterson, "'Obama's Foreign Policy Report Card': Juan Cole Grades His President—and Very Positively," *MR Zine*, November 9, 2009, at www.monthlyreview.org/mrzine/hp091109.html, citing Jeremy Scahill, "Obama Has 250,000 Contractors in Iraq and Afghan Wars, Increases Number of Mercenaries," *Rebel Reports*, June 1, 2009. See also Moshe Schwartz, *Department of Defense Contractors in Iraq and Afghanistan: Background and Analysis* (Washington, DC: Congressional Research Service, September 21, 2009 [posted to the Web site of the Federation of American Scientists]); Peter Grier, "US Use of Private Contractors in War Hits Record High," *Christian Science Monitor*, September 1, 2009; and James Glantz, "Contractors Outnumber U.S. Troops in Afghanistan," *New York Times*, September 2, 2009.

19. Steven Lee Meyers and Helene Cooper, "In Baghdad, Obama Presses Iraqi Leaders to Unite Factions," *New York Times*, April 7, 2009.

20. Tom Engelhardt, "The Corpse on the Gurney: The Success Mantra in Iraq," *Antiwar.com*, January 18, 2008, at www.antiwar.com/engelhardt/ ?articleid=12229.

21. Nir Rosen, "The Death of Iraq," *Current History*, December 2007, 31.

22. "Noam Chomsky on US Expansion of Afghan Occupation," *Democracy Now*, April 3, 2009, at www.democracynow.org/2009/4/3/noam.

23. Julian Borger, "Pressure on Harmad Karzai to Scrap Afghan Women's Law," *The Guardian*, April 1, 2009, at www.truthout.org/040209WA.

24. ABC News, "President Obama Calls New Women-Oppressing Afghan Law Abhorrent—but Suggests It Won't Change U.S. Mission," April 4, 2009, at http://blogs.abcnews.com/politicalpunch/2009/04/president-oba-4.html.

25. Ibid.

26. Glen Ford, "First Black President Defeats U.S. Antiwar Movement," *Black Agenda Report*, April 15, 2009, at www.blackagendareport.com/?q=content/first-black-president-defeats-us-antiwar-movement.

27. Dennis Sullivan, "Kerry: Administration Lacks 'Real Strategy' for Handling Pakistan," ABC News, April 22, 2009, at http://abcnews.go.com/story?id=7400721.

28. Agence France-Presse, "Obama Makes Pakistan Center of Al-Qaeda War," March 28, 2009, at http://au.news.yahoo.com/a/-/world/5460242/obama-makes-pakistan-center-alqaeda-war/.

29. Juan Cole, "Obama's Domino Theory," *Salon*, March 30, 2009, at www.salon.com/opinion/feature/2009/03/30/afghanistan/.

30. James Traub, "Can Pakistan Be Governed?" *New York Times Magazine*, April 5, 2009, 28; Cole, "Obama's Domino Theory."

31. James Blitz et al., "Swat Outlook 'Pretty Bleak' for Pakistan," *Financial Times*, May 13, 2009.

32. David Kilcullen and Andrew McDonald Exum, "Death from Above, Outrage Down Below," *New York Times*, May 17, 2009.

33. Jane Mayer, "The Predator War," *New Yorker*, October 26, 2009, 36–37.

34. Ibid., 37.

35. Ibid., 37–38.

36. Ibid., 40.

37. Kathy Kelly, "Visitors and Hosts in Pakistan," *CounterPunch*, June 10, 2009; Kathy Kelly and Dan Pearson, "Down and Out in Shah Mansoor," *CounterPunch*, June 11, 2009; Kathy Kelly, "Now We See You, Now We Don't," *CounterPunch*, June 25, 2009; Dan Pearson and Kathy Kelly, "The Rotten Fruits of War," *CounterPunch*, October 22, 2009.

38. Herman and Peterson, "'Obama's Foreign Policy Report Card.'"

39. "Exclusive: Al Jazeera-Pakistan Survey," *Al Jazeera*, August 13, 2009, at http://english.aljazeera.net/focus/2009/08/2009888238994769.html; Owen Fay, "Pakistanis See US as Big Threat," *Al Jazeera*, August 13, 2009, at http://english.aljazeera.net/news/asia/2009/08/20098910857878664.html; Herman and Peterson, "'Obama's Foreign Policy Report Card.'"

40. "Secretary of State Hillary Rodham Clinton Participates in 'Townterview' with Prominent Women Journalists," Islamabad, Pakistan, October 30, 2009, cited and quoted in Herman and Peterson, "'Obama's Foreign Policy Report Card.'"

41. Justin Raimondo, "Hillary's Ill-Will Tour," *Antiwar.com*, November 2, 2009, cited in Herman and Peterson, "'Obama's Foreign Policy Report Card.'"

42. Michael Phillips, "'Army Deploys Old Tactic in PR War," *Wall Street Journal*, June 1, 2009.

43. Ibid.

44. Carlotta Gall and Taimoor Shah, "Civilian Deaths Imperil Support for Afghan War," *New York Times*, May 6, 2009.

45. Ibid.

46. Christina Boyle, "President Obama Calls Air Force One Flyover 'Mistake' After Low-Flying Plane Terrifies New York," *New York Daily News*, April 28, 2009; Michel Muskai, "Presidential Plane's Photo-Op over New York Cost as Much as $357,000," *Los Angeles Times*, May 9, 2009; Peter Nicholas, "Louis Caldera Resigns over Air Force One Flyover Fiasco," *Los Angeles Time*, May 9, 2009.

47. Paul Street, "Niebuhr Lives, Civilians Die in the Age of Obama," *ZNet*, June 15, 2009, at www.zmag.org/znet/viewArticle/21701.

48. Alexander Cockburn, "How Long Does it Take?" *CounterPunch*, May 23 2009, at www.counterpunch.org/cockburn05222009.html.

49. Tom Engelhardt, "The Pressure of an Expanding War," *TomDispatch.com*, May 21, 2009, at www.tomdispatch.com/post/175074/the_pressure_of_an_expanding_war.

50. "Obama Requests $83.4 Billion More for War Spending," *Los Angeles Times*, April 10, 2009, at www.google.com/search?hl=en&q=obama+and+supplemental+funding&start=0&sa=N.

51. Barack Obama, "Remarks by President and Wreath-Laying Ceremony at the Pentagon Memorial," September 11, 2009, at www.whitehouse.gov/the_press_office/Remarks-by-the-President-at-Wreath-Laying-Ceremony-at-the-Pentagon-Memorial/.

52. Obama Speech to New Yorkers, September 11, 2009, at www.nydailynews.com/opinions/2009/09/11/2009-09-11_obamas_message_on_911.html.

53. Stephen Walt, "The Safe Haven Myth," *Foreign Policy*, August 18, 2009, at http://walt.foreignpolicy.com/posts/2009/08/18/the_safe_haven_myth; Stephen Walt, interview by Amy Goodman, *Democracy Now*, August 25, 2009, at www.democracynow.org/2009/8/25/the_safe_haven_myth_harvard_prof.

54. Paul R. Pillar, "Who's Afraid of a Terrorist Haven," *Washington Post*, September 16, 2009, at www.washingtonpost.com/wp-dyn/content/article/2009/09/15/AR2009091502977_pf.html.

55. ABC Television, March 3, 2008.

56. Debate transcript archived by the *Austin Chronicle* at www.austinchronicle.com/gyrobase/News/Blogs/?oid=oid:595243.

57. Noam Chomsky, *Hegemony or Survival: America's Quest for Global Dominance* (New York: Metropolitan Books, 2003), 199–206. See also Rajul Mahajan, *The New Crusade: America's War on Terrorism* (New York: Monthly Review Press, 2002), 21.

58. Marjorie Cohn, "End the Occupation of Iraq and Afghanistan," *Znet*, July 30, 2008, at www.zcommunications.org/znet/viewArticle/18303.

59. Mahajan, *The New Crusade*, 21.

60. Abid Aslam, "Polls Question Support for Military Campaign," Inter Press Service, October 8, 2001; Gallup International, Gallup International Poll on Terrorism, September 2001; Herman and Peterson, "'Obama's Foreign Policy Report Card.'"

61. Noam Chomsky, "The World According to Washington," *Asia Times*, February 28, 2008.

62. Jennifer Agiesta and Jon Cohen, "Public Opinion in U.S. Turns Against War," *Washington Post*, August 20, 2009, at www.washingtonpost.com/wp-dyn/content/article/2009/08/19/AR2009081903066.html.

63. Yochi Dreazen, "Call for an Afghan Surge: Pentagon Endorses More Troops, Obama Finds Allies in GOP," *Wall Street Journal*, September 16, 2009.

64. Agiesta and Cohen, "Public Opinion."

65. Quoted in Dreazen, "Call for an Afghan Surge."

66. Peter Baker, "Palin Sides with Obama on Pakistan," at http://thecaucus.blogs.nytimes.com/2009/09/08/palin-sides-with-obama-on-afghanistan.

67. Ross Douthat, "A War President?" *New York Times*, September 28, 2009, at www.nytimes.com/2009/09/28/opinion/28douthat.html.

68. Gabriel Kolko, "Escalation Is Futile," *The Age* (Australia), September 23, 2009.

69. Gabriel Kolko, *Confronting the Third World: United States Foreign Policy, 1945–1980* (New York: Pantheon Books, 1988); Gabriel Kolko, *Century of War: Politics, Conflicts, and Society Since 1914* (New York: New Press, 1994); Gabriel Kolko, *Another Century of War?* (New York: New Press, 2002).

70. Kolko, *Another Century of War.*

71. I am quoting from an e-mail communication from Portland, Oregon–based progressive activist Kelly Gerling, September 24, 2009.

72. Alexander Cockburn, "War and Peace," *CounterPunch*, October 9, 2009, at www.counterpunch.org/cockburn10092009.html; www.tomdispatch.com/post/175118.

73. Ibid.

74. Jennifer Loven and Anne Gearan, "Afghan Buildup Involves 30,000 Troops," Associated Press, December 1, 2009.

75. David Lindorff, "Barack Obama as the Manchurian Candidate," *CounterPunch*, November 30, 2009, at www.counterpunch.org/lindorff11302009.html.

76. Martin Luther King Jr., "A Time to Break the Silence," April 4, 1967, in James M. Washington, ed., *A Testament of Hope: The Essential Writings and Speeches of Martin Luther King Jr.* (San Francisco: HarperCollins, 1991).

77. Christi Parsons and Julian E. Barnes, "Pricing an Afghanistan Troop Buildup Is No Simple Calculation," *Los Angeles Times*, November 23, 2009.

78. Bob Herbert, "A Tragic Mistake," *New York Times*, December 1, 2009.

79. Please see Paul Street, *Empire and Inequality: America and the World Since 9/11* (Boulder, CO: Paradigm Publishers, 2004), which was written at the height of the self-described "war president" George W. Bush's reign, but is equally applicable to the first year of the "progressive" presidency of Barack Obama. winner of the Nobel Peace Prize.

80. Tom Engelhardt, " A Military That Wants its Way," *TomDispatch*, September 24, 2009, at www.tomdispatch.com/post/175118.

81. "Text of Obama's Speech on Afghanistan," December 1, 2009, at www.cbsnews.com/blogs/2009/12/01/politics/politicalhotsheet/entry5855894.shtml.

82. As Cohn noted in the summer of 2008, "Resolutions 1368 and 1373 condemned the September 11 attacks, and ordered the freezing of assets; the criminalizing of terrorist activity; the prevention of the commission of and support for terrorist attacks; the taking of necessary steps to prevent the commission of terrorist activity, including the sharing of information; and urged ratification and enforcement of the international conventions against terrorism." See Cohn, "End the Occupation of Iraq and Afghanistan."

83. Chomsky, "The World According to Washington." See also Chomsky, *Hegemony or Survival*, 200.

84. "Text of Obama's Speech on Afghanistan."

85. See Mahajan, *The New Crusade*, 28–31; and Chomsky, *Hegemony or Survival*, 198–202.

86. *The Guardian*, October 14, 2001.

87. Rothschild, "Obama Steals Bush's Speech Writers." Rothschild compared Obama's airbrushed historical account with the following passage from Bush's 2004 State of the Union address: "America is a Nation with a mission, and that mission comes from our most basic beliefs," he said. "We have no desire to dominate, no ambitions of empire. Our aim is a democratic peace—a peace founded upon the dignity and rights of every man and woman. America acts in this cause with friends and allies at our side, yet we understand our special calling: This great Republic will lead the cause of freedom."

88. Herman and Peterson, "'Obama's Foreign Policy Report Card.'"

89. CNN, "NATO: Airstrike Killed Afghan Women, Children," October 1, 2009, at http://www.cnn.com/2009/WORLD/asiapcf/10/01/afghanistan.nato.airstrike/.

90. Ibid.

91. Saeed Shah and Warren P. Strobel, "Iraq Redux? Obama Seeks Funds for Obama Super-Embassy," *McClatchy Newspapers*, May 27, 2009, at http://www.mcclatchydc .com/251/story/68952.html; Noam Chomsky, "War, Peace, and Obama's Nobel," *In These Times*, November 5, 2009.

92. Paul Craig Roberts, "Another War in the Works," Information Clearing House, September 29, 2009; Mark Hosenball, "Intelligence Agencies Say No New Nukes in Iran," *Newsweek*, September 16, 2009, at www.newsweek.com/id/215529; John Pilger, "Media Lies and the War Drive Against Iran," *Pakistan Daily*, October 15, 2009, at www.daily.pk/media-lies-and-the-war-drive-against-iran-12189/.

93. "UN Nuclear Agency Head Denies Withholding Information on Iran's Nuclear Program," United Nations Radio, September 7, 2009, at www.unmultimedia.org/radio/english/detail/81066.html.

94. "Ultimate Bunker Buster: U.S. Military Speeds Planning for 13-Ton Bomb," *Daily Mail*, October 13, 2009; Chomsky, "War, Peace, and Obama's Nobel."

95. Mamoon Alabbasi, "No Change in USA's 'Mafia Principle,'" *Media Lens Message Board*, November 3, 2009, at http://members5.boardhost.com/medialens/msg/1257 200905.html.

96. Ibid.

97. John Pilger, "Iran's Nuclear Threat Is a Lie," *New Statesman*, October 1, 2009, at www.newstatesman.com/international-politics/2009/10/iran-nuclear-pilger-obama.

98. For comprehensive reflections, see Noam Chomsky, "Turning Point?" *ZNet*, June 8, 2009, at http://www.zcommunications.org/znet/viewArticle/21649. Herman and Peterson, "'Obama's Foreign Policy Report Card.'"

99. Phyllis Bennis, "Netanyahu Speaks: The Israel-Palestine Ball Remains in Obama's Court," Institute for Policy Studies, June 16, 2009, at http://www.ips-dc.org/articles/netanyahu_speaks_the_israel-palestine_ball_remains_in_obamas_court; Chomsky, "Turning Point?"

100. Sonja Karkar, "Letter to Obama," *ZNet*, October 13, 2009, at www.zcommunications.org/znet/viewArticle/22865.

101. UN News Center, "UN Missions Finds Evidence of War Crimes," September 15, 2009, at http://www.un.org/apps/news/story.asp?NewsID=32057&Cr=palestin&Cr1=.

102. Naomi Klein, "Obama's Bad Influence," *The Nation*, October 14, 2009.

103. Glen Greenwald, "Charles Freeman Fails the Loyalty Test," *Salon*, March 10, 2009, at www.salon.com/opinion/greenwald/2009/03/10/freeman/.

104. Noam Chomsky, "Elections 2008 and Obama's Vision," *Z Magazine*, February 2008.

105. Seymour Hersh, "Syria Calling," *New Yorker*, April 9, 2009.

106. "President Obama's Inaugural Address: The Full Text," January 20, 2009, at http://www.time.com/time/politics/article/0,8599,1872715,00.html.

107. Chomsky, "Elections 2008"; Chomsky, "Turning Point?"

108. Herman and Peterson, "'Obama's Foreign Policy Report Card.'"

109. Chomsky, "War, Peace, and Obama's Nobel."

110. Pilger, "Iran's Nuclear Threat."

111. Chomsky, "War, Peace, and Obama's Nobel."

112. Eli Lake, "Obama Agrees to Keep Israel's Nukes Secret," *Washington Times*, October 2, 2009, at http://www.washingtontimes.com/news/2009/oct/02/president-obama-has-reaffirmed-a-4-decade-old-secr/.

"The chief nuclear understanding was reached," Lake noted,

at a summit between President Nixon and Israeli Prime Minister Golda Meir that began on Sept. 25, 1969. Avner Cohen, author of "Israel and the Bomb" and the leading authority outside the Israeli government on the history of Israel's nuclear program, said the accord amounts to "the United States passively accepting Israel's nuclear weapons status as long as Israel does not unveil publicly its capability or test a weapon."

There is no formal record of the agreement nor have Israeli nor American governments ever publicly acknowledged it. In 2007, however, the Nixon library declassified a July 19, 1969, memo from national security adviser Henry Kissinger that comes closest to articulating U.S. policy on the issue. That memo says, "While we might ideally like to halt actual Israeli possession, what we really want at a minimum may be just to keep Israeli possession from becoming an established international fact."

113. Michael Brull, "Obama Just Updated U.S. Double-Speak," *New Matilda*, June 11, 2009, at http://newmatilda.com/print/6154; U.S. Liberals, "Barack Obama's Stirring 2002 Speech Against the Iraq War," October 2002, at http://usliberals.about.com/od/extraordinaryspeeches/a/Obama2002War.htm.

114. John Pomfret, "Obama's Meeting with the Dalai Lama Is Delayed," *Washington Post*, October 5, 2009, at www.washingtonpost.com/wp-dyn/content/article/2009/10/04/AR2009100403262_pf.html; Maureen Dowd, "Fie, Fatal Flaw!" *New York Times*, October 18, 2009; Alex Spillus, "Barack Obama Cancels Meeting with Dalai Lama to 'Keep China Happy,'" *Telegraph*, October 5, 2009, at www.telegraph.co.uk/news/world news/northamerica/usa/barackobama/6262938/Barack-Obama-cancels-meeting-with -Dalai-Lama-to-keep-China-happy.html#.

115. Gilbert Achcar, "Obama's Cairo Speech," *ZNet*, June 6, 2009, at www.zcommu-nications.org/znet/v: iewArticle/21635.

116. Jon Alterman quoted in Michael Scherer, "Obama Seeks to Win Muslim Hearts and Minds," *Time*, June 3, 2009, at www.time.com/time/nation/article/0,8599,1902334,00.html.

117. Jackie Calmes and Robert Pear, "Obama Plans Major Shift in Spending," *New York Times*, February 27, 2009.

118. Winslow T. Wheeler, "The Pentagon Spigot Is Wide Open," *CounterPunch*, June 17, 2009, at www.counterpunch.org/wheeler060172009.html.

119. Katherine McIntire Peters, "Defense Budget Portends Difficult Trade-Offs," *Government Executive*, August 12, 2009, at www.govexec.com/dailyfed/0809/081209 kp1.htm. *Government Executive* describes itself as "government's business news daily and the premier Web site for federal managers and executives."

120. Matthew Cardinale. "Nukes Agency Pushes New Bomb Production," Inter Press Service, September 30, 2009, at www.ipsnews.net/print.asp?idnews=48654; Anthony Dimaggio, "Nuclear Hypocrisy," *ZNet*, October 10, 2009.

121. *New York Times* Editors, "The Fallout of a Reversal on Missile Defense," *New York Times*, September 17, 2009, at http://roomfordebate.blogs.nytimes.com/2009/09/17/the-fallout-of-a-reversal-on-missile-defense/?hp.

122. Pilger, "Iran's Nuclear Threat Is a Lie."

123. Alexander Cockburn, "NATO: Still Mission-Creeping at 60," *The Nation*, March 18, 2009; Herman and Peterson, "'Obama's Foreign Policy Report Card'"; Alexander Cockburn, "From Twin Towers to Twin Camelots," *CounterPunch*, April 4, 2009, at www.counterpunch.org/cockburn04032009.html; Rick Rozoff, "ABC of West's Global Military Network," *Stop NATO*, October 28, 2009, at http://rickrozoff.wordpress.com/.

124. John Pilger, "Power, Illusion, and America's Last Taboo," *International Socialist Review*, November–December 2009, 26.

125. Juan Cole, "Obama's Foreign Policy Report Card," *Salon*, October 27, 2009; Herman and Peterson, "'Obama's Foreign Policy Report Card.'"

126. Herman and Peterson, "'Obama's Foreign Policy Report Card.'"

127. Tom Fawthrop, "'New Beginning' on Cuba Is a Dead End," *The Guardian*, October 28, 2009, at www.guardian.co.uk/commentisfree/2009/oct/28/cuba-obama-us-sanctions-embargo.

128. Rory Carroll, "Obama Offers Olive Branch to Chavez, Ortega, and Latin America," *The Guardian*, April 19, 2009, at www.guardian.co.uk/world/2009/apr/19/obama-latin-america.

129. John Pilger, "War Is Peace. Ignorance Is Strength," *The Guardian*, October 17, 2009.

130. Teresa Arreaza, "ALBA: Bolivarian Alternative," *Venezuelanalysis*, January 30, 2004, at www.venezuelanalysis.com/analysis/339. Paraguay (currently under left-leaning political leadership) may well enter ALBA in the near future. See "Destacan posible incorporación de Paraguay al Alba," *Agencia Bolivariana de Noticia*, October 17, 2009, at www.abn.info.ve/noticia.php?articulo=203394&lee=16.

131. Raul Zibechi, "Massacre in the Amazon: The U.S.-Peru Free Trade Government Sparks a Battle over Land and Resources," *America's Program Special Report*, June 16, 2009, at http://americas.irc.online.org/am/6191; Julio Cesar Tello, "Obama Ignores Peru," *Karikuy*, January 30, 2009, at http://karikuy.blogspot.com/2009/01/obama-ignores-peru.html; John Gibler, "Indigenous Protest and State Violence in the Amazon," *Huffington Post*, June 19, 2009, at www.huffingtonpost.com/john-gibler/indigenous-protest-and-st_b_214901.html.

132. TomP, "Obama Supports Peru Trade Pact That Unions and Many Progressives Oppose," *Daily Kos*, October 11, 2007, at www.dailykos.com/story/2007/10/11/62226/860; Tricia Miller and Mark Murray, "Edwards Opposes Obama on Peru," MSNBC, November 4, 2007, at http://firstread.msnbc.msn.com/archive/2007/11/04/447267.aspx; David Sirota, "Obama Says He Will Vote for NAFTA Expansion," *Huffington Post*, October 9, 2007, at www.huffingtonpost.com/david-sirota/breaking-obama-says-he-wi_b_67780.html.

133. George Ciccareillo-Maher, "The Counter-Revolution Will Not be Tweeted," *CounterPunch*, July 5, 2009, at www.counterpunch.org/maher07032009.html.

134. Albert Vallente Thoreson, "Why Zelaya's Actions Were Legal," *CounterPunch*, July 1, 2009, at www.counterpunch.org/thorensen07012009.html; Mark Weisbrot, "Does the U.S. Back the Honduran Coup?" *The Guardian*, July 1, 2009, at www.guardian .co.uk/commentisfree/cifamerica/2009/jul/01/honduras-zelaya-coup-obama.

135. Eva Gollinger, "Obama's First Coup d'Etat: Honduran President Has Been Kidnapped," *Venezuelanalaysis*, June 29, 2009, at www.venezuelanalysis.com/analysis/4554; Nicholas Kozloff, "The Coup in Honduras: Obama's Real Message to Latin America?" *CounterPunch*, June 29, 2009, at www.counterpunch.org/kozloff06292009.html.

136. Mary Beth Sheridan, "U.S. Condemns Honduran Coup: Still, Administration Steps Lightly," *Washington Post*, June 30, 2009, at www.washingtonpost.com/wp-dyn/ content/article/2009/06/29/AR2009062904239.html.

137. Roberto Lovato, "Obama Has the Power and Responsibility to Restore Democracy in Honduras," *Huffington Post*, June 29, 2009, at www.huffingtonpost.com/roberto-lovato/ obama-has-the-power-and-r_b_222170.html; Mark Weisbrot, "Deal or No Deal in Honduras?" *The Guardian*, November 4, 2009.

138. Noam Chomsky, *Interventions* (San Francisco: City Lights Books, 2007), 89–92.

139. Eva Gollinger, "Washington and the Coup in Honduras: Here's the Evidence," *Postcards from the Revolution*, July 15, 2009, at www.chavezcode.com/2009/07/washington -coup-in-honduras-here-is.html.

140. Sheridan, "U.S. Condemns Honduran Coup."

141. "U.S. Lobbyists with Clinton Ties Hired to Defend Honduran Coup Regime," *Democracy Now*, July 15, 2009, read at www.democracynow.org/2009/7/15/honduras; Bill Van Auken, "Ex-Clinton Aides Advising Honduran Coup Regime," World Socialist Web Site, July 15, 2009, at www.wsws.org/articles/2009/jul2009/hond-j15.shtml.

142. Ivan Castro and Sean Mattson, "Ousted Zelaya Sets Foot Back in Honduras— Briefly," Reuters, July 24, 2009, at www.reuters.com/article/marketsNews/idINN 2445650720090725?rpc=44.

143. "Obama Calls for Order," FOX News, June 28, 2009, at www.foxnews.com/ politics/2009/06/28/obama-calls-order-military-arrests-honduran-president/; Jeremy Scahill, "A Few Thoughts on the Coup in Honduras," *Common Dreams*, June 30, 2009, at www.commondreams.org/view/2009/06/29-11; Greg Grandin, "Democracy Derailed in Honduras," *The Nation*, June 30, 2009, at www.thenation.com/doc/20090713/ grandin/single; Reuters, "U.S. Could Cut Off Aid to Honduras After Coup," *AlterNet*, June 29, 2009, at http://www.alertnet.org/thenews/newsdesk/N29384895.htm.

144. Mark Weisbrot, "Does the U.S. Back the Honduran Coup?" *The Guardian*, July 8, 2009, at http://progreso-weekly.com/2/index.php?option=com_content&view= article&id=1069:fidel-obama-y-nosotros&catid=2:ultima-edicion&Itemid=7.

145. Bill Conroy, "Money Talks in U.S. Policy Toward Honduran Putsch Regime," *The Narcosphere*, September 13, 2009, at http://narcosphere.narconews.com/notebook/ bill-conroy/2009/09/money-talks-us-policy-toward-honduran-putsch-regime; Amy Goodman, "President Zelaya and the Audacity of Action," *Truthdig*, September 22,

2009, at www.truthdig.com/report/item/20090922_president_zelaya_and_the_audacity _of_action/?ln.

146. Weisbrot, "Does the U.S. Back the Honduran Coup?"

147. Herman and Peterson, "'Obama's Foreign Policy Report Card.'"

148. Scahill, "A Few Thoughts." See also Gollinger, "Washington and Honduras."

149. Weisbrot, "Does the U.S. Back the Honduran Coup?" See also Eva Gollinger, "Obama's First Coup d'Etat: Honduran President Has Been Kidnapped," *Venezuelanalaysis*, June 29, 2009, at www.venezuelanalysis.com/analysis/4554; Grandin, "Democracy Derailed in Honduras."

150. Goodman, "President Zelaya."

151. Weisbrot, "Does the U.S. Back the Honduran Coup?"

152. Latin America Working Group, "Zelaya Is Back," at www.lawg.org/index.php ?option=com_content&task=view&id=509&Itemid=64.

153. Ginger Thompson and Ron Nixon, "Leader Ousted, Honduras Hires U.S. Lobbyists," *New York Times*, October 8, 2009.

154. Pilger, "War Is Peace."

155. Eva Gollinger, "Honduras: A Victory for Smart Power," *Postcards from the Revolution*, November 2, 2009, at www.chavezcode.com/2009/11/honduras-victory-for -smart-power.html.

156. Ethan Katz, "Cunning Micheletti Determined to Outfox Zelaya," Council on Hemispheric Affairs, November, 6, 2009, at www.creative-i.info/?p=11864; Herman and Peterson, "'Obama's Foreign Policy Report Card.'"

157. Ginger Thompson, "U.S. Tries to Salvage Honduras Accord," *New York Times*, November 11, 2009.

158. Jean Guy Allard, "The Sordid History of Lewis Amselem, " *Machetera*, September 29, 2009, at http://machetera.wordpress.com/2009/09/29/the-sordid-history-of -lewis-amselem-deputy-u-s-permanent-representative-to-the-oas/.

159. Gollinger, "Honduras."

160. Eva Gollinger, "The Fraud of the Obama Administration's Policies Revealed (Yet Again) in Honduras," *Postcards from the Revolution*, November 6, 2009, at www .chavezcode.com/2009/11/fraud-of-obama-administrations-policies.html.

161. Mary Beth Sheridan, "U.S. and Some Allies at Odds over Honduras Election," *Washington Post*, December 1, 2009; Eva Gollinger, "Bogus Honduran Elections Today: Hypocrites Washington, Costa Rica, Panama, Colombia, and Israel the Only Nations to Recognize the Illegal Elections," *Postcards from the Revolution*, November 29, 2009, at www.chavezcode.com/2009/11/bogus-honduran-elections-today.html; Tamara Pearson, "Venezuela Refuses to Recognize Honduran Elections," *Venezuelanalysis*, November 30, 2009, at www.venezuelanalysis.com/news/4967.

162. Eva Gollinger, "Breaking News: Official U.S. Air Force Document Reveals the True Intentions Behind the U.S.-Colombia Military Agreement," *Postcards from the Revolution*, November 5, 2009, at www.chavezcode.com/2009/11/breaking-news-official -us-air-force.html.

163. "Colombia Wants Greater U.S. Military Presence," *The Guardian*, October 30, 2009.

164. Gollinger, "Breaking News"; Department of the United States Air Force, *Military Construction Program: FY 2010 Budget Estimates, Justification Data Submitted to Congress* (May 2010), at http://www.centrodealerta.org/documentos_desclasificados/original_in_english_air_for.pdf.

165. Gollinger, "Breaking News."

166. Shaun Joseph, "The Coup in Honduras: Perspectives and Prospects," *International Socialist Review*, November–December 2009, 14.

167. Barack Obama, *The Audacity of Hope* (New York: Crown, 2006), 315.

168. Mark Weisbrot, "The Mirage of Progress," *American Prospect*, January 1, 2002, at www.prospect.org/cs/articles?article=the_mirage_of_progress; Mark Weisbrot, "Globalization Fails to Deliver the Goods," *Common Dreams*, August 29, 2002, at www.commondreams.org/views02/0829-05.htm.

169. Alexander Cockburn, "Into the Tunnel," *CounterPunch*, September 5, 2009, at www.counterpunch.org/cockburn09042009.html.

170. Anthony Dimaggio, "Star Wars Redux: Full Spectrum Dominance and Obama's Missile Shield," *ZNet*, September 20, 2009, at www.zmag.org/znet/viewArticle/22647.

171. Jeremy Scahill and Anthony Arnove, "Rebranding War and Occupation," *Socialist Worker*, June 17, 2009, at http://socialistworker.org/2009/06/17/rebranding-war-and-occupation.

172. Ibid.

173. Pilger, "Media Lies."

174. Scahill and Arnove, "Rebranding War and Occupation."

175. Pew Research Center, "Confidence in Obama Lifts U.S. Image Around the World," *Pew Research Center Publications*, July 23, 2009, at http://pewresearch.org/pubs/1289/global-attitudes-survey-2009-obama-lifts-america-image; Peter Baker, "Good Will, but Few Foreign Policy Benefits for Obama," *New York Times*, September 19, 2009.

176. Dominique Moisi, "Obama's American Revolution," *The Guardian*, December 24, 2007.

177. Baker, "Good Will."

178. "Analysis: Chicago's Blow Is a Blow to Obama Too," Associated Press, October 26, 2009, at www.kltv.com/global/story.asp?s=11248703#; Jeff Zeleny and Peter Baker, "For Obama, an Unsuccessful Campaign," *New York Times*, October 2, 2009.

179. Katie Thomas et al., "Critics Assail U.S.O.C After Chicago's Loss," *New York Times*, October 2, 2009.

180. *Common Dreams*, November 9, 2009.

181. Professor Inderjeet Parmar, Dr. Mark Ledwidge, Professor Rob Singh, and Dr. Tim Lynch, "Letter: Scrutiny of U.S. Foreign Policy," *The Guardian*, September 18, 2009, at www.guardian.co.uk/world/2009/sep/18/us-foreign-policy-obama-afghanistan.

182. Karl Ritter and Matt Moore, "President Barack Obama Wins Nobel Peace Prize," Associated Press, October 9, 2009, at http://news.yahoo.com/s/ap/eu_nobel_peace.

183. "Remarks by the President at the Acceptance of the Nobel Peace Prize," Oslo, Norway, December 10, 2009, at www.whitehouse.gov/the-press-office/remarks-president-acceptance-nobel-peace-prize.

184. Ben Feller, "Obama Accepts Nobel Peace Prize with Robust Defense of War," Associated Press, December 10, 2010.

185. "Remarks by the President."

186. *Al Jazeera English*, "Afghans Anger at Obama's Nobel Peace Prize," YouTube, December 10, 2009, at www.youtube.com/watch?v=OBHrnQTinGY&feature=related.

187. "U.S. Kill 63 Civilians, 28 Children in Yemen Air Strikes," Press TV Video Report, December 18, 2009, at www.informationclearinghouse.info/article24226.htm.

188. Barry Grey, "Obama Ordered U.S. Air Strikes on Yemen," World Socialist Web Site, December 21, 2009, at www.wsws.org/articles/2009/dec2009/yeme-d21.shtml. Compare the forthright treatments from Press TV and the World Socialist Web Site with the following propagandistic milquetoast from the *New York Times*: "The United States provided firepower, intelligence and other support to the government of Yemen as it carried out raids . . . to strike at suspected hide-outs of Al Qaeda within its borders, according to officials familiar with the operations. . . . The officials said that the American support was approved by President Obama." Tom Shanker and Mark Landler, "U.S. Aids Yemeni Raids on Al Qaeda,' Officials Say," *New York Times*, December 19, 2009, at www.nytimes.com/2009/12/19/world/middleeast/19yemen.html.

189. "Yemen Opposition Says Government Attack Killed Civilians," Reuters, December 18, 2009.

190. Street, *Barack Obama*.

191. Feller, "Obama Accepts Nobel Peace Prize."

192. http://www.wgal.com/politics/21917001/detail.html.

193. "Norwegian Press Comments on Obama's Acceptance Speech," *Norway Post: Doorway to Norway*, December 13, 2009, at www.norwaypost.no/content/view/22892/26/.

194. *Wall Street Journal* Editors, "Barack Hussein Bush," *Wall Street Journal*, December 5, 2009, at http://online.wsj.com/article/SB124416109792287285.html.

Notes to Chapter Three

1. Quoted in Kevin Sack, "For Public, Obama Didn't Fill in Health Blanks, *New York Times*, July 23, 2009.

2. Chad Terhune and Keith Epstein, "The Health Insurers Have Already Won," *Business Week*, August 6, 2009, at www.businessweek.com/print/magazine/content/09_33/b4143034820260.htm.

3. For a critique of the common liberal narrative claiming that Obama's rapid ascendancy was a remarkably improbable longshot, see Paul Street, "Obama, as Predicted," *ZNet* (November 21, 2009), at http://www.zcommunications.org/obama-as-predicted-by-paul-street.

4. Jeff Zeleny, "Health Debate Fails to Ignite Obama's Grass Roots," *New York Times*, August 15, 2009.

5. Ibid.

6. Edward S. Herman and David Peterson, "Riding the 'Green Wave' at the Campaign for Peace and Democracy and Beyond," *Electric Politics*, July 22, 2009.

7. Sheldon S. Wolin, *Democracy Incorporated: Managed Democracy and the Specter of Inverted Totalitarianism* (Princeton, NJ: Princeton University Press, 2008).

8. Noam Chomsky, *Interventions* (San Francisco: City Lights Books, 2007), 97–100.

9. Charles Derber, *Hidden Power: What You Need to Know to Save Our Democracy* (San Francisco: Berrett-Koehler, 2005), 6–9. See also Adolph Reed Jr., "Sitting This One Out," *The Progressive*, November 2007.

10. Kevin Baker, "Barack Hoover Obama: The Best and the Brightest Blow It Again," *Harper's*, July 2009, 37.

11. Sack, "For Public, Obama Didn't Fill in Health Blanks."

12. On corporate regimes in U.S. history and the distinction between corporate regime Democrats and progressive Democrats, see Derber, *Hidden Power*.

13. Christopher Hitchens, *No One Left to Lie To: The Values of the Worst Family* (New York: Verso Books, 2000), 17–18.

14. Paul Street, "Obama's Corporatist Health Care Speech," *ZNet*, September 12, 2009, at www.zcommunications.org/znet/viewArticle/22580.

15. David Brooks, "The Dime Standard," *New York Times*, September 11, 2009, at http://www.nytimes.com/2009/09/11/opinion/11brooks.html?pagewanted=print.

16. Hitchens, *No One Left to Lie To*, 18.

17. Roger Bybee, "Obama's Health Reform," *Z Magazine*, July–August 2009; Paul Street, "Employment-Based Health Care v. Democracy: Hidden Dimensions of Business Rule," *ZNet*, September 2, 2009, at www.zcommunications.org/znet/viewArticle/22495; Paul Street, "Corporate-Managed Democracy: Health Reform in the Age of Obama," *Z Magazine*, September 2009.

18. Eric Schlosser, *Fast Food Nation: The Dark Side of the All-American Meal* (New York: Perennial, 2002).

19. Brooks, "The Dime Standard."

20. *New York Times*, September 10, 2009.

21. John Bellamy Foster, Hannah Holleman, and Robert W. McChesney, "The U.S. Imperial Triangle and Military Spending," *Monthly Review*, October 2008, at www.monthlyreview.org/081001foster-holleman-mcchesney.php.

22. David Cecere, "New Study Finds 45,000 Deaths Linked Annually to Lack of Health Insurance," *HarvardScience*, September 17, 2009, at www.harvardscience.harvard.edu/medicine-health/articles/new-study-finds-45000-deaths-annually-linked-lack-health-coverage. On the broader hypocrisy, see Paul Street, "Perverted Priorities: One Year Later," *ZNet*, November 5, 2009, at www.zcommunications.org/znet/viewArticle/23068; and Glen Greenwald, "'America's Priorities,' by the Beltway Elite," *Salon*, October 24, 2008, at www.salon.com/news/opinion/glenn_greenwald/?page=2.

23. "Politics Today: Health Reform Meets New Resistance," CBS News, September 15, 2009, at www.cbsnews.com/blogs/2009/09/15/politics/politicalhotsheet/entry531 1990.shtml; Paul Street, "Time to Scrape the Kerry Sticker Off: On Democrats, Values, and the Lakoff Thesis," *ZNet Sustainer Commentary*, June 17, 2005, at www.zmag.org/Sustainers/Content/2005-06/17street.cfm.

24. Terhune and Epstein, "The Health Insurers Have Already Won."

25. Robert Reich, "The Ersatz Public Option," *Huffington Post*, November 19, 2009, at www.huffingtonpost.com/robert-reich/the-ersatz-public-option_b_364396.html.

26. Baker, "Barack Hoover Obama."

27. *New York Times*/CBS Poll, "Confusion over Health Care," September 19–23, 2009, questions 31, 32, and 38, at http://documents.nytimes.com/new-york-times-cbs -news-poll-confusion-over-health-care-tepid-support-for-war#p=15.

28. Mike Allen, "Pelosi Lacks the Votes for Most Sweeping Public Option," *Politico*, October 23, 2009, at www.politico.com/news/stories/1009/28651.html; Ben Pershing, "Obama's 'Trigger' Stance Irks the Hill," *Washington Post Blog*, October 26, 2009, at http://voices.washingtonpost.com/44/2009/10/26/obamas_trigger_stance_irks_the.html.

29. David Sirota. "We've Seen This Trigger Before," *In These Times*, September 12, 2009, at www.inthesetimes.com/article/4885/weve_seen_this_trigger_before/.

30. Ibid.

31. J. Taylor Rush and Alexander Bolton, "Senator Reid Bows to Centrists," *The Hill*, December 14, 2009, at http://thehill.com/homenews/senate/72187-reid-gives-in-to -centrists-on-healthcare-senators-say.

32. ABC News, December 16, 2009, at http://blogs.abcnews.com/politicalpunch/ 2009/12/white-house-says-howard-deans-arguments-against-democrats-health-care -reform-simply-werent-true-sugg.html.

33. John Heilemann, "Obama Lost, Obama Found," *New York*, December 7, 2009, 39.

34. Baker, "Barack Hoover Obama." For some more details on the limits of Obama's approach and public option (what MSNBC's Keith Olbermann calls "public optional"), see Street, "Corporate-Managed Democracy."

35. Heilemann, "Obama Lost."

36. Street, *Barack Obama*; Baker, "Barack Hoover Obama;"; John R. MacArthur, "Obama Is Far from a Radical Reformer," *Providence Journal*, March 19, 2009, at www.projo.com/opinion/contributors/content/CT_rick18_03-18-09_1SDM2BF_v26 .3e689c2.html.

37. Kevin Zeese's comment appeared on my Facebook page after I posted there D. Herszenhorn and C. Hulse, "Democrats Clinch Deal for Deciding Vote on Health Care," *New York Times*, December 19, 2009. Zeese was referring to a March 5th Health Care Summit at the White House, held prior to the legislative process. On Baucus's crit- ical corporate-sponsored and outsized role, see Street, "Corporate-Managed Democracy."

38. *New York Times*/CBS Poll, "Confusion over Health Care," question 57.

39. Data from the Center for Responsive Politics "Open Secrets" Web site.

40. "Obama on Single Payer Health Insurance," June 30, 2003, YouTube video clip, at www.1payer.net/All-Videos/obama-on-single-payer.html. See also YouTube link at www.youtube.com/watch?v=fpAyan1fXCE.

41. "Obama on Single Payer Health Insurance."

42. "Eisenhower's Farewell Address," January 17, 1961, at http://en.wikisource.org/ wiki/Military-Industrial_Complex_Speech.

43. Arundhati Roy, "Democracy's Fading Light," *Outlook India Magazine*, July 13, 2009, at www.outlookindia.com/article.aspx?250418.

Notes to Chapter Four

1. E-mail communication, February 12, 2009.

2. See Paul Street, *Barack Obama and the Future of American Politics* (Boulder, CO: Paradigm Publishers, 2008), 73–121.

3. Richard Wolffe and Darren Briscoe, "Across the Divide: Barack Obama's Road to Racial Reconstruction," *Newsweek*, July 16, 2007.

4. "Barack Obama and the African American Community: A Debate with Michael Eric Dyson and Glen Ford," *Democracy Now*, January 9, 2008.

5. Paul Street, "Obama's Latest 'Beautiful Speech,'" *ZNet Magazine*, March 20, 2008, at www.zcommunications.org/znet/viewArticle/16947; Bill Fletcher, "Obama Race Speech Analysis," *Black Commentator*, March 20, 2008, at www.blackcommentator .com/269/269_cover_obama_race_speech_analysis_ed_bd.html. For more on Obama's race neutralism during the campaign, see these essays of mine: "The Pale Reflection: Barack Obama, Martin Luther King Jr., and the Meaning of the Black Revolution," *ZNet Magazine*, March 16, 2007, at www.zmag.org/content/showarticle.cfm?ItemID =12336; "Barack Obama's White Appeal and the Perverse Racial Politics of the Post– Civil Rights Era," *Black Agenda Report*, June 20, 2007, at www.blackagendareport .com/index.php?option=com_content&task=view&id=254&Itemid=34; "Race and Class in the Democratic Primaries," *ZNet*, April 25, 2008, at www.zcommunications .org/znet/viewArticle/17509.

6. "The Two Nations of Black America: Interview with Henry Louis Gates Jr.," *Frontline*, n.d., at www.pbs.org/wgbh/pages/frontline/shows/race/interviews/gates.html; Paul Street, "Skipping Past Structural Racism: Center Trumps Left in Recent PBS Series on Race in America," *Black Commentator*, April 8, 2004, at www.blackcommentator .com/85/85_think_street.html; Steve Johnson, "Behind Gates: How the Harvard Scholar Is Using His 'Color-Line' PBS as a Wake-Up Call," *Chicago Tribune*, February 3, 2004.

7. "Speech to the NAACP," July 17, 2009, at www.whitehouse.gov/.

8. Ibid.

9. Mumia Abu-Jamal, "Imagine Being Van Jones," *ZNet*, September 22, 2009, at http://axisoflogic.com/artman/publish/Article_57003.shtml.

10. Justin Hyde and Richard Wolf, "President Says He Shouldn't Put Focus on Blacks' Troubles," *USA Today*, December 4, 2009.

11. Glenn Beck, "Obama Has a Deep-Seated Hatred for White People," July 28, 2009, at www.youtube.com/watch?v=MIZDnpPafaA; Amy Goodman, "Van Jones and the Boycott of Glenn Beck," *Huffington Post*, September 8, 2009.

12. "Carter: Wilson's Outburst Based on Racism," Associated Press, September 15, 2009, at www.foxnews.com/politics/elections/2009/09/15/carter-wilsons-outburst -based-racism/; "White House Disputes Carter's Analysis," MSNBC, September 16, 2009, at http://www.msnbc.msn.com/id/32869276/; Steve Holland, "Obama Disagrees with Carter on Race Issue," Reuters, September 16, 2009, at http://news.yahoo.com/ s/nm/20090916/pl_nm/us_usa_carter_racism.

13. Tim Wise, "Socialism as the New Black Bogeyman—Red-Baiting and Racism," *Progressives for Obama*, August 12, 2009, at http://progressivesforobama.blogspot.com/.

14. For a critique and partial appreciation of Wise's thesis, see my essay, "The Racist Red-Baiting of Obama Is About More Than Race Alone," *ZNet*, August 23, 2009. Wise's essay was far too strong. It was a good reminder, along with Carter's statement (which received hearty approval from many U.S. liberals and leftists), that it isn't only the right that drives racialized politics in America. The "left" makes its own contributions.

15. Greg Bluestein, "White House: Criticism of Obama Not Based on Race," Associated Press, September 16, 2009, at www.wwlp.com/dpp/news/politics/whitehouse/nat_ap_dc_white_house_criticism_of_obama_not_based_on_race_200909161522_2872396.

16. John Pilger, "Obama and Empire" (speech to International Socialist Organization, San Francisco, California, July 4, 2009). View and hear the segment at http://louisproyect.wordpress.com/2009/08/18/john-pilger-obama-is-a-corporate-marketing-creation/.

17. Paul Krugman, "Big Table Fantasies," *New York Times*, December 17, 2007; Paul Street, "Angry John Edwards v. KumbayObama," *SleptOn Magazine*, December 28, 2007, at www.slepton.com/slepton/viewcontent.pl?id=1234; Mike Davis, "Obama at Manassas," *New Left Review*, March–April 2009.

18. Celine-Marie Pascale and Katie Beran, "Nowhere to Fall," *Z Magazine*, October 2009, 31.

19. Paul Street, "Race Cowardice from the Top Down," *Black Agenda Report*, April 22, 2009.

20. David Zirin, "Olympics in Chicago: 'Obama's Folly'?" *The Nation*, September 22, 2009; No Games Chicago, Press Release, April 2, 2009, at http://nogames.files.wordpress.com/2009/03/rally_press_release.pdf; "Michelle, Oprah Arrive in Copenhagen," ABC 7 News, September 30, 2009, at http://abclocal.go.com/wls/story?section=news/local&id=7040148; Paul Street, *Racial Oppression in the Global Metropolis: A Living Black Chicago History* (New York: Rowman and Littlefield, 2007), 51, 107, 164, 172, 260, 293, 296.

21. "Police Seek 3 More in Teen's Death," CNN, September 29, 2009, at www.cnn.com/2009/CRIME/09/29/chicago.teen.beating/index.html#cnnSTCText.

22. "Remarks by the President and First Lady to the International Olympic Committee," Copenhagen, Denmark, October 2, 2009, at www.whitehouse.gov/the_press_office/Remarks-By-the-President-And-the-First-Lady-to-the-International-Olympic-Committee.

23. J. Coyden Palmer, "Are Chicago Public School Policies to Blame for Melee That Killed Derrior Albert?" *Chicago Crusader Newspaper*, October 5, 2009, at www.theskanner.com/article/view/id/10458; Street, *Racial Oppression in the Global Metropolis*.

24. Deborah Lynch, "'Turnaround'—the Deadliest Reform of All," *Substance: The Newspaper of Public Education in Chicago*, October 2009, 1, 13.

25. Rubin Navarette Jr., "Obama's Silence on Chicago Crime," CNN (special to CNN), October 2, 2009, at http://edition.cnn.com/2009/POLITICS/10/02/navarrette.chicago.obama.olympics/index.html.

26. Quoted in Maureen Dowd, "Fie, Fatal Flaw!" *New York Times*, October 18, 2009.

27. Peter Baker and Campbell Robertson, "Obama Tells New Orleans Progress Is Being Made," *New York Times*, October 16, 2009.

28. Ibid.

29. Naomi Klein, *The Shock Doctrine: The Rise of Disaster Capitalism* (New York: Metropolitan Books, 2007), 5.

30. Baker and Robertson, "Obama Tells New Orleans."

31. Dowd, "Fie, Fatal Flaw!"

32. Derrick Bell, *Silent Covenants: Brown v. Board of Education and the Unfulfilled Hopes for Racial Reform* (New York: Oxford University Press, 2004), 77–78.

33. Sheryl Cashin, *The Failures of Integration* (New York: PublicAffairs, 2004), xi–xii. See also Leonard Steinhorn and Barbara Diggs-Brown, *By the Color of Our Skin* (New York: Penguin, 2000), 7; Stanley Aronowitz, "Race: the Continental Divide," *The Nation*, March 12, 2001; Paul Street, "A Lott Missing: Rituals of Purification and Deep Racism Denial," *Black Commentator*, December 22, 2002._

34. Marc Lamont Hill, "Not My Brand of Hope: Obama's Politics of Cunning, Compromise, and Concession," *CounterPunch*, February 11, 2008.

35. Quoted in John B. Judis, "American Adam: Obama and the Cult of the New," *New Republic*, March 12, 2008, 24.

36. Jorge Ramos, "The Promise," August 19, 2009, at ImmigrationProf Blog, http://lawprofessors.typepad.com/immigration/2009/08/latino-discontent-with-dhs-and-obama-delay.html.

37. Julia Preston, "Immigration Crackdown with Firings, Not Raids," *New York Times*, September 30, 2009.

38. Ibid.

39. Seth Galinsky, "Health Reform Plan Aimed Against Workers: Measures Target Abortion Rights, Immigrants," *The Militant* 73, no. 37 (September 28, 2009), at www.themilitant.com/2009/7337/733702.html.

40. George Stephanopoulos, "Latino Lawmaker Rips Obama for Making It Harder for Illegals to Buy Private Insurance," ABC News, September 15, 2009, at http://blogs.abcnews.com/george/2009/09/latino-lawmaker-rips-obama-for-making-it-harder-for-illegals-to-buy-private-insurance.html.

41. Galinksy, "Health Reform Plan."

42. Sharon Smith, "Obama and Abortion Rights," *CounterPunch*, May 26, 2009, at www.counterpunch.org/sharon05262009.html.

43. For details and commentary, see Natasha Chart, "This Round Goes to Terrorists, Intractable Believers," *Open Left*, June 10, 2009, at www.openleft.com/tag/Alexia%20Kelley.

44. Sarah Posner, "Abortion Foe to Lead HHS Faith-Based Office," *American Prospect*, June 4, 2009, at www.prospect.org/csnc/blogs/tapped_archive?base_name=abortion_foe_to_lead_hhs_faith&month=06&year=2009.

45. Sarah Posner, "Obama's Faithful Flock," *The Nation*, July 15, 2009, at www.thenation.com/doc/20090803/posner.

46. Ben Fisher, "Obama Flops on Gay Marriage," *Columbia (South Carolina) City Paper*, July 23, 2009, at http://columbiacitypaper.com/index.php/News-Commentary/Commentary/Obama-flops-on-gay-marriage.html; "Obama Facing Gay Groups' Growing Anger," ABC News, June 15, 2009.

47. John Cloud, "Obama, the Gay-Marriage Flip-Flopper," *Time*, August 19, 2009, at www.time.com/time/printout/0,8816,1917344,00.html.
48. "Obama Facing Gay Groups."
49. Ibid.
50. Peter Baker, "Favorites of Left Don't Make Obama's Court List," *New York Times*, May 26, 2009.
51. Sheryl Stolberg, "Obama Invites Gay Rights Activists to White House," *New York Times Caucus Blog*, June 22, 2009, at http://thecaucus.blogs.nytimes.com/2009/06/22/obama-invites-gay-rights-advocates-to-white-house/.
52. Cloud, "Obama."

Notes to Chapter 5

1. Jack Goldsmith, "The Cheney Fallacy: Why Barack Obama Is Waging a More Effective War on Terror Than George W. Bush," *New Republic*, May 18, 2009, at www.tnr.com/story_print.html?id=1e733cac-c273-48e5-9140-80443ed1f5e2. Goldsmith was an assistant attorney general in the Bush II administration.
2. Matt Gonzales, "The Obama Craze: Count Me Out," *BeyondChron: San Francisco's Online Daily*, February 28 2008, at www.beyondchron.org/news/index.php?itemid=5413.
3. Henry A. Giroux, *The Terror of Neoliberalism: Authoritarianism and the Eclipse of Democracy* (Boulder, CO: Paradigm Publishers, 2004), 8.
4. Susan Davis, "Obama Tilts Toward Center," *Wall Street Journal*, June 25, 2008; Michael Powell, "For Obama, a Pragmatist's Shift Toward the Center," *New York Times*, June 27, 2008; Janet Hook, "Obama Moving Toward Center: Democrat Edging Away from Left on Some Issues in Effort to Woo Independent Voters," *Los Angeles Times*, June 27, 2008.
5. Paul Kane, "Obama Supports FISA Legislation, Angering Left," *The Trail: A Daily Diary of Campaign 2008*, June 20, 2008, at http://blog.washingtonpost.com/44/2008/06/20/obama_supports_fisa_legislatio.html.
6. Glen Greenwald, "Obama and Habeas Corpus: Then and Now," *Salon*, April 11, 2009, at www.salon.com/opinion/greenwald/2009/04/11/bagram/.
7. *New York Times*, April 21, 2009.
8. "Remarks by the President to CIA Employees," April 20, 2009, at www.whitehouse.gov/the_press_office/Remarks-by-the-President-to-CIA-employees-at-CIA-Headquarters.
9. *New York Times*, April 17, 2009.
10. Scott Horton, "Investigating Bush's Crimes," *The Nation*, February 18, 2009; Paul Krugman, "Reclaiming America's Soul," *New York Times*, April 23, 2009.
11. Jeff Zeleny and Thom Shanker, "Obama Moves to Bar Release of Detainee Abuse Photos," *New York Times*, May 13, 2009; Bill Van Auken "Obama Bows to Republican Right and Military on Torture Photos," World Socialist Web Site, May 14, 2009, at www.wsws.org/articles/2009/may2009/tort-m14.shtml; Michael Doyle, "In Stark Legal

Turn Around, Obama Now Resembles Bush," *McClatchy Newspapers*, June 19, 2009, at www.mcclatchydc/227/story/70383.html.

12. Paul Street, *Barack Obama and the Future of American Politics* (Boulder, CO: Paradigm Publishers, 2008), 146–155.

13. Ibid., 155–161.

14. "Remarks at Memorial Service at Fort Hood," November 19, 2009.

15. "Remarks to CIA Employees."

16. Jane Mayer, "The Secret History," *New Yorker*, June 22, 2009.

17. For details and sources, see Glen Greenwald, "Obama Administration Threatens Britain to Keep Torture Evidence Concealed," *Salon*, May 12, 2009, at www.salon.com.

18. Ibid.

19. See Attachment (from the U.S. Department of Justice) to *Claim No. CO/4241/ 2008 In the High Court of Justice, Queen's Bench Division, Divisional Court, Between The Queen (on the application of Binyam Mohamed, Claimant) v. The Secretary of State for Foreign and Commonwealth Affairs, Defendant)*, posted (by Glen Greenwald) to http:// www.salon.com/news/opinion/glenn_greenwald/2009/05/12/obama/obama.pdf and linked at Greenwald, "Obama Administration Threatens."

20. Goldsmith, "The Cheney Fallacy"; Doyle, "In Stark Legal Turn Around."

21. Goldsmith, "The Cheney Fallacy;" Greenwald, "Obama Administration Threatens England."

22. Doyle, "In Stark Legal Turn Around."

23. Jeremy Scahill, "The Black Shirts of Guantanamo," *CounterPunch*, May 15, 2009, at www.counterpunch.org/scahill05152009.html; Goldsmith, "The Cheney Fallacy."

24. Ibid.

25. Glen Greenwald, "Obama's Civil Liberties Speech," *Salon*, May 21, 2009, at http://www.salon.com/opinion/greenwald/2009/05/21/obama/index.html.

26. In her essay "Obama's Bad Influence," *The Nation*, October 14, 2009, Klein noted how Obama's progressive imagery gave European elites something of a green light to behave in imperial and regressive ways in regard to key global issues such as climate change (carbon emissions), Palestinian rights, and slavery/African reparations.

27. Bob Herbert, "Who Are We?" *New York Times*, June 22, 2009.

28. Goldsmith, "The Cheney Fallacy."

29. See my discussion of trumped-up charges against Iran in Chapter 2.

30. John Pilger, "War Is Peace. Ignorance Is Strength," *The Guardian*, October 17, 2009. For a truly haunting video and sound of the first use of LRAD in the United States, in Pittsburgh in September 2009, see "Long Range Acoustic Device," September 26, 2009, at www.youtube.com/watch?v=QSMyY3_dmrM; and "G20—Confronted by LRAD Acoustic Weapon," YouTube, September 24, 2009, at www.youtube.com/ watch?v=DAwmX5O-FAE&feature=related.

31. Mike Ferner, "With Shot and Shell, or 'Modular Crowd Control Munitions,'" *ZNet*, December 15, 2008, at www.zcommunications.org/znet/viewArticle/19953; Antifascist, "Compliance by Design: The Continuing Allure of 'Non-Lethal Weapons," *Antifascist Calling*, September 18, 2009, at http://antifascist-calling.blogspot.com/2009/

09/compliance-by-design-continuing-allure.html; N. Lewer and N. Davison, "Non-Lethal Technologies: An Overview," *Disarmament Forum*, no. 1 (2005): 36–52.

32. Ed Pilkington, "New York Man Accused of Using Twitter to Direct Protestors During G 20 Summit," *The Guardian*, October 4, 2009.

33. "Remarks of the President at Memorial Service at Fort Hood," November 10, 2009, at www.whitehouse.gov.

34. William Fisher, "Obama Quietly Backs Patriot Act Provisions," Inter Press Service, November 25, 2009, at http://ipsnorthamerica.net/news.php?idnews=2694.

35. Jeff Cohen, "Get Ready for the Obama/GOP Alliance," *ZNet Sustainer Commentary*, November 29, 2009, at www.zcommunications.org/zspace/commentaries/4058.

36. The hellish Guantanamo channel house remains open as of this books completion, half a year later.

37. Barack Obama quoted in Jason Leopold, "Blistering Indictment Leveled Against Obama over His Handling of Bush-Era War Crimes," *Truthout*, December 12, 2009.

Notes to Chapter 6

1. Scott Horton, "Finding Ways to Stay in Iraq," Antiwar.com, March 4, 2009.

2. Tom Hayden, "I'm Stripping the Obama Bumper Sticker Off My Car," December 3, 2009, at www.thefoxnation.com/tom-hayden/2009/12/03/im-stripping-obama-bumper-sticker-my-car.

3. Glen Ford, "Progressives for Obama Changes Their Name to Omit Their President," *Black Agenda Report*, December 15, 2009, at http://tns3.blackagendareport.com/?q=content/progressives-obama-change-name-omit-their-president.

4. Matthew Rothschild, "Obama Steals Bush's Speech Writers," *The Progressive*, December 2, 2009, at www.progressive.org/wx120209.html.

5. On MoveOn.org's opposition to the health reform bill in mid-December 2009, see "MoveOn Calls on Members to Help Block Health Care Bill," CNN Politics, December 18, 2009, at http://politicalticker.blogs.cnn.com/2009/12/18/moveon-calls-on-members-to-help-block-health-care-bill/.

6. Jason Leopold, "Blistering Indictment Leveled Against Obama over His Handling of Bush-Era War Crimes," *Truthout*, December 12, 2009.

7. Justin Hyde and Richard Wolf, "President Says He Shouldn't Put Focus on Blacks' Troubles," *USA Today*, December 4, 2009.

8. Horton, "Finding Ways to Stay in Iraq."

9. An excellent reflection from the primary election period is Glen Ford, "Obama Stumbles on His Own Contradictions: Pop Goes the Race-Neutral Campaign!" *Black Agenda Report*, April 30, 2008. See also Chapter 4 of the present study; and Paul Street, *Barack Obama and the Future of American Politics* (Boulder, CO: Paradigm Publishers, 2008), chap. 3.

10. That's exactly what I saw during my many years in and around Chicago and Illinois politics and policy circles. See Paul Street, "Statehouse Days: The Myth of Obama's 'True

Progressive' Past," *ZNet*, July 20, 2008, at www.zcommunications.org/znet/viewArticle/ 18224; and Paul Street, "'Getting Things Done' with Obama," *ZNet*, December 21, 2008, at www.zcommunications.org/znet/viewArticle/20015.

11. Maureen Dowd, "Fie, Fatal Flaw!" *New York Times*, October 18, 2009.

12. Larissa MacFarquhar, "The Conciliator: Where Is Barack Obama Coming From?" *New Yorker*, May 7, 2007.

13. David Brooks, "Obama, Gospel and Verse," *New York Times*, April 26, 2007; Robert Kagan, "Obama the Interventionist," *Washington Post*, April 29, 2007; Jason Linkins, "Christopher Buckley Resigns from *National Review* After Obama Endorsement," *Huffington Post*, October 14, 2008, at www.huffingtonpost.com/2008/10/14/ christopher-buckley-resig_n_134628.html.

14. William Kristol, "GOP Dog Days?" *New York Times*, November 10, 2008.

15. Sam Stein, "Obama Defends Cabinet: The Change Will Come from Me," *Huffington Post*, November 26, 2008, at www.huffingtonpost.com/2008/11/26/obama -defends-cabinet-the_n_146648.html; Thomas B. Edsall, "The Obama Test: Personnel Is Policy," *Huffington Post*, November 26, 2008, at www.huffingtonpost.com/2008/ 10/24/the-obama-test-personnel_n_137757.html.

16. "Obama Breaks Fundraising Records," *Voice of America News*, October 21, 2009, at www1.voanews.com/english/news/a-13-2008-10-21-voa47-66601732.html; Street, *Barack Obama and the Future*, 19–22.

17. Ken Silverstein, "Barack Obama, Inc.: The Birth of a Washington Machine," *Harper's*, November 2006.

18. Barack Obama, *The Audacity of Hope* (New York: Crown, 2006), 149–150.

19. David Sirota, "Mr. Obama Goes to Washington," *The Nation*, June 7, 2006.

20. Paul Street, "Profit Surge," *ZNet Magazine*, February 10, 2007, at www.zmag.org/ content/showarticle.cfm?ItemID=12089.

21. For a sample of such unbalanced reflections, see Paul Street, *Empire and Inequality: America and the World Since 9/11* (Boulder, CO: Paradigm Publishers, 2004), 143–184. See also Robert Howard, *Brave New Workplace* (New York: Viking, 1986); Edward N. Wolff, *Top Heavy: A Study of the Increasing Inequality of Wealth in America* (New York: New Press, 2002); Joel Bakan, *The Corporation: The Pathological Pursuit of Profit and Power* (New York: Free Press, 2004); Juliet Schor, *The Overworked America: The Unexpected Decline of Leisure* (New York: Basic Books, 1992); Godfrey Hodgson, *More Equal Than Others: America from Nixon to the New Century* (New York: Century Foundation, 2004); David Gordon, *Fat and Mean: The Corporate Squeeze of Working Americans and the Myth of Managerial Downsizing* (New York: Free Press, 1996); Paul Street, "Labor Day Reflections: Time as a Democracy Issue," *ZNet Daily Commentaries*, September 3, 2002, at www.zmag. org/ sustainers/content/ 2002-08/01street.cfm; Barbara Ehrenreich, *Nickel and Dimed: On (Not) Getting By in America* (New York: Metropolitan Books, 2001); and Barbara Ehrenreich, *Bait and Switch: The (Futile) Pursuit of the American Dream* (New York: Henry Holt, 2005). For Obama on the Founders' democracy legacy, see Obama, *Audacity*, 87–88.

22. For background data, see Janny Scott and David Leonhardt, "Shadowy Lines That Still Divide," *New York Times*, May 15, 2005; Lawrence Mishel, Jared Bernstein, and

Heather Boushey, *The State of Working America 2002–2003* (Ithaca, NY: Economic Policy Institute and Cornell University Press, 2003), 414–422.

23. One term used by some left analysts to describe really existing U.S. "democracy" is "polyarchy," what left sociologist William I. Robinson called "a system in which a small group actually rules and mass participation in decision making is confined to leadership choices carefully managed by competing [business and business-sanctioned] elites. The polyarchic concept of democracy," noted Robinson, "is an effective arrangement for legitimating and sustaining inequalities within and between nations (deepening in a global economy) far more effectively than authoritarian solutions." William I. Robinson, *Promoting Polyarchy: Globalization, US Intervention, and Hegemony* (Cambridge: Cambridge University Press, 1996), 385.

24. Alex Carey, *Taking the Risk Out of Democracy: Corporate Propaganda Versus Freedom and Liberty* (Urbana: University of Illinois Press, 1997), 11–86, 133–139.

25. Barack Obama, "Our Common Stake in America's Prosperity," NASDAQ Headquarters, New York, September 17, 2007.

26. Jeff Faux, *The Global Class War: How America's Bipartisan Elite Lost Our Future and What It Will Take to Win it Back* (New York: Wiley, 2006), 87, 168, 179–200; Leslie Sklair, *The Transnational Capitalist Class* (Malden, MA: Blackwell, 2000).

27. Bob Herbert, "Crisis on Many Fronts," *New York Times*, October 25, 2008.

28. "Biden to Run Middle Class Task Force," CBS News, December 21, 2008, at www.cbsnews.com/stories/2008/12/21/politics/main4680733.shtml?source=RSSattr =HOME_4680733.

29. For an interesting "List of Left Wing Articles Critical of Obama," see www .dkosopedia.com/wiki/List_of_Left-wing_articles_critical_of_Obama.

30. Paul Street, "Keynote Reflections," *ZNet*, July 29, 2004, at www.zmag.org/ content/showarticle.cfm?SectionID=41&ItemID=5951.

31. Sheldon Wolin, *Democracy Incorporated: Managed Democracy and the Specter of Inverted Totalitarianism* (Princeton, NJ: Princeton University Press, 2008). For a critical but appreciative review, see Paul Street, "It Can Happen Here," *Dissident Voice*, August 23, 2008, at www.dissidentvoice.org/2008/08/totalitarianism-it-can-happen-here/.

32. The prize for earliest left identification of Obama as a fake-progressive neoliberal centrist goes without question to black political scientist Adolph Reed Jr., who penned a retrospectively fascinating account of Obama in the *Village Voice* at the beginning of Obama's political career in 1996. See Adolph Reed Jr., "The Curse of Community," *Village Voice*, January 16, 1996, reproduced in Adolph Reed Jr., *Class Notes: Posing as Politics and Other Thoughts on the American Scene* (New York: New Press, 2000).

33. John Pilger, "After Bobby Kennedy (There Was Barack Obama)," *Common Dreams*, May 31, 2008, at www.commondreams.org/archive/ 2008/05/ 31/9327/.

34. Susan Davis, "Obama Tilts Toward Center," *Wall Street Journal*, June 25, 2008; Michael Powell, "For Obama, a Pragmatist's Shift Toward the Center," *New York Times*, June 27, 2008; Janet Hook, "Obama Moving Toward Center: Democrat Edging Away from Left on Some Issues in Effort to Woo Independent Voters," *Los Angeles Times*, June 27, 2008.

35. The Hamilton Group is a leading "conservative" (business-friendly) economic think tank. Furman was linked closely to Robert Rubin, a top Wall Street financial

mogul and former Clinton economics advisor and Treasury secretary. Rubin's regressive views on behalf of "free trade" (including the North American Free Trade Agreement, investor's rights, wages, welfare and "deficit reduction") gave the Clinton administration "credibility" in the halls of corporate and financial power.

36. See also Alexander Cockburn, "Change? What Change?" *CounterPunch*, June 13–15, 2008, at www.counterpunch.org/cockburn06132008.html.

37. Sara Baxter, "Barack Obama May Recruit Defence Chief Robert Gates," *Sunday Times*, June 29, 2008, at www.timesonline.co.uk/tol/news/world/us_and_americas/us_elections/article4232070.ee.

38. "Remarks of Senator Obama: Council for Faith-Based and Neighborhood Partnerships," Zanesville, Ohio, July 1, 2008, at www.barackobama.com/2008/07/01/remarks_of_senator_barack_obam_86.php.

39. Leutisha Stills, "Obama Charges Rightward," *Black Agenda Report*, June 25, 2008, at www.blackagendareport.com/index.php?option=com_content&task=view&id=674&Itemid=1.

40. "Change We Can Believe In: An Open Letter to Barack Obama," *The Nation*, July 30, 2008, at www.thenation.com/doc/20080818/open_letter.

41. Michael Powell, "Obama Addresses Critics on 'Centrist' Moves," *New York Times*, July 8, 2008, at http://thecaucus.blogs.nytimes.com/2008/07/08/obama-addresses-critics-on-centrist-moves/.

42. See Street, *Barack Obama and the Future*, for a detailed historical account.

43. Nevertheless, there was more than a hint of bad faith in Obama's lecture to his "friends on the left." Obama and his marketers worked effectively to create a false left impression among certain targeted voters. He posed as a left-leaning antiwar and social justice progressive, donning deceptive rebel's clothing in numerous speeches, town hall meetings, and television commercials across the primary season. There was an ugly undercurrent of blaming the victim in Obama's criticism of his leftmost backers.

44. Brooks, "Obama, Gospel and Verse."

45. Quoted in Danny Shea, "David Brooks: Sarah Palin Represents a Fatal Cancer on the Republican Party," *Huffington Post*, October 8, 2008, at www.huffingtonpost.com/2008/10/08/david-brooks-sarah-palin_n_133001.html.

46. Noam Chomsky, "Reinhold Niebuhr," *Grand Street* 6, no. 2 (Winter 1987).

47. Reinhold Niebuhr, *The Nature and Destiny of Man: A Christian Interpretation* (1941), quoted in Chomsky, "Reinhold Niebuhr."

48. Noam Chomsky, *Keeping the Rabble in Line: Interviews with David Barsamian* (Monroe, ME: Common Courage, 1994), 96–97.

49. David Brooks, "The Insiders' Crusade," *New York Times*, November 21, 2008; "Brooks and Markus on Obama's Cabinet Picks, Economy Woes," *PBS NewsHour*, November 21, 2008, at www.pbs.org/newshour/bb/politics/july-dec08/bmeconomy_11-21.html; Bruce Miroff, *Pragmatic Illusions: The Presidential Politics of John Fitzgerald Kennedy* (New York: Longman's, 1976); Paul Street, "David Brooks' Pragmatic Illusions and the New Administration," *ZNet Sustainer Commentary*, November 25, 2008, at www.zmag.org/zspace/commentaries/3692.

50. Chomsky, "Reinhold Niebuhr."

51. Reinhold Niebuhr quoted in Noam Chomsky, "Force and Opinion," *Z Magazine*, July–August 1991, at www.chomsky.info/articles/199107--.htm.

52. "Transcript of Obama Interview on CNN," July 25, 2008, *The Page*, at http://thepage.time.com/transcript-of-obama-interview-on-cnn/.

53. It has been truly tiresome to hear candidate, President-elect and President Obama repeatedly refer to the United States as living "in a time of war." The United States is engaged in one-sided imperial violence against Iraq and Afghanistan. At the very least, it should be admitted that the United States is waging colonial war on relatively defenseless others and that there is no war with foreign states or people being fought or waged on U.S. soil.

54. For some details, see Paul Street, "Obama's Good and 'Proper' War," *ZNet*, March 5, 2008, at www.zcommunications.org/znet/viewArticle/16760.

55. John Pilger, *Freedom Next Time: Resisting the Empire* (New York: Nation Books, 2007), 284–285.

56. Ibid., 285–286.

57. Ibid., 286.

58. Ibid., 287–293; John Pilger, "Obama, the Prince of Bait and Switch," *New Statesman*, July 26, 2008.

59. Jason Linkins, "Dirty Secrets of the Bailout: 32 Words None Dare Utter," *Huffington Post*, September 22, 2009, at www.huffingtonpost.com/2008/09/22/dirty-secret-of-the-bailo_n_128294.html.

60. Jeff Zeleny, "Obama: No Blank Check on Bailout," *New York Times*, September 22, 2009, at http://thecaucus.blogs.nytimes.com/2008/09/21/obama-no-blank-check-on-bailout/.

61. www.votenader.org/bailout/.

62. "Nader/Gonzales Warn Against Blank-Check Bailout," KSFY Television News, Sioux Falls, South Dakota, October 2, 2008, at www.ksfy.com/explorepolitics/?feed=bim&id=30195834.

63. Morgan Stanley Research, Aerospace & Defense, Heidi Wood et al., "Early Thoughts on Obama and Defense" (November 5, 2008), read at www.washingtonpost.com/wp-srv/business/governmentinc/documents/ObamaDefense.pdf.

64. Noam Chomsky, "Elections 2008 and Obama's Vision," *Z Magazine*, February 2008.

65. "President Obama's Inaugural Address: The Full Text," January 20, 2009, at www.time.com/time/politics/article/0,8599,1872715,00.html.

66. "Obama Victory Speech—Video, Text," *Huffington Post*, November 4, 2008, at www.huffingtonpost.com/2008/11/04/obama-victory-speech_n_141194.html.

67. See Noam Chomsky, *Failed States: The Abuse of Power and the Assault on Democracy* (New York: Metropolitan Books, 2006), chap. 5, 205–250.

68. MacFarquhar, "The Conciliator."

69. Barack Obama, "E-mail Message to His Supporters This Evening," November 4, 2008, at http://isaac.blogs.com/isaac_laquedem/2008/11/barack-obamas-e-mail-message-to-his-supporters-this-evening.html.

70. Chomsky, "Elections 2008."

71. Mike Dorning and Christi Parsons, "Carefully Crafting the Obama Brand," *Chicago Tribune,* June 12, 2007.

72. For left critiques of the centrist Obama's 2004 Democratic Convention Keynote Address, his March 2008 Philadelphia race race Speech, his August 2008 Berlin speech, and his election night victory speech, see Paul Street, "Keynote Reflections," *ZNet,* July 29, 2004, at www.zmag.org/content/showarticle.cfm?SectionID=41&ItemID=5951; Paul Street, "Obama's Latest 'Beautiful Speech,'" *ZNet,* March 22, 2008, at www.zcommunications.org/znet/viewArticle/16947; Paul Street, "His High Imperial Holiness Obama Does Berlin," *Black Agenda Report,* July 30, 2008, at www.blackagendareport .com/index.php?option=com_content&task=view&id=717&Itemid=34; and Paul Street, "'Anyone Out There?'" *ZNet,* November 10, 2008, at www.zcommunications.org/znet/viewArticle/19414.

For an extensive review and left critique, see Paul Street, "Obama's Audacious Deference to Power," *ZNet,* January 24, 2007, at www.zmag.org/content/showarticle.cfm ?ItemID=11936.

73. There was precedent in Obama's already vast rhetorical record for this sort of strange and reactionary historical conflation. An especially nauseating part of Obama's first famous speech—the 2004 Democratic Convention keynote address, which turned him into an overnight sensation—came when he said the following about his repeatedly invoked concept of "hope":

> I'm not talking about blind optimism here—the almost willful ignorance that thinks un-employment will go away if we just don't talk about it, or the health care crisis will solve it-self if we just ignore it. I'm talking about something more substantial. It's the hope of slaves sitting around a fire singing freedom songs; the hope of immigrants setting out for distant shores; the hope of a young naval lieutenant bravely patrolling the Mekong Delta; the hope of a mill worker's son who dares to defy the odds; the hope of a skinny kid with a funny name who believes that America has a place for him, too. . . . In the end, that is God's great-est gift to us, the bedrock of this nation; a belief in things not seen; a belief that there are better days ahead.

The "young naval lieutenant line" was a reference to Democratic presidential candidate John F. Kerry's participation in a previous imperialist adventure, one that took millions of Vietnamese lives. It took no small and reactionary chutzpah for Obama to lump African American slaves' struggles and spirituality with the imperial and racist U.S. assault on Southeast Asia under the image of noble Americans wishing together for a better future. Perhaps "God" (the officially highly religious Obama's keynote address made re-peated references to "God" and "the Creator") gave Nazi executioners and Nazi victims the shared gift of hoping for "better days ahead." It was not clear who or what told Obama that the Mekong Delta was Kerry and his superiors' territory to "patrol"—the same arrogant, nationalist, and racist sensibilities, perhaps, that gave nineteenth-century white Americans permission to own slaves and steal land from Mexico and Native Americans and that allowed the Bush administration to seize Iraq as a neocolonial possession?

74. Mike Albert, *PARECON: Life After Capitalism* (New York: Verso Books, 2003), 65.

75. Laurence H. Shoup, "Obama and McCain March Rightward," *Z Magazine*, September 2008, 27.

76. For a thoughtful critique of that pervasive notion from within the foreign policy national security establishment, see "Anonymous" (Michael Scheuer), *Imperial Hubris: Why the West Is Losing the War on Terror* (Washington, DC: Potomac Books, 2004).

77. Noam Chomsky, "'Exterminate All the Brutes': Gaza 2009," *ZNet*, January 20, 2009.

78. Paul Street, "'We Will Not Apologize for Our Way of Life': Left Reflections on Barack Obama's Not-So-Non-Ideological Inaugural Address," *ZNet*, January 23, 2009, at www.zcommunications.org/we-will-not-apologize-for-our-way-of-life-by-paul-street.

79. Alfred Young, ed., *The American Revolution: Explorations in the History of American Radicalism* (DeKalb: Northern Illinois University Press, 1976).

80. "A nation that continues year after year to spend more money on military defense than on programs of social uplift is approaching spiritual death." Martin Luther King Jr., "A Time to Break the Silence," Riverside Church, New York City, April 4. 1967.

Afterword

1. Susan Page, "Obama's Election One Year Later," *USA Today*, October 28, 2009.

2. David D. Kirkpatrick, "Financial Giants Donating Little to Obama Party," *New York Times*, October 20, 2009.

3. *Washington Post*, October 24, 2009.

4. Interview with Colonel Andrew Bacevich [Ret.], *Frontline*/PBS, September 21, 2009, at www.pbs.org/wgbh/pages/frontline/obamaswar/interviews/bacevich.html.

5. David Cecere, "New Study Finds 45,000 Deaths Linked Annually to Lack of Health Insurance," *HarvardScience*, September 17, 2009, at www.harvardscience.harvard.edu/medicine-health/articles/new-study-finds-45000-deaths-annually-linked-lack-health-coverage.

6. Glen Greenwald, "'America's Priorities,' by the Beltway Elite," *Salon*, October 24, 2009, at www.salon.com/news/opinion/glenn_greenwald/?page=2.

7. David Garrow, *Bearing the Cross: Martin Luther King and the Southern Christian Leadership Conference* (New York: HarperCollins, 1986), 562.

8. Martin Luther King Jr., "Where Do We Go from Here?" 1967, in James M. Washington, ed., *A Testament of Hope: The Essential Writings and Speeches of Martin Luther King Jr.* (San Francisco: HarperCollins, 1991), 250; Michael Eric Dyson, *I May Not Get There with You: The True Martin Luther King Jr.* (New York: Touchstone Books, 2000), 82–89; Paul Street, "The Pale Reflection: Barack Obama, Martin Luther King Jr., and the Meaning of the Black Revolution," *ZNet*, March 16, 2007, at www.zmag.org/content/showarticle.cfm?ItemID=12336; Paul Street, "Martin Luther King Jr,: Democratic Socialist," *ZNet Sustainer Commentary*, January 14, 2006, at http://www.zmag.org/Sustainers/Content/2006-01/14street.cfm, and at *Black Commentator*, February 2, 2006, at www.blackcommentator.com/169/169_street_mlk_democratic_socialist.html; Paul Street, "'Until We Get a New Social Order': Reflections on the Radicalism of Martin

Luther King Jr.," *ZNet*, January 16, 2007, at www.zmag.org/content/showarticle.cfm ?ItemID=11871.

9. For more on U.S.-imposed mass death and devastation in Southeast Asia, see William Blum, *Rogue State: A Guide to the World's Only Superpower* (Monroe, ME: Common Courage, 2005), 66, 114, 117–118, 138–139, 174; Noam Chomsky, *Year 501: The Conquest Continues* (Boston, MA: South End Press, 1993), 251–274; Ward Churchill, *On the Justice of Roosting Chickens: Reflections on the Consequences of U.S. Imperial Arrogance and Criminality* (Oakland, CA: AK Press, 2003), 132–149.

10. Garrow, *Bearing the Cross*, 562.

11. King, "Where Do We Go from Here?,"; ibid.

12. See Larissa MacFarquhar, "The Conciliator: Where Is Barack Obama Coming From?" *New Yorker*, May 7, 2007; Paul Street, *Barack Obama and the Future of American Politics* (Boulder, CO: Paradigm Publishers, 2008); Paul Street, "Obama's Audacious Deference to Power," *ZNet*, January 24, 2007; and Kevin Baker, "Barack Hoover Obama: The Best and the Brightest Blow It Again," *Harper's* (July 2009).

13. See the Introduction and Chapter 3.

14. See Chapter 6, pages 188–189.

15. Psalms 146:3.

16. Laurence H. Shoup, "The Presidential Election 2008," *Z Magazine*, February 2008; Edward S. Herman and David Peterson, "Riding the 'Green Wave' at the Campaign for Peace and Democracy and Beyond," *Electric Politics*, July 22, 2009.

17. Noam Chomsky, *Interventions* (San Francisco: City Lights, 2007), 99–100.

18. Noam Chomsky, *Failed States: The Abuse of Power and the Assault on Democracy* (New York: Metropolitan Books, 2006), 262.

19. Street, *Barack Obama*, 193–220.

20. Ibid., 206.

21. John K. Wilson, *Barack Obama: This Improbable Quest* (Boulder, CO: Paradigm Publishers, 2008), 126.

22. As intrepid left Obama critic Glen Ford noted in the summer of 2009: "The president and his supporters often throw around the old cliché about not letting the 'perfect become the enemy of the good.' That's their way of defending the fatal compromises Obama keeps making with the right-wing before the fight has even begun. Whether because of lack of gumption or lack of real commitment on Obama's part, this refusal to confront Power is what has brought us to the current health care debacle in Congress. It's not a matter of the perfect being the enemy of the good, but that the health care legislation shaped by the White House and its allies in Congress is *just no damn good.*" Glen Ford, "John Conyers: 'There Is No One More Disappointed Than I Am in Barack Obama," *Black Agenda Report*, August 4, 2009, at www.blackagendareport.com/?q=content/conyers-%E2%80%9C there-no-one-more-disappointed-i-am-barack-obama%E2%80%9D.

23. For details and sources, see Street, *Barack Obama*, 40–54; and Paul Street, "Michael Moore and Barack Obama: A Love Story," *ZNet*, October 9, 2009, at www.zmag.org/ znet/viewArticle/22823.

24. Fred Magdoff and Michael D. Yates, "What Needs to Be Done: A Socialist View," *Monthly Review*, November 2009, 90.

25. Massachusetts Institute of Technology, "Climate Change Odds Much Worse Than Thought: New Analysis Shows Warming Could Be Double Previous Estimates," *MIT News*, May 19, 2009, at http://web.mit.edu/newsoffice/2009/roulette-0519.html#; Christian Schwagerl, "Obama Has Failed the World on Climate Change," *Spiegel Online*, November 17, 2009, at www.spiegel.de/international/world/0,1518,661678,00.html.

26. Ricardo Levins-Morales, "Revolution in the Time of Hamsters," *ZNet*, September 1, 2009.

27. For a chilling and comprehensive reflection by the environmental editor of the leading French newspaper *Le Monde*, see Herve Kempf, *How the Rich Are Destroying the Earth* (White River Junction, VT: Chelsea Green, 2007). For recent data that ought to give pause, see Massachusetts Institute of Technology, "Climate Change Odds Much Worse." Istvan Meszaros, *Socialism or Barbarism: From the "American Century" to the Crossroads* (New York: Monthly Review Press, 2001).

28. David Germain, "Michael Moore: I May Quit Documentaries," *Huffington Post*, September 15, 2009, at www.huffingtonpost.com/2009/09/15/michael-moore-i-may-quit-_n_286854.html.

29. See Chapter 2; and Paul Street, "To Save the Capitalist System: Reflections on Orin Kramer's Understanding of Barack Obama's Duty to America," *Z Magazine*, December 2009.

30. I originally expected to follow *Barack Obama and the Future of American Politics* (2008) with a volume titled "It's the Capitalism, Stupid." Rightly or wrongly, I concluded that the project of advancing radical criticism and movements within and beyond the United States would benefit from a prior effort to demystify the Obama phenomenon— an effort that tackled Obama's first year in the White House.

"Philosophers had merely interpreted the world," Karl Marx once wrote; "the point is to change it."

Postscript

1. John Pilger, "After Bobby Kennedy (There Was Barack Obama)," *Common Dreams*, May 31, 2008, at www.commondreams.org/archive/2008/05/31/9327/.

2. Paul Street, *Barack Obama and the Future of American Politics* (Boulder, CO: Paradigm Publishers, 2008), xxii–xxviii, 161–163, 173–176.

3. On the back dust jacket of ibid.

4. Ibid., 203–206.

5. George Orwell, *An Age like This, 1920–1940* (New York: Harcourt Brace Jovanovich, 1968), 353.

6. Ricardo Levins-Morales, "Revolution in the Time of Hamsters," *ZNet*, September 18, 2009, at www.zmag.org/znet/viewArticle/22498.

7. John Judis, "End the Honeymoon," *New Republic*, February 13, 2009, at www.tnr.com/politics/story.html?id=5bff5e94-6fa6-4a69-9ff2-8f08cb437ccc.

8. John Pilger, "Power, Illusion, and America's Last Taboo," July 4, 2009, at www.johnpilger.com/page.asp?partid=545.

9. Justin Raimondo, "Springtime for Obama and the Death of the Old Left," Antiwar.com, March 22, 2010, at http://original.antiwar.com/justin/2010/03/21/spring time-for-obama/.

10. "Headlines for September 24, 2009," *Democracy Now*, at http://i3.democracynow .org/2009/9/24/headlines.

11. Comment quoted in Glen Ford, "First Black President Defeats Antiwar Movement," *Black Agenda Report*, April 15, 2009, at www.blackagendareport.com/?q=content/ first-black-president-defeats-us-antiwar-movement.

12. Dana Priest, "U.S. Military Intelligence Deeply Involved in Yemen Air Strikes," *Washington Post*, January 27, 2010.

13. Glenn Greenwald, "Obama Threatens to Veto Greater Intelligence Oversight," *Salon*, March 16, 2010.

14. Glenn Greenwald, "The Obama DOJ's Warrantless Demand for E-mails," *Salon*, April 15, 2010.

15. Glenn Greenwald, "What the Whistleblower Prosecution Says About the Obama DOJ," *Salon*, April 16, 2010.

16. Glenn Greenwald, "Presidential Assassination of U.S. Citizens," *Salon*, January 27, 2010.

17. Glenn Greenwald, "Olbermann on Obama's Assassination Program," *Salon*, April 8, 2010.

18. See the chilling account in Christopher Hayes, "Tuesdays with Rahm," *The Nation*, October 26, 2009.

19. Lance Selfa, "Can the Right Stage a Comeback?" *International Socialist Review* 69 (January–February 2010).

20. *New York Times*/CBS Poll, "Confusion over Health Care," survey of 1,042 adults, September 19–23, 2009, question 57, at http://documents.nytimes.com/new-york-times -cbs-news-poll-confusion-over-health-care-tepid-support-for-war#p=15.

21. For more details and sources right after the bill's passage, see Paul Street, "Health Reform: Theirs and Ours," *ZNet*, March 24, 2010, at www.zcommunications.org/health -reform-theirs-and-ours-by-paul-street; Paul Street, "Corporatist Health 'Reform,'" *ZNet*, March 31, 2010, at www.zcommunications.org/corporatist-health-reform-as-an -attack-on-wealth-inequality-by-paul-street.

22. www.allyourtv.com/index.php?option=com_content&view=article&id=1058 :transcript-rahm-emanuel-on-pbs-newshour-03252010&catid=1:latest-news.

23. Sam Stein, "David Axelrod: Health Care Lobbyists Descending like 'Locusts' on Congress," *Huffington Post*, March 14, 2010, at www.huffingtonpost.com/2010/03/14/ david-axelrod-health-care_n_498290.html?page=5; Jonathan Chait, "The Insurance Industry Doesn't Want Its 'Giveaway,'" *New Republic*, March 1, 2010, at www.tnr.com/ blog/jonathan-chait/the-insurance-industry-doesnt-want-its-giveaway; Ezra Klein, "Twilight of the Interest Groups," *Washington Post*, March 19, 2010, at http:// voices.washingtonpost.com/ezra-klein/2010/03/twilight_of_the_interest_group.html. Klein actually went to the preposterous length of saying that the Obama administration "succeeded in neutralizing every single industry" in the health care sector.

24. Phil Galewicz, "Doctors, Hospitals, Insurers, Pharma Come Out Ahead with Health Care Bill," *Kaiser Health News*, March 22, 2010, at www.kaiserhealthnews.org/Stories/2010/March/22/winners-losers-health-reform.aspx; Glenn Greenwald, "Industry Interests Are Not in Their 'Twilight,'" *Salon*, March 20, 2010.

25. Firedog Lake, March 18, 2010, at http://seminal.firedoglake.com/diary/35866.

26. Sabrina Eaton, ""Rep. Dennis Kucinich Draws Fire from the Left over Health Care Reform," *Cleveland Plain Dealer*, March 12, 2010, at www.cleveland.com/open/index.ssf/2010/03/rep_dennis_kucinich_draws_fire.html.

27. Glenn Greenwald, "Has Rahm's Assumption About Progressives Been Vindicated?" *Salon*, March 18, 2010, at www.salon.com/news/opinion/glenn_greenwald/2010/03/18/progressives/index.html.

28. Klein, "Twilight of the Interest Groups."

29. Glenn Greenwald, "More on Those 'Neutralized' Special Interests," *Salon*, March 23, 2010. Liberal commentator Matthew Yglesias noted that Ezra Klein's claim about interest groups losing out in the health "reform" was just wrong: "Interest groups were able to get their way on most key points without needing to seriously attempt to deliver votes in exchange. . . . The interest groups were able to get 85 percent of what they wanted in exchange for absolutely nothing." Matthew Yglesias, "Interests Group Alive and Well," *Yglesias*, March 20, 2010, at http://yglesias.thinkprogress.org/archives/2010/03/interest-groups-alive-and-well.php.

30. Jane Hamsher, "The Progressive Movement Is Officially Dead," Firedog Lake, April 30, 2010, at http://fdlaction.firedoglake.com/2010/04/30/the-progressive-movement-is-officially-dead/; Jane Hamsher, "Progressive Caucus Outlines Its Plan to Give Coal Lobby Everything It Wants," Firedog Lake, April 7, 2010, at http://fdlaction.firedoglake.com/2010/04/07/progressive-caucus-outlines-their-plan-to-give-coal-lobby-everything-it-wants/; Jane Hamsher, "Durbin Says 'Bleeding Heart Liberals' Should Be Open to Medicare and Social Security Cuts," Firedog Lake, April 29, 2010, at http://fdlaction.firedoglake.com/2010/04/29/durbin-says-bleeding-heart-liberals-should-be-open-to-medicare-and-social-security-cuts/. Durbin is also quoted in Jackie Calmes, "Obama Tells Debt Commission 'Everything Has to Be on Table,'" *New York Times*, April 27, 2010.

31. Paul Street, "What's the Matter with the Democrats? Post-Massachusetts Reflections on Popular Resentment, the Liberal-Left Vacuum, and the Right Comeback," *ZNet*, January 24, 2010; Selfa, "Can the Right Stage a Comeback?"

32. Lance Selfa, "How Did This Guy Win?" *Socialist Worker*, January 20, 2010, at http://socialistworker.org/print/2010/01/20/how-did-this-guy-win?

33. Brian Mooney, "Suburbs Carried Brown to Victory: Low Turnout Recorded in Most Cities," *Boston Globe*, January 21, 2009, at www.boston.com/news/local/massachusetts/articles/2010/01/21/suburbs_carried_brown_to_victory/. Thank you to Noam Chomsky for alerting me to this story.

34. Bob Herbert, "They Still Don't Get It," *New York Times*, January 23, 2010.

35. Noam Chomsky and Diane Krauthamer, "Worker Occupations and the Future of Radical Labor: An Interview with Noam Chomsky," *Z Magazine*, February 2010, 22.

Index

Paul Street is an independent journalist, policy advisor, and historian. Formerly he was vice president for Research and Planning at the Chicago Urban League. Among his recent books are *Barack Obama and the Future of American Politics* (Paradigm, 2008), *Racial Oppression in the Global Metropolis: A Living Black Chicago History* (Rowman & Littlefield, 2007), and *Segregated Schools: Educational Apartheid in Post–Civil Rights America* (Routledge, 2005). His many articles have appeared in the *Chicago Tribune, In These Times, Dissent, Z Magazine, Black Commentator, Monthly Review, Journal of American Ethnic History, Journal of Social History,* and other publications.